For H.M.F.
and
Friends in Orkney

THE ISLANDS SERIES

ORKNEY

THE ISLANDS SERIES

†Achill
 Alderney
†The Aran Islands
 The Isle of Arran
 The Island of Bute
*Canary Islands: Fuerteventura
*Cape Breton Island
*Corsica
*‡Cyprus
*The Falkland Islands
†Gotland
*Grand Bahama
†Harris and Lewis
†The Isle of Mull
 Lundy
 The Maltese Islands
†Orkney
*Puerto Rico
 St Kilda and other Hebridean Islands
*‡The Seychelles
†Shetland
*‡Singapore
‡Skye
*‡The Solomon Islands
*Vancouver Island

   in preparation
   Bermuda
   Fiji
   Mauritius
   Rhodes
   St Helena
   Tasmania
   Tobago
   Uists and Barra

* Published in the United States by Stackpole
† Published in the United States by David & Charles
‡ The series is distributed in Australia by Wren

ORKNEY

by *PATRICK BAILEY*

DAVID & CHARLES

NEWTON ABBOT : NORTH POMFRET (VT)

ISBN 0 7153 5000 5

First published 1971
Reprinted 1974

Set in eleven on twelve point Baskerville
and printed in Great Britain
by W J Holman Limited Dawlish
for David & Charles (Holdings) Limited
South Devon House Newton Abbot Devon

CONTENTS

ILLUSTRATIONS

ILLUSTRATIONS

All photographs and drawings by the author unless otherwise acknowledged

Key:

- ━━ 'A' Roads
- 741 Spot heights in feet
- Land over 250 feet
- Lakes
- Cliffed coast
- + Church
- olm Parish
- ■ Archaeological site

Miles 10

Kilometres 15

NORTH RONALDSAY

Mull Head

PAPA WESTRAY

Burrian Broch

Noup Head

SANDAY

Noltland Castle ■ Pierowall

Westray Firth

WESTRAY

Kettletoft   Tres Ness
Cross and Burness   Els Ness
Lady
Stove

ROUSAY

EDAY

PAPA STRONSAY

Westness   + St. Magnus

▲821   Whitehall

Brough of Birsay   Birsay   Evie   Eynhallow Sound   EGILSEY   STRONSAY

Earl's Palace   A967   Trumland   WYRE

Marwick Head   A966   GAIRSAY

Dounby   Rendall   Stronsay Firth

Harray   AUSKERRY

Bay of Skaill   A986   Balfour   SHAPINSAY

Skara Brae   Sandwick   Bay of   The String

Borwick   Firth   FINSTOWN

Yesnaby   Maeshowe ■   A966   ▲741   KIRKWALL   Brough of Deerness

▲518   Stenness   ▲721

Black Craig   A964   ▲881   A964   Deerness

STROMNESS ■   A965   Scapa Bay   A960   St. Andrews

Hoy Sound   Orphir   Holm   MAINLAND

St. John's Head   ▲Cuilags   St. Mary's

Ward Hill ▲1565   Bay of   Scapa

Old Man of Hoy   Houton   Flow

Rora Head   Rackwick   BURRAY   Churchill Barriers

HOY   Lyness   Hoxa Sound   A961   St. Margaret's Hope

The Berry   Walls   Long Hope   SOUTH RONALDSAY

Melsetter ■   ▲389

Ferry

Pentland   Firth

SHETLANDS

Bergen

Dunnet Head   STROMA   Thurso   ORKNEYS   NORWAY

Inverness   North Sea

John o' Groats   Ducansby Head   Stacks of Ducansby

rabster   CAITHNESS   BRITISH   Miles 200   DENMARK
A836   Freswick Bay   ISLES   Kms 300
THURSO

1 THE ORKNEY ISLANDS

IFTY miles south of the latitude of Cape Farewell at the southern tip of Greenland, and level with Churchill on Hudson Bay, Skagway in Alaska and other very northern-sounding places on latitude 59° north, lie the Orkney islands, one of Britain's most northerly outposts, bunched loosely together within a rectangle of sea some 56 miles from north to south and 29 miles east to west. Flying in to Grimsetter airport on Mainland, the principal island, one sees a land where low hills are surrounded by broad, cultivated lowlands, rather than of lowlands shut in between sea and hill—which is the first impression from seaward. These lowlands have been inhabited and tilled from time immemorial and many of the farms stand on sites which have been occupied for tens of centuries. Some may indeed occupy sites chosen by the very first settlers in Orkney over four thousand years ago.

The islands are the home of a working community and no mere holiday spot. Visitors are made very welcome but they must expect mainly to find their own amusement. Orkney is no place for a seaside holiday of swimming and sunbathing; the sea is too chilly to be enjoyed by either visitors or Orcadians—with certain stalwart exceptions,—and the winds make sunbathing an unusual pastime.

Orkney has a tremendous amount to offer whether to the armchair explorer or to the visitor. For the former there is a considerable literature. For the latter there are explorations that need not be strenuous, along splendid empty coastlines and over low hills with extensive views of sea and island; trips by small boat across sounds and firths, perhaps to some skerry uninhabited by man but alive with seabirds; the pleasures of free fishing, a relic of the old Norse legal system; a wonderfully clean, clear atmosphere with long summer days, spectacular sunsets and a very

13

fair chance of fine summer weather; and an array of ancient monuments unequalled in Europe. A week can easily be spent just visiting these last; their study could occupy a lifetime. Indeed so rich is Rousay in ancient remains that it has been named with some justification the Egypt of the North. Above all there is a feeling of relaxation and friendliness, and the stresses of urban living seem very far away. Food and accommodation are good and hospitably given; on the outer isles especially the visitor is still regarded as a guest.

The islands are somewhat smaller in area than the Hebrides; their total land area is 376 square miles, about twice as large as Rutland. Their extent is often a surprise to southern visitors, and map-makers are much to blame for this. For years it has been customary to place Orkney and Shetland as insets to a main map of Britain and often at half the scale of the rest of the map, in order to meet the exigencies of the size of the map sheet.

THE ISLAND GROUPS

The Orkneys lie immediately north of the north-east corner of Scotland, from which they are separated by the Pentland Firth. There are about sixty islands all told, though this number varies according to the minimum size of rock one calls an island; authors of books on Orkney have had many different ideas on this detail. They are divided into three groups by broad firths and sounds which, like the islands, have a pronounced north-west to south-east alignment. More than half the land area is concentrated in Mainland, the largest island, 23 miles from west to east, on which stand Kirkwall and Stromness. Kirkwall is the chief town and administrative capital of the County of Orkney. Its population is only about 4,500 but, because it is the capital, it has more and better shops than one might expect in so small a town. Mainland used to be called Pomona through an ancient literary error and this name still appears occasionally on modern maps. The eastern third of Mainland is joined to the western part by the isthmus of Scapa, at the northern end of which Kirkwall is situated, the most strategic location in Orkney. Further east again, the Deerness peninsula is separate from Mainland but for a narrow spit of shingle and sand.

North of Mainland are the North Isles, divisible into those which are close-in and reached by small local boats and those further out across the Stronsay and Westray Firths. These more distant islands are reached by inter-island ship from Kirkwall. The inner isles include Rousay, Egilsay, Wyre, Gairsay and Shapinsay; the last mentioned is so close to Kirkwall as to be called the suburban island. It alone is well populated; Gairsay is now quite empty and the others have few people for their size. The outer isles include Westray and Papa Westray, Sanday, North Ronaldsay and Stronsay, all of which are well populated, and Eday which is seriously depopulated. Most of these islands, except for Papa Westray and North Ronaldsay, can be seen in clear weather from Wideford Hill near Kirkwall.

South of Mainland are the South Isles, composed of Hoy which is hilly (the name means 'high island') and an eastern group of Burray and South Ronaldsay. Since the second World War the last two have been joined to Mainland by the four Churchill Barriers, which carry a main road. A scatter of low islands between Hoy and South Ronaldsay encloses the sheltered inland sea of Scapa Flow, 50 square miles of deep water which served as a naval anchorage in two world wars. On Hoy, only forty people remain, including three who live on the Atlantic coast at Rackwick. The eastern South Isles are well populated.

Although Orkney is smaller than Shetland, 50 miles further north, it has a population slightly higher—about 17,100 in 1970 as against Shetland's 17,000.

MAINLAND PARISHES

The usual way to describe the location of a place in Mainland is by reference to the parish in which it stands. There are fourteen of these and they represent fairly clear and in many cases very obvious natural divisions of the country; some may have been pre-Christian administrative units. Their names mostly derive from the Old Norse tongue and describe some feature characteristic of each.

Kirkwall means 'church bay'. Most probably the name records the existence of a Celtic church at this place when the Norsemen landed. Around Kirkwall is the parish of St Ola or Olav, named after a notable Norwegian royal saint who once visited Orkney. East of Kirkwall is the parish of Holm, pronounced 'ham'; this name probably refers to the small islands or holms which lie between its southern shore and the island of Burray, or it may simply mean 'remote place'. Most of it was heathland until the present century. St. Andrews and Deerness occupy the extreme east of Mainland; the deer referred to were red deer, whose bones lie in Orkney peat-bogs.

West of Kirkwall, Firth parish consists mainly of the coastal lowland around the Bay of Firth. At the head of this bay stands the village of Finstown, founded by an Irishman called Phinn. Nearby is the home of the Rt Hon Jo Grimond, member of parliament for Orkney and Shetland for many years and re-founder of the liberal party after World War II. To the north, Evie and Rendall face the island of Rousay across Eynhallow (Holy Island) Sound. Evie means 'swirl' and undoubtedly refers to the fierce tidal eddies off shore. Rendall probably means 'cleared valley'. Inland, the central depression of West Mainland is occupied by parts of three parishes: Harray, the only parish without a sea coast, meaning 'hunting territory', Birsay in the north meaning 'fortress island' (the Brough of Birsay, brough being pronounced in the same way as broch) and Stenness, named from the standing stones near the peninsula or ness of Brodgar. Sandwick on the Atlantic coast takes its name from the sand dunes of Skaill Bay, and Stromness from the ness which juts out into the tidal stream or roost of Hoy Sound. Turning back east towards Kirkwall along the shore of Scapa Flow, Orphir parish signifies 'place of ebbing' and seems to refer to the tidal islet called Holm of Howton.

So far, no explanation has been given of the name Orkney itself; indeed its meaning is difficult to establish with certainty. It appears to consist of two words drawn from two quite different languages. The first syllable probably comes from the Celtic word *orc*, meaning a wild boar, and it is thought that this animal, which once lived in Orkney, must have been some kind of totem or symbol for the island people. The second syllable is the Old Norse *ey*, an island, which is often written -ay or -a in other island names in Orkney. The name Orkney therefore seems to mean 'islands of the wild boar people'.

Page 17 Old Man of Hoy, a 450ft sandstone pillar, with MV *St Ola* off shore

Page 18 West Mainland cliffs, Yesnaby

GETTING TO ORKNEY

There are two interesting ways of reaching Orkney from the south and one rather dull one. The best and least expensive is by the passenger and vehicle ferry from Scrabster (Thurso) to Stromness across the Pentland Firth. Thurso has a rail link with Inverness. There is a 27 mile sea crossing which can be a memorable delight in summer and memorable for quite different reasons in winter. The route is a spectacular one, past the 450ft Old Man of Hoy, the largest sea-stack in Britain, and the towering cliffs of St John's Head. Alternatively one may go by air from Wick to Kirkwall's airport of Grimsetter by BEA. Cars may be left at Wick aerodrome. The flight is made at a very low altitude and takes only a few minutes; it affords unrivalled views of the splendid cliffs and sea-stacks of Duncansby, the Pentland Firth and Stroma and Scapa Flow. The flights are made daily and Wick has daily air connections with Glasgow via Inverness and Edinburgh via Aberdeen. From Grimsetter some planes fly on to Shetland.

Much less interesting from a scenic point of view is the approach by ship from Aberdeen, on which route cars can be taken. There is little to be seen until the ship passes through the String between Shapinsay and Mainland and turns into Kirkwall Bay.

Once in Orkney it is absolutely essential to have or to hire transport of one's own, be it car or cycle. Without this it is almost impossible to reach most places of interest, since there is little public transport. Roads are excellent throughout Orkney. Areas of good moorland or coastal walking are widely separated from each other and none can be reached at all conveniently from either Kirkwall or Stromness without transport.

ORKNEY LANDSCAPES

As one approaches Orkney from Scrabster past the palisades of Hoy, one's first impression is of high and hilly islands. In fact, Orkney is generally a country of broad lowlands and low, gentle hills. Except in Hoy no hill reaches the 1,000ft contour. Mainland's highest summit is the Ward Hill in Orphir, only

B

881ft. In the North Isles, Blotchniefiold in Rousay reaches 821ft.

Generally speaking, Orkney is a land of western hills and eastern lowlands, though there are a good many exceptions to this rule. The hills always seem higher than they really are because of their nearness to the sea. To find the finest stretches of cliffed coast-line one goes first to the west where the higher ground faces the Atlantic. The lowlands of the east run down to curving bays and low headlands looking out to sheltered sea channels, a very different though equally spacious and inspiring kind of coastal scenery.

Looking at the map it would almost seem that certain hilly islands such as Rousay and Eday have been sundered from their lowland sections in some far-off time, leaving them inhospitable to man. Other islands, such as Sanday and North Ronaldsay, are wholly low-lying. In consequence they lack the peat which was until recently the only available fuel for most Orkney house-holds. The people of Sanday had to cut their peat in Eday and bring it home by boat. Of all the outer islands, Westray is that with the most perfect combination of upland and lowland.

In Mainland there is subtle landscape variety rather than strong contrast. There is for example a clear difference between the parishes of Sandwick and Harray in the number, size and dis-tribution of farms and houses. In Sandwick the farm buildings are evenly spread over the countryside and are surrounded by large, very regular fields. In Harray and also in the neighbouring parts of Birsay and Stenness, the heart of the west Mainland depression, the landscape is much less regular and tidy. There, a very large number of small houses are scattered over the land in no apparent order. This difference has nothing to do with soil fertility or any other physical condition; it results from the per-sistence of ancient Norse property and inheritance arrangements in Harray and their virtual extinction in Sandwick, and this in turn can only be explained by reference to events and conditions in the sixteenth and seventeenth centuries.

Hardly any part of Orkney is out of sight of the sea. The main exception is the low central plain of west Mainland mainly in the parish of Harray. This plain is enclosed by low hills and contains the shallow lochs of Harray, which is fresh, and Stenness which

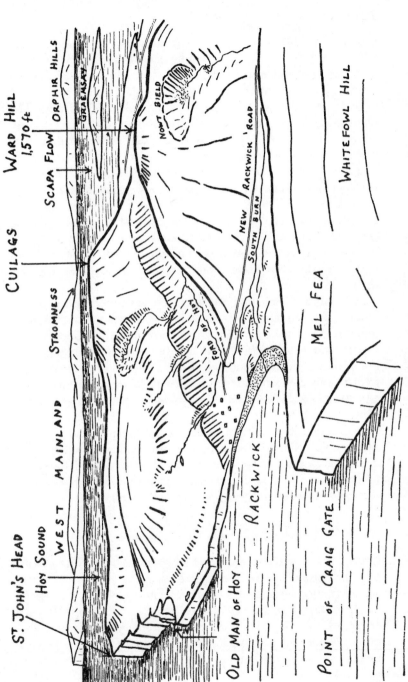

A panorama of the hills and coast of north Hoy, looking northward over Rackwick bay

ST. JOHN'S HEAD

HOY SOUND

WEST MAINLAND

STROMNESS

CUILAGS

SCAPA FLOW

WARD HILL
1,570 ft

ORPHIR HILLS

GRAEMSAY

NOWT BIELD

OLD MAN OF HOY

RACKWICK

ASH

FORD OF

NEW RACKWICK ROAD

SOUTH BURN

MEL FEA

WHITEFOWL HILL

POINT OF CRAIG GATE

is tidal. The central plain is a mysterious place, especially on days when cloud lies on the surrounding hills and seems to make its isolation from the world outside absolute. Much of the plain is farmed, but there are tracts of moor and bog which are sombre even on sunny days and are quite untypical of Orkney. The plain has a history of remoteness, inaccessibility, independence and poverty. The air of mystery is enhanced by the splendid pre-historic monuments which stand here, relics of a culture totally forgotten, stranded among modern fields. Maeshowe is a mighty neolithic burial mound; we cannot tell who raised it or for whom it was prepared. The henge monuments of Stenness and Brodgar with their attendant standing stones suggest that the principal centre of a Bronze Age religious ceremonial once lay here; but of the nature of that religion or the purpose of the great stone circles we know almost nothing, and it seems unlikely that we ever shall.

Hoy stands in splendid and spectacular contrast to the rest of Orkney. Its southern end is low-lying, but predominantly it is an island of steep heathery hills. At its northern end stand the two shapely summits of Ward Hill, 1,570ft and the Cuilags, a little lower. The distinctive outlines of these two hills, separated by a trench-like valley, dominate almost every southward view in Orkney Mainland. Where the Cuilags meet the Atlantic some of Britain's most breathtaking cliffs occur. St John's Head towers 1,140ft above the sea and is the highest perpendicular cliff in Britain. The cliffs of Foula in Shetland are higher but they are much less sheer. Two miles south of St John's Head stands the Old Man of Hoy. To be appreciated in their full majesty both cliffs and sea-stack need to be seen from the land.

FARMS AND SETTLEMENTS

Orkney is a country of dispersed farms and houses. The absence of villages usually strikes the English visitor as rather odd. Houses are distributed more or less evenly over the lowlands, with small, loose clusterings at strategic points, usually a crossroads. In these crossroad clusterings one finds usually at least one general shop, a public house and perhaps a garage. Churches tend to stand by themselves out in the country. The nearest approach to a village in the English sense is probably Dounby in west Mainland. It is mainly a twentieth-century creation and straddles the boundaries of three parishes.

Small clusterings of houses occur at various points around the coast, and most used to look to the sea rather than to the land for their livelihood. St Margaret's Hope in South Ronaldsay once shared the commerce of Kirkwall and Stromness, and is now experiencing some revival of its seaborne trade. Most other small settlements are much newer than this and represent deliberate attempts during the nineteenth century to develop fishing in the islands. Whitehall in Stronsay, once a great base for the herring fishery, Pierowall in Westray and Finstown in west Mainland originated in this way. Finstown is now a dormitory suburb for Kirkwall and is much favoured by retired people.

Crofting as the term is understood in Shetland or the Hebrides is unknown, though Orkney counts as one of the Crofting Counties of Scotland for administrative purposes. Its farming, however, is in general modern. Aberdeen-Angus beef cattle are the mainstay of the farming and are shipped in large numbers from Kirkwall and Stromness for sale live in Aberdeen. To feed the cattle, most cultivated land in Orkney is under grass for grazing, hay or silage, or fodder crops, mainly oats and roots. There are some dairy cattle in Mainland; cheese and milk products, but not fresh milk, are exported. Sheep are kept in some numbers but on the farms, not on the hill land. The sheepless uplands of Orkney are a great surprise to visitors from Shetland, where thousands of sheep roam the hill commons under the control of clerks of the grazings. In Orkney the uplands have not been common for over a century, except in Hoy. Until recently hens were kept on every Orkney farm and eggs were a principal export, but numbers and exports are now much reduced.

Fishing is not at present very important. It is roughly correct to think of the Orcadian as a farmer who occasionally fishes, in contrast with the Shetlander who is a fisherman with a smallholding. Most Orcadians have nothing directly to do with fishing. Nevertheless there are today some quite significant new fishing developments in Orkney, notably in Stromness where local fishermen have established a co-operative to handle crab and lobster, in Stronsay where there is fishing for white-fish as well as for lobster and crab, and in Westray, where lobster and crab processing are also important.

THE ORCADIANS

Who are the Orkney people? Orcadians do not have a Scots accent as the term is commonly understood. If anything their speech is reminiscent of County Antrim; it is of course similar to that of Shetland. Its distinctive cadence derives from the Old Norse tongue. Orkney is not part of the Gaelic west; its strongest ethnic and historical links are with Norway and with the Scottish lowlands.

Roughly a thousand years ago Orkney was colonised by the Norsemen, but before they came there was a substantial population in the islands. The monuments of this early people dot the land in rich profusion, suggesting that the islands were both populous and prosperous according to the standards of the times. Before the coming of the Norwegians Orkney was brought under the political domination of the Picts and within the sphere of influence of the Celtic Christian church. And yet, except for the archaeology, nothing remains of these early peoples, who presumably spoke a Celtic language. So far as we can tell the Norsemen came in such numbers as to erase the entire culture of their predecessors.

Today Orkney still bears a strong Norse imprint. Virtually every ancient place-name is Norse. Despite close scrutiny no certain example of a pre-Norse farm-name has yet been identified. The dispersed form of settlement is distinctively Scandinavian. Many Orkney personal names are of Norse origin. The old part of Kirkwall still has the look of a Norwegian town, especially if one mentally substitutes timber for stone as the building material. Stromness, though much newer, has a similar aspect; its pattern of development compares very closely with Norwegian coastal towns such as Måløy.

The traditional Orkney house derives directly from the Norse long-house; there are a great number of examples falling to ruin scattered throughout the Orkney countryside. Norse law and custom were established to the exclusion of all other, and some aspects of both survive today; free fishing has already been mentioned. In Norse times the land was held by yeomen farmers, called odallers, who held their farms in absolute freehold and owed allegiance in the feudal sense to no man. There are still some odallers in modern Orkney. Under the Norwegian crown, government in Orkney was exercised by a line of earls, some of whom were men of great distinction. Some made themselves in effect rulers of an independent principality. Details of their exploits have come down to us in the Orkneyinga Saga, one of the most eventful and readable of the surviving Norse sagas. When the Norsemen eventually became Christian they built churches in many parts of Orkney. The finest of these was St Magnus Cathedral in Kirkwall, a building of exceptional size and beauty for its time and place. Bishops of Orkney were subject to the See of Nidaros. The Orkney people spoke the Norn, a variant of Old Norse, now extinct.

For the better part of five hundred years, Norse influence and rule were supreme in Orkney. But the sea lanes back to Norway were long and liable to interruption by storms in winter. It was therefore hardly surprising that, as political power and organisation developed in mainland Scotland, the situation of the Norsemen in their off-shore islands became more and more precarious. Scots immigration into Orkney gathered momentum. Finally in 1468 Orkney was pledged by King Christian I of Denmark and Norway to the Scots Crown, in the person of James III. Strictly speaking the islands have remained 'in pawn' ever since and theoretically redeemable by Denmark. The Scottish parliament chose to ignore this fact and formally annexed the islands to Scotland in 1471.

It is a far cry from those days to ours. In the intervening centuries Orkney first lapsed into a profound remoteness and obscurity in consequence of its terminal position at the farthest end of Scotland. Although there were here and there faint glimmerings of light engendered by overseas trade, this dark age continued until the nineteenth century. Then, a number of progressive estate owners introduced the ideas of 'High Farming' and estate management which had been developed by the Earl of Leicester and others and began the transformation of the Orkney countryside. Two great wars in our own century greatly accelerated the transforming process. Scapa Flow became a naval base in both wars while in the second much capital was pumped into the islands by the stationing of a large garrison there. Beginning in the 1920s Orkney changed from being a land of estates and tenant-farmers into a land of owner-occupiers working family farms.

It is hard to say whether the present-day Orcadians have a distinctive appearance. A considerable number are rather squarely built and of medium height, with somewhat broad faces, fresh complexions which often become deeply lined in later life, and fair, wavy hair. Otherwise there seem to be no general physical characteristics common to a large number of people.

There are the strong Norse and Scottish strains which were introduced by the two major colonisations of the islands in historic times. The Norsemen introduced such distinctive Orkney surnames as Flett, Scarth, Firth, Heddle, Sclater, Skea, Foubister and Linklater, while from Scotland came names such as Spence, Craigie, Leask, Fraser, Pottinger, Reid, Louttit and Bell.

There are in addition many people whose ancestors were shipwrecked mariners, and in view of the thousands of wrecks which have occurred on Orkney coasts it would be astonishing if this were not so. It is also said that the Hudson Bay connection brought some North American Indian blood into the Stromness district, and that the crew of a Spanish galleon wrecked at the time of the Armada were responsible for some distinctive physical characteristics in Westray.

The general impression of a people whose origins are very mixed is, as we shall see, supported by the history of these islands.

O RKNEY is a land of flagstones. It is also very old, in geological terms. Except in a few limited areas in south-west and west Mainland, the islands are built entirely of sedimentary rocks of Devonian (Old Red Sandstone) age. In this respect Orkney closely resembles the lowland county of Caithness across the Pentland Firth and is quite different from the Scottish highlands, the Hebrides and most of Shetland, which are built for the most part of ancient rocks of volcanic origin or of ancient sedimentaries that have been much altered by heat and pressure. In fact, these more ancient rocks—granites and schists, which are estimated to be thousands of millions of years old—are the foundation on which the Orkney sandstones lie, and they appear at the surface, in Orkney, only in small outcrops chiefly near Stromness, on the west Mainland coast and in Graemsay.

None of the younger sedimentary rocks are now to be found in Orkney, though this area of Britain has certainly had such deposits laid down upon it and subsequently stripped off by erosion. Only a few small volcanic dykes, injected from below into fissures of the sandstone and some small areas of basalt on Hoy remain to bespeak the geological history of the islands. Otherwise there are only very recent deposits indeed—the relics left by ice sheets, blown sand, and peat.

THE SANDSTONES

The Old Red Sandstones are among the oldest sediments in Britain, dating from a time when the fishes first rose to prominence, the earliest trees and the first spiders appeared, and ammonites and primitive amphibians came into existence—some 350–400 million years ago. They are often red in colour—as they are in Devonshire and Herefordshire—but in Orkney the colour can easily be exaggerated. If one comes to the islands by sea from Scrabster, the initial impression is of the magnificent red cliffs of Hoy. In Kirkwall, the red stones in St Magnus Cathedral are likely to make an immediate impression. But wider acquaintance with the landscapes of Orkney shows that browns, greys and ochres are more usual colours.

Many of the rocks are true flagstones divided into thin and regular beds. Some are so finely divided that the layers can be split off and used as roofing flags. Others are thicker and make good paving stone. Others again are more solid and slabby and yield easily fashioned blocks of building stone. These are true sandstones, and one of the most attractive comes from the island of Eday. It also occurs in Mainland, and the stone of St Magnus Cathedral, which is of this type, is thought to have been quarried at Head of Holland east of Kirkwall.

The Orkney rocks are not generally very hard; though grindstones could be made from some of them, they were only hard enough to grind bere, a relatively soft grain. Grindstones of Millstone Grit from the Pennines had to be imported to deal with oats. From prehistoric times down to the present day, Orcadian builders both public and domestic have made skilful use of the available building stones. The use of thinly laminated flagstone as a substitute for wood has been a characteristic and persistent feature of building in treeless Orkney.

The Old Red Sandstones are divided by geologists according to their age—and position—into three groups; only the Middle and Upper Old Red Sandstones are represented in Orkney. The Middle group is subdivided in turn into three series, differing somewhat in colour and characteristics, thus giving differences in landscape and in the building materials that we have already remarked.

Mainland and the North Isles are built of Middle Old Red sediments laid down in shallow fresh water. By totalling the thicknesses of all the layers of sediment it can be shown that at least a 14,000ft thickness was deposited. This is a minimum estimate because some beds may have been eroded away before those above were laid down. The growing weight of the muds and sands being deposited seems to have caused the floor of the ancient lake to sink, thus allowing the whole tremendous thickness of deposits to be accumulated in shallow water. The complete sequence of beds cannot, of course, be observed at any one place, otherwise the hills of Orkney would be very much higher than they are. In fact they never overlapped completely, and the erosion, tilting and faulting which have taken place since they were deposited makes it necessary to travel from place to place throughout the whole island group to find examples from the various levels.

The lowest of the sandstones belong to, the Stromness series and occur mainly in west Mainland. They are mostly ochreous, thinly laminated flagstones which weather into excellent soils and produce splendid cliff architecture. Above the Stromness series lie the Rousay flagstones, generally more slabby and grey in colour. They underlie the peat-covered uplands of Rousay and the forbidding moors of Harray. However, the Rousay series also includes sediments which produce lowlands and good soils, and the fertile islands of Shapinsay, Westray and Sanday, and also east Mainland, are founded upon Rousay beds. Similar variations occur in the Eday series of rocks which overlie the Rousay. Eday sandstones and flagstones occur in Eday itself, Deerness and South Ronaldsay. Clearly, the threefold division of Orkney rocks into Stromness, Rousay and Eday series goes only part of the way to explaining the arrangement of hills and lowlands. Differences within the series themselves are nearly as important.

The Stromness sequence includes the fish beds, long famous for their fossil remains. These are quite thin deposits which have been much quarried for building and road stone in west Mainland. A notable fossil specimen is preserved in Stromness museum. Today it is hard to find good fossils, because most of the small quarries are abandoned and flooded and because of the use of mechanical diggers in the large quarry on Cruaday Hill in Sandwick. But one may be lucky.

Hoy is scenically quite distinct from the rest of Orkney because it is almost wholly built in Upper Old Red Sandstones. These are found nowhere else in Orkney, are extremely hard and massive and for the most part are distinctively reddish or orange colour. They form the hills which rise north-westward from Melsetter towards the summits of Ward Hill, the highest point in Orkney, and the Cuilags. Their hard and slabby strata, exposed to

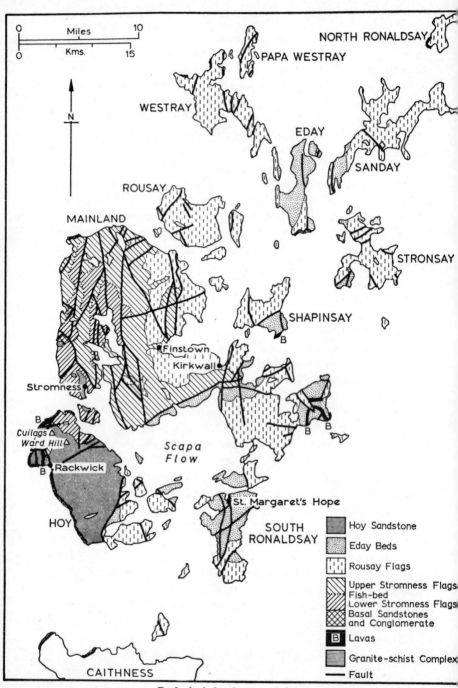

Geological sketch map of Orkney

the fury of Atlantic storms, have been weathered into the fantastic cliffs of western Hoy.

SEQUENCE OF OLD RED SANDSTONE
(becoming progressively older downwards)

Upper Old Red Sandstone

Hoy Sandstones	At least 3,500ft thick	Confined to Hoy and forming the hills and cliff scenery of the island
Hoy Volcanics	400ft thick	Basalt lavas deposited on an ancient land surface. Visible in cliff sections and forming a pedestal beneath the Old Man of Hoy

Between the deposition of the Upper and the Middle Sandstone groups there was a gap in time, of unknown duration, since the younger rocks lie unconformably and not successively upon the older.

Middle Old Red Sandstone

Eday Beds	At least 4,000ft thick	Occurring in Eday, east Mainland, and South Ronaldsay; a series of flagstones and sandstones, the latter providing the building stones for St Magnus Cathedral
Rousay Beds	At least 5,500ft thick	Sandstones which have weathered into low hills, as in west Mainland and Rousay; flagstones which produce lowlands, often scenically monotonous as in Shapinsay and east Mainland
Stromness Beds	At least 4,600ft thick	Finely laminated flagstones weathering to good soils and forming fine cliff scenery of west Mainland

On the east of the island there is a low platform of cultivated country at the hill foot. This is a detached portion of the Stromness flagstone terrain of Mainland. The abrupt break of slope between it and the hills shows that here also a major break occurs in the sequence of deposits. After the Stromness flags had been laid down in the Devonian lake, the land was uplifted and for thousands and perhaps millions of years exposed to denudation by the agencies of weather and streams. There was a period of intense volcanic activity which produced a thick covering of ash and lavas in certain areas; this period is represented today by the Hoy Volcanics. Thereafter there was a renewed submergence and the Upper Old Red Sandstones were laid down on what had already become an old and eroded land surface.

OTHER ROCKS

Exposures of the ancient rocks of the basement foundation of Orkney have already been referred to as being very limited in extent. The largest exposures are around Stromness, near Yesnaby on the west coast of Mainland, and in north Graemsay. Behind Stromness town is a quite steep hill called Brinkies Brae. From the top of this hill a superb view opens out, taking in the southwest coast of Mainland, Hoy Sound and the Hoy hills and Scapa Flow. But in the foreground some very un-Orcadian walls are to be seen, made from rounded boulders instead of flagstones. The local terrain is also distinctly un-Orcadian in appearance; 'knobbly' might be an appropriate description. There are rounded outcrops of bare, smooth rocks in the fields. Closer inspection of walls and outcrops shows both to consist of a hard grey-and-pink non-sedimentary rock, much like the rocks of the central Highlands. This is the so-called granite-schist complex of the immensely old Pre-Cambrian foundation of Orkney. Moreover, evidence of its greater age—in the light of knowledge of the structural history of northern Britain—can be seen quite close by.

If one walks to the shore beyond Stromness golf course the granite may be seen exposed on the beach close to a gaunt wartime lookout tower. Westward a short distance from this point, the finely bedded sandstones, which are here yellowish-brown, abut against the granite, and the granite disappears beneath them a few yards further west. The break in sequence between the two rocks represents a vast gulf of time—all the aeons that came between the formation and metamorphosis of the Pre-Cambrian rocks and the settlement of the sediments that hardened into the Middle Old Red Sandstone as we know it now. Any intervening deposits that were laid down were entirely eroded.

Tens of millions of years are represented here by a gap of less than an inch.

Between the solid granite and the flagstones is a zone of less solid granitic rock which looks very much like a concrete conglomerate. Looking closely one may see lumps of pinkish granite embedded in a kind of matrix or cementing material. Here it seems the granite once stood up as low rocky islands in a stormy sea or lake and this concrete-like rock is an ancient beach material consolidated by great pressure in later times, when it was buried beneath the Old Red sediments. One may also see that the granite islands had steep sides, for the granite disappears from sight at a steep angle both here and at other places on the west coast of Mainland.

The younger volcanic rocks include those of Hoy, interposed between the eroded surface of the Middle Old Red Sandstones and the Hoy Sandstone, and a number of volcanic dykes which were intruded into fissures in the Middle Old Red Sandstones. These dykes do not create the typical upstanding or trench features that are associated with dykes in other parts of Scotland. They generally lie along NE–SW axes, typical of the grain of the folds and pressures exerted upon the country in these early geological times. Good examples may be seen on the cliff top at Yesnaby.

SHAPING THE LAND

Although the characteristics of the various rocks are important in determining the character of the Orcadian landscapes, the structural processes of earth movements, folding and faulting and the effects of glaciation and weathering have been the significant factors in fashioning the details of the present-day landscape. Even a casual inspection of the sandstones shows that the strata have been tilted from their original more or less horizontal position. This tilting is very striking along the cliffs of west Mainland where the whole country seems about to slide down into the sea below. Tilting in various directions may be seen elsewhere. It results from deep-seated and slow movements in the crust of the earth which have folded the sediments of Orkney into a number of gentle arches and troughs. West Mainland is today a depression, with low hills to west and east. The tilt or dip of the strata shows that this depression was originally an upfold, the higher central parts of which have been worn away by weathering and stream action so that the area that was once highest is now low.

Although the folding was gentle it nevertheless caused much cracking and faulting in the brittle Orkney sandstones and flags. Fault lines often stand out clearly in the modern scenery, for example along the north shores of Scapa Flow. Approaching Kirkwall by road from Orphir, from Stromness by the old high road over Wideford Hill or from the Churchill Barriers, one may

Development of cliff architecture: from left to right, caves; a geo or inlet; a gloup or blow-hole; natural arch; sea-stack; stump

see the clear lines of the faults which form the shores of Scapa Bay and converge to produce the Scapa Gap, at the north end of which Kirkwall stands. Faulting is also partly responsible for many of the sharpest cliff lines in Orkney, and for the spectacular clefts which cut right through the island of Hoy on either side of Ward Hill. The great cliffs of Hoy are almost certainly fault-guided features.

Where cracking, folding and fissuring occur near the sea, the scene has been set by nature for the production of splendid cliff architecture. On the west coast of Mainland from Black Craig northwards there is a seemingly endless succession of headlands, bays and narrow trench-like inlets called geos, together with caves, gloups or blow-holes, arches and sea-stacks in every stage of development and destruction. Excellent cliff scenery is to be found on the north coast of Mainland, in Deerness, the east coast of South Ronaldsay, and in Westray and Rousay. For sheer scale,

Page 35 (above) The Dwarfie Stone, Hoy, a neolithic rock-hewn tomb; (below) the entrance passage to the chambered cairn of Maeshowe

Page 36 *(above)* Skara Brae, a neolithic village on the Bay of Skaill, showing built-in cupboard contrived out of sandstone slabs and boulders. The shoreline is now encroaching on the village site; *(below)* the Broch of Borwick, an Iron Age fort about 1½ miles south of Skara Brae on west coast of Mainland, showing low entrance

however, Hoy cliffs are without parallel, and a walk along them from Rackwick to the Old Man of Hoy and St John's Head is one of the great walks of Britain.

The folding and fissuring of the rocks happened long ago, even in terms of geological time. Since then, the portion of the earth's surface we now call Orkney has undergone many changes. At times it was buried beneath thousands of feet of rocks which have since been stripped off by erosion. At other times it lay submerged far beneath the sea. Once the tops of the Hoy hills may have formed part of a broad plain near sea level. Later, there seems to have been land, perhaps a continent now vanished, away to the north-west, from which flowed large rivers, cutting deep valleys which are now the sounds and firths between the islands. Eynhallow Sound between Mainland and Rousay, Hoy Sound and perhaps the Pentland Firth itself may be drowned sections of these ancient valleys. But much of this is supposition which cannot be proved. Too much evidence has vanished without trace for the complete story of Orkney's scenery to be reconstructed.

The events of a more recent period—glaciation during the Ice Age—can be more precisely charted. About one million years ago, as the earth's climate began to cool and the polar ice-caps began to grow, first snow and then ice must have gathered on the Hoy hills and gradually spread to the lower ground. As the climate grew more frigid, ice sheets spread to Orkney from Scandinavia and later from the mainland of Scotland. The moving ice smoothed the Orkney hills into their present shapes, a relatively easy and probably quite rapid process upon the sandstones.

On Hoy true glaciers developed, creating the deep corries we see today. The finest examples are the Kame of Hoy, shaped like an arm-chair in the north-western Cuilags opposite Stromness, into which one looks from the ferry boat from Scrabster, Quoyawa which faces Graemsay, and the Nowt Bield opposite the Dwarfie Stone, both in Ward Hill. The two most northerly valleys of Hoy exhibit most of the classical glacial landforms of U-shape, hanging tributaries and truncated spurs.

When the ice at last melted it left a deposit of clay over most of Orkney. So complete is this clay cover that solid rock is rarely to be seen inland; the steep Hoy hills are the main exceptions.

c

During the melting stage, when the ground was still without vegetation, there was a long period of very cold climate and it is from this cheerless time that the bare rocky 'pavements' on the summits of the Hoy hills originate, as well as the great gashes cut by torrents of meltwater on the flanks of these same hills. Oddly enough, these precipitous gulleys are called glens in Orkney; large valleys never carry this name, as they do in mainland Scotland.

The existence of the glacial deposits has been of the utmost significance to Orkney's agricultural development. In combination with the underlying sandstone, they have produced a fertile, often easily drained soil of good structure that is the basis of the island's farming.

The most significant differences between the landscapes immediately after the Ice Age and those of today are in the height of sea level and the extent of low ground available for settlement. During the Ice Age the level of the sea was lowered by about 300ft through the engrossing of vast quantities of ocean water into the ice sheets. With the melting of the ice the waters thus released rose, probably over a long period of time to judge by the fact that trees had time to become established on some shorelines before they were submerged. Submerged remnants of trees *in situ* have been found at several places around the coasts, such as at Finstown and Skaill Bay. However, simultaneously with a gradual rise in sea level there was in northern Scotland an accompanying uplift of the land. It would appear that the great weight of ice depressed the land during the Ice Age by an unknown amount, and that when the ice melted a process of recovery or uplift took place. It is not known to what extent this depression and recovery affected Orkney, which never carried as great a thickness of ice as, say, the Highlands. If there was little postglacial uplift in Orkney, then the Pentland Firth must have been flooded at a relatively early date, destroying the land link with Caithness. Any uplift would of course delay its flooding. As to climatic conditions in prehistoric times, we have little direct evidence from Orkney, but much is known about the general pattern of events around the North Atlantic and North Sea margins, mainly from researches in Scandinavia and Britain. The main doubts lie in the exact dating of the various changes.

It seems clear that a chilly late-glacial climate persisted in the north of Scotland until around 8000 BC. Then, a warming-up occurred. By about 7500 BC the so-called Boreal phase was established which lasted some 2,000 years. Conditions were more 'continental' than today, with considerably warmer summers, probably less rain and less wind, and trees such as rowan, elder, birch and hazel grew in Orkney, apparently in some profusion. An Atlantic phase followed, from about 5500 to 2500 BC, during which conditions were still probably warmer than at present, but there was an increase in rain and a decrease in temperature-range between winter and summer. By this time, it is assumed, groups of people of stone age culture had reached Orkney. Relatively warm conditions seem to have continued, with fluctuations, until about 700 BC when there was an onset of cooler weather. Climatic fluctuations have continued down to modern times. During the wetter and colder climatic phases, thick accumulations of peat developed on the Orkney uplands, and at times spread onto lower ground. Warmer and drier conditions resulted in the erosion and retreat of the peat margins.

Relating the sea-level adjustments and the climatic fluctuations, it would appear that the Pentland Firth was dry land as late as the Boreal period, and that the sea was then about 150ft below its present level. Both animals and plant seeds were spreading northwards as the climate improved and could still cross freely into Orkney. Then the Pentland land-bridge vanished beneath the rising waters, so that man, when he came first in the Atlantic period, had a sea crossing to make much as that of today. He almost certainly found open woodland of small trees on the Orkney lowlands, and general conditions would be rather less wet than they are today. Sea level was a little lower than at present, and it is probable that many early settlement sites, mere camps in fact, were coastal and have since disappeared beneath the waves.

Within historical times, the sea has encroached on some shores, exploring the weaknesses of the rock structure, on a large scale as in the Bay of Skaill, and on a small scale as in the Old Man of Hoy. Some authorities suggest that Orkney itself has subsided slightly, relative to sea level and to the land level of northern Scotland. It is certainly difficult to find clear traces of the raised beaches that mark the uplift of other Scottish coasts. However, despite this widespread appearance of subsidence and coastal drowning, there are sections of cliff which have undoubtedly been raised above the present level of wave attack in relatively recent times. One such section is the south-west coast of Mainland between Black Craig and Stromness which has examples of slightly raised clifflines and, near Billia Croo, a small uplifted sea-stack.

There seem to be two widely held views about Orkney weather. One was expressed succinctly in a wartime poem by Captain Hamish Blair, *Bloody Orkney*—'All bloody clouds and bloody rains'; the other is summarised in a more recent author's description of Orkney as a 'fairy archipelago set in a summer sea'. The visitor to Orkney should on no account allow himself to be deterred by the first view, with its dark hints of storm-lashed, cheerless islands, nor should he allow the second view with its suggestions of brilliant sun, seas of Mediterranean blue and balmy airs persuade him that Orkney is warmer, and its weather more certain, than it is.

The islands are in fact slightly nearer to the Arctic Circle than they are to London, and in consequence they are cool in summer, which is the season in which most people visit them. However, they are completely open to the Atlantic to the west and south-west and therefore they benefit from the south-westerly winds and ocean currents, both of tropical origin, which move across the North Atlantic thoughout the year. Because of these winds and currents, frost and snow are unusual in Orkney, and when they do occur are of short duration. But the mild westerlies also bring rain, which falls in every month of the year.

Average summer temperatures in Orkney are similar to those of west Norwegian fjords—about 13°C in July. Average winter temperatures, however, are remarkably mild. In January the islands have almost the same sea-level temperatures (about 4°C) as Morecambe Bay and the Sussex coast—and even further south, the northern Adriatic and Aegean shores and the southern islands of Japan. Since visitors rarely choose Orkney for a Christmas holiday in preference to the Sussex or Dalmatian coasts, there are clearly deterrent features of the Orcadian climate. The phenomena that distinguish it are wind, cloud and rain. Yet another factor of significance is a consequence of high latitude—extreme variations in day-length and in sun angle between summer and winter.

Wind is an ever-present feature of the Orkney scene. The air is almost never still, no matter how fine the day, hence the coolness of Orkney summers and the cutting edge of Orkney winters. This coolness and breeziness is enhanced by the general lack of natural shelter on the islands. There are no surviving native trees, except for some very small examples in the Hoy glens, and the hills are normally too low and smooth to give much protection. Thus wind is an important ingredient in virtually every Orkney weather mixture. Although the Norwegian fjords have similar temperatures to Orkney, their summers often seem much warmer because of the shelter of steep mountain sides and forest.

Evidence for the strength, persistence and dominant direction of the wind is supplied by the occasional plantings of trees which have been established in the lee of walls and houses. The trees grow sturdily enough up to the height of the protecting structure, then bend over almost at a right-angle towards the north-east. One usually thinks of trees sheltering houses; in Orkney houses shelter trees, and the largest trees on the islands are to be found in central Kirkwall. Some nineteenth-century estate owners intent on improvement tried to establish shelterbelts around their mansions, but the trees seldom reach as high as the first-floor windows. Balfour Castle on Shapinsay is a case in point. The Ordnance maps have no symbols to depict the special character of Orkney woodlands. Studying the map of Shapinsay, one has a brief vision of a great house in the south-west corner of the island, probably in Scots baronial style, glimpsed through a handsome belt of trees. In fact the trees are only a few feet high and the house stands up in full view, quite unprotected.

There is a small wood in Mainland, set in the narrow Binscarth valley above Finstown. The trees were planted following a careful survey of exposure and relative shelter by means of flags, which were set in all parts of the valley and observed for a year. This 'Binscarth' method has since been used by the Forestry Commission and other bodies concerned to establish trees in windy locations. It is interesting to compare this successful

41

planting with a small coniferous plantation at Hoy Lodge near the north-east corner of Hoy. The situation seems sheltered enough, yet the trees which were planted in 1953 are still very small indeed.

Wind sometimes comes in gale force, usually from the Atlantic, less frequently but perhaps more violently from the north-east. On average, gale-force winds blow for 24 days each year. Tremendous rollers crash against the cliffs, sending spray hundreds of feet into the air. This salt spray is carried to every part of Orkney; even in the central lowland of west Mainland, the most inland part of the county, the air carries a strong tang of salt. Salinity of the air combines with strong winds to inhibit plant growth of every kind, and growing crops are always subject to late springs, slow growth and late harvest. Salinity is thought to be at least as important as strong winds in preventing the growth of trees.

Unfortunately, Orkney gales can occur in any month of the year. Gales at harvest-time are rare, but have been disastrous, and that of August 1778 practically destroyed the whole food supply for the year, so that the enormous sum of £15,000 had to be spent on food imports. However, the summer visitor need not anticipate anything more drastic than awaking to the sounds of wind and driving rain, seeing the sun come out at breakfast time and enjoying a day of sun and occasional showers. There may in fact be no more rain that day, that week or even that month.

Most of the great twentieth-century gales have come in midwinter, those of 1952, 1953, 1962 and 1969 being especially memorable. The gale of January 1952 is always spoken of as the worst in living memory, and some salient details of it are recorded in *The New Orkney Book*. A wind-speed of 135 mph was recorded. This was exceeded by 1 mph at Kirkwall airport on 7 February 1969, and on that occasion the gale, which came from the north-east, was accompanied by much snow. 'Snow entombs Orkney . . . all roads blocked : ploughs escort hospital cases : ships aground : schools close'—so read *The Orcadian*. It remains to be seen whether this unusually heavy snowfall is the prelude to a series of colder winters. Evidence from Iceland, where the pack-ice returned to the north coast in 1965 after an absence of forty years, rather suggests a general cooling of the North Atlantic winter climate, but such evidence is inconclusive as yet. Meanwhile prophets of a new ice age may note that, when Murdoch Mackenzie made his great survey of Orkney in the 1750s he measured his base-line on the frozen waters of the Loch of Stenness.

Cloud is a dominant element in Orkney weather. In winter, only a small proportion of the total possible sunshine actually reaches the ground, and the persistent grey overcast can be depressing. In summer there is less cloud, and the constant winds produce splendid skyscapes and a fair proportion of sunny days. In still weather there can be dense white sea-fog, a hazard to sea and air navigation. In recent years, summers have been unusually dry and sunny in consequence of the North Atlantic depressions taking a more southerly course than normal and dropping most of their rain south of the Highlands. Fine summers may be another part of the possible climatic change referred to above, in which case Orkney may expect more summer visitors; but unfortunately there is no guarantee that the seemingly endless sunny days of 1967–9 will be regularly repeated.

Rainfall varies considerably in different parts of Orkney. The Hoy hills generate great banks of cloud when the wind is from the Atlantic, and are clearly much wetter than other parts, but there are no precise rainfall measurements for them; 60–100 inches (1,500–2,500mm) in a year may be somewhere near the mark. The rest of Orkney receives between 35 and 45 inches (880–1,150mm) of annual rainfall, the eastern parts of Mainland being drier than the west. Deerness is probably the driest part of all. Rainfall is often very local, and there is so much variation from year to year that a graph showing average figures for each month has little meaning. May and June are the driest months, and an early summer holiday in Orkney can be a delight, with little rain, sufficient sunshine and fresh spring-like colours in the landscape.

Finally, there is the question of day-length. In latitude 59° north this varies greatly between winter and summer, and this variation has a profound effect upon the whole 'feel' of Orkney weather. In January the sun rises shortly after 1000 hours and sets about 1615 hours (BST). When the sun is visible it is low in

43

the sky and the days are dark and dismal. However, the very long days of summer do much to compensate for winter darkness. On 21 June the sun is up before 0400 hours and does not set until after 2230 hours. On cloudless nights it never gets dark at all. Members of Stromness golf club often play until half an hour before midnight, while visitors from the south who have never previously read a newspaper at midnight out of doors have no difficulty in doing so. A feature of the lingering summer day is the Orkney sunset. Examples occur most regularly in May, June and July and their brilliance and wealth of colour have to be seen to be believed.

The severer aspects of Orkney's weather are to some extent offset by its distinctive pleasures. The splendour of summer sunsets has been mentioned; there is also a great purity and clarity of atmosphere and an ever-changing design of cloud and sunlight which give variety and a tremendous sense of space to the generally rather level Orkney landscapes. Living in the towns of the south one seldom notices the sky; in Orkney it is the dominant part of every prospect. The combination of sea, a smoothly rounded open land and an infinite variety of skyscape together constitute the unique character and charm of Orkney.

NATURAL HISTORY

The birds, animals, flowers and insects of Orkney are fit subjects for a separate book. It is impossible in a few words to do more than mention them. Naturalists and others who wish to follow their own special interests in the islands would be well advised to make initial contact with the Orkney Field Club, a very active body, or with the local representative of the Royal Society for the Protection of Birds, whose address may be had from the Orkney Tourist Organisation.

Hoy is the greatest treasure house of plant life in Orkney. It contains a rich variety of flowers including some rare alpines, and in the deep clefts (glens) cut by streams descending from Ward Hill and Cuilags grow the only indigenous trees in the islands: rowan (*Sorbus aucuparia*), hazel (*Corytus avellana*), birch (*Betula pubescens*), aspen (*Populus tremulus*) and sallow (*Salix atrocinerea*). But the visitor who has walked the hills of Sutherland will at once notice the absence of certain species, such as the sweet-scented bog myrtle (*Myrica gale*) which are common south of the Pentland Firth. Such absences may be explained by the early submergence of the Pentland land-bridge, by unfavourable climatic fluctuations since that submergence which eliminated the island colonies, or by an initial introduction in numbers so small as to make survival in isolation genetically impossible. In the case of bog myrtle, the second and third of these suggested explanations seem best fitted to explain its absence from Hoy; the species did reach Orkney, and has managed to survive on Eday. Dunes and shorelines have many splendid plants. The blue-flowered oyster plant is a rarity worth looking for. Angelica is another characteristic Orcadian plant which resembles hogweed, though it flowers later in the year. It is reputed to have been introduced by the Norsemen.

Of the insect life of the islands, it may be noted that midges can be a sore trial on Hoy on the rare summer days when it is warm and humid and there is no wind. More pleasantly, the lepidoptera (butterflies and moths) are well represented, and many migrants such as the Painted Lady (*Vanessa cardui*) make their way north along the lowland corridor of eastern Scotland. A collection of species so far recognised in Orkney was placed in Stromness museum in 1969. Much work remains to be done before the list is completed. No sooner had the collection been exhibited than a fine specimen of the Convolvulus Hawk Moth (*Sphinx convolvuli*), formerly unknown in Orkney, was taken by a young member of the Field Club.

One of the great glories of Orkney is in its colonies of sea-birds, which occur in great numbers and variety. Nowhere is their presence more spectacular than along the Atlantic cliffs of Hoy, where a profusion of gulls, guillemots, terns, kittiwakes, cormorants and skuas are to be seen, together with many other birds. The great skua, a huge brown bird with white markings, has recently multiplied in Orkney after a period of great rarity; now it is the terror of lesser birds.

There are even place-names which show that the Norse settlers, when they went round naming the features of the land, were well aware of the bird life. In Orkney the word 'chun' means a small lake; it is the equivalent of 'tarn' in northern England. The name

Loomachun occurs in several places, meaning the tarn of the red-throated diver. The species lives on most of these tarns today.

Around the coasts both grey and common seals abound, and they too have made their mark in Orkney place-names. Out in Scapa Flow there is a rock nearly submerged called the Barrel of Butter. This curious name records the form of annual rent paid by the people of Orphir in medieval times to their lord for the privilege of killing seals on the rock.

Orkney's mammals include a number which appear to have reached the islands themselves after the Ice Age and may therefore be termed native; there are several species known to have been introduced, and one, the Orkney vole, which is unique to the islands. There are some noteworthy absences of species found on the south side of the Pentland Firth, while at least one large animal, the red deer, is known to have become extinct since early Norse times. Reindeer antlers have been found in Orkney peat-bogs.

Native animals include the pygmy shrew, the rabbit which was formerly much more numerous than at present, having been drastically reduced by myxamatosis in the 1950s, the house mouse, otter and toad. Presumably these species crossed the Pentland land-bridge before rising post-glacial sea levels made it impassable. Frogs, newts and adders are absent; they seem to have reached northern Scotland too late to make the crossing to Orkney.

Of the introduced mammals the hedgehog is the most recent incomer. A few specimens were brought to Orkney about 1870 by a minister's sons. The subsequent history of this colony is unknown, but very probably it established itself as did a colony in Shetland at about the same date. A further introduction occurred during World War II, apparently by members of the garrison, and the animal is now widespread and fairly numerous in the islands.

On Hoy, the blue or alpine hare (*Lepus timidus*) may be a re-introduction, probably in the eighteenth century, following the extinction of a native race by hunting. This striking animal lives on the heathery hills in the north of the island, which are seamed with its arrow-straight tracks. In winter its greyish-brown coat turns to white, and this condition persists long after the snow has gone. In March and April the hares make brilliant flecks of white against the dark heather. Elsewhere in Orkney the brown hare is common, and has recently multiplied rapidly. It is not known whether or not it is a native species; it may have entered, or been brought to, Orkney later than the blue hare and displaced the latter in all islands save Hoy. Two other introduced mammals are the black rat, which found its way to Europe from the East in medieval times, and the brown or Norway rat, which reached Orkney in the eighteenth century.

Another animal long thought to be native but almost certainly present through human agency is the long-tailed field mouse (*Apodemus sylvaticus*). This species occurs widely in Europe and the British Isles; in recent years R. J. Berry and others have demonstrated by detailed skeletal examination that mice living in Shetland, the Hebrides and St Kilda, as well as other North Atlantic islands, are more nearly related to Norwegian than to Scottish mainland mice. At least fifteen races or subspecies have been identified on various islands, and each appears to descend from a very small group of initial mouse colonists, the peculiar genetic characteristics of which have affected the whole island population. There would appear to be little doubt that these island races were founded by mice which travelled with the food, domestic animals and bedding of Norse settlers. Unfortunately there have so far been no intensive skeletal examinations of Orkney mice, but it seems very likely that they also are closely related to the Norwegian form.

The one mammal species unique to Orkney is the Orkney vole (*Microtus orcadensis*), a subspecies, or perhaps a series of subspecies, of the European vole (*Microtus arvalis*), a species found in the British Isles only in Guernsey. The Orkney vole was first noted by the minister of Shapinsay in 1805, described for science by J. G. Millais, son of the painter, in 1904, and divided into five subspecies by G. S. Miller and M. A. C. Hinton shortly before World War I. Recent work has cast doubt upon the reality of these subdivisions.

In order to explain the occurrence of this animal in Orkney and nowhere else it has been suggested that it was the first species of vole to colonise the British Isles in the wake of the melting ice, and that it crossed to Orkney while the Pentland Firth was still dry land. Once there, it was protected by the post-glacial rise of sea level from the competition of two other vole species which displaced it throughout mainland Britain.

Unfortunately there is no evidence to support this theory, and the fact that Orkney voles appear to be related to Spanish forms of the animal suggests they may have been introduced accidentally in relatively recent times, perhaps from the Armada shipwreck on Westray. The distinctiveness of the Orkney subspecies would naturally result from the genetic peculiarities of a few individual animals being established throughout the island race. Such an explanation has one major objection, that voles are not normally to be found on board ships. The origin of these tiny but fascinating creatures therefore remains mysterious.

3   PREHISTORIC ORKNEY

ORKNEY contains, in its array of prehistoric monuments, a vast amount of evidence of its very early occupation by man. The islands, along with Caithness, have in them some of the most celebrated sites of neolithic times in the whole of Britain. If one could encompass in the imagination both the chronology and the significance of the many different kinds of sites, there would be revealed an astonishing sequence of human activity on these remote, windswept islands for at least 2,000 years before Christ. Yet we do not know when, by what means or by what route the first men reached Orkney, what language they spoke, or the name of a single individual among them. And it is impossible—as yet—to decipher from the evidence the exact relationships both in time and in culture between the various groups of prehistoric remains.

Of one type of monument alone—the chambered mounds— about fifty have been accounted for; several are known to have been destroyed during the past fifty to a hundred years. It is highly likely that very many more mounds as well as other remains have been destroyed during past centuries as men have sought stone for their houses and broken new ground for farmland. Archaeological interest in Orkney dates back to about 1850— Wideford Hill cairn was excavated by Petrie in 1849—and there is a fairly substantial literature published about it, though there remain gaps, unsolved as yet, in the time record. Only a few of the sites can be mentioned here; their selection is inevitably a personal one, of those which are more exciting and evocative of the past than others. Greater detail of some of the monuments is given in chapter 10, Places to Visit.

It is possible that primitive hunters, fishermen and food gatherers found their way to this northern extremity of Britain in the amelioration of weather conditions that followed the glacial period and long before the later Stone Age people who built the monuments. But no record of the most primitive cultures has so far been found; if such ever existed here it may have been destroyed through the encroachment of the sea upon the shoreline that has occurred within historical time.

BUILDERS IN STONE

The first inhabitants of whom we have knowledge were expert builders in stone. Their culture was neolithic and they seem to have been both pastoralists and hunters, gatherers of shellfish and cultivators. They tended cattle and sheep, both of which they presumably brought with them into Orkney. They hunted red deer and wild boar and made good use of the occasional stranded whale, not least for its bones. The grain they grew was very much like bere, the variety of barley which was a staple of Orkney agriculture until the present century and is still grown here and there. The buildings they raised, and especially their tombs, denote connections with the Atlantic margins of western Europe and the Mediterranean, but we do not know whether the actual individuals who reached Orkney came from Mediterranean bases. In view of their undoubted competence in navigation, there seems to be no reason why not. However, the culture they developed in this far northern corner of the world was in some respects distinctively Orcadian. Our knowledge of their culture is based chiefly on the discovery and interpretation of two kinds of remains : stone-built tombs and dwellings.

CHAMBERED CAIRNS

The stone-built tombs are generally called chambered cairns, but this is a different use of the word 'cairn' from that denoting a pile or pyramid of stones. For many years the tombs hidden beneath great, in some cases massive, earthen mounds were the only visible neolithic monuments in Orkney though the fact that they belonged to the neolithic period long remained unknown. The mounds are oval or round, in two cases crescent-shaped ('horned'), and Maeshowe is as much as 115ft in diameter. They were dated with fair certainty after the excavation of Onston

Cairn in west Mainland in 1884. There a large assemblage of grave-goods and pottery was unearthed and the pottery was related to the Windmill Hill ware of Wiltshire, which had already been dated as early neolithic. Allowing for a time-lag of a few centuries for a drift of the culture from southern to northern sites, it has been argued that this and similar cairns were built not later than about 1500 BC. In fact since travel by sea must have been at least as quick as travel by land in the neolithic period, the time-lag allowances would appear to be an unnecessary refinement.

Maeshowe

Successive excavations revealed two main types of cairn. All have a central chamber reached by a low tunnel. One type has this chamber divided into recesses or 'stalls' by large slabs of flagstone placed vertically; the second has stone-built cells opening off the central chamber. The most spectacular examples of the first type have their central chambers enlarged and greatly elongated, with a great many burial stalls. The finest examples are to be found in Rousay at Midhowe and Yarso. The second type is best exemplified by the superb Maeshowe. Onston itself has features of both the two main types and is unique in this respect.

Many variants of the two types have been identified, including a

51

two-storey development of the second type at Taiverso Tuick in Rousay and Huntersquoy in Eday. The elaborate subtleties of cairn development are discussed by V. Gordon Childe in *The Northern Isles*, edited by F. T. Wainwright.

It is believed that chambered cairns were communal burial chambers, one might say family vaults. It can only be conjectured that they served a neolithic family or tribal group and that they were used—or re-used—probably over quite a long period of time, though the number of human remains identified in them is in fact limited. One might hazard a guess that the two types represent different patterns of such tombs, or possibly a hybrid development of designs, that reached Orkney by a route through the western isles of Scotland and another through the eastern lowlands and Caithness. Some of the mounds were probably built, used and deserted before others were constructed, over several hundred years, as small groups of people arrived in Orkney either to settle or to migrate yet again across the sea to Denmark.

No metal objects have so far been recovered from the chambered cairns. It cannot be inferred with certainty from this negative evidence that metallurgy was unknown to any of the megalith builders who constructed or used the tombs, particularly those which were built at later dates, for metal objects might have been destroyed or plundered in the intervening 3,500–4,000 years.

STONE-BUILT DWELLINGS

It was always thought improbable that any of the supposedly frail domestic dwellings of neolithic times could have survived down to the present day. With the benefit of hindsight, one may ask why the excellence of prehistoric tomb-building in stone was not matched by equal competence in domestic building; but in fact it was believed that the early peoples were probably exclusively pastoralists and hunters, probably living in temporary dwellings. It was only as recently as 1939 that Dr Hans Holbaek demonstrated that imprints of grain were in fact identifiable in Orkney neolithic ware, and that by implication some of them at least were cultivators.

In 1928–29 the late Professor Gordon Childe carried out one of the classic excavations of British archaeology at the site known

Page 53 Brough of Birsay: *(above)* the excavated ruins of Earl Thorfinn's Christ Church, an eleventh-century 'minster'; *(below)* an air view of the excavations on the eastern end of the islet

Page 54 Brough of Deerness in extreme east of Mainland. Nearby are the ruins of a chapel in this retreat of Celtic saints

as Skara Brae on Skaill Bay in west Mainland. Sand dunes line the shore at this point, holding back a freshwater loch. In 1850 a great gale from the west had swept much of the dune sand inland, and revealed the remains of a number of stone-built huts. There was some preliminary excavation up to 1868, under the direction of the laird of Skaill. The buildings were then thought to be medieval, dating from the early Christian period, an error occasioned by a cross-inscribed stone from a neighbouring site being wrongly attributed to Skara Brae.

Professor Childe's work revealed that the inhabitants of the huts had a purely stone age culture. Not a trace of metal of any kind was discovered. Some crude pottery was found, but this could not be related to any known culture. In view of the remoteness of Orkney and the supposed probability that ancient cultures might have lingered on in the islands long after they had been superseded on the British mainland, the earliest date that could be proposed for Skara Brae was about 500 BC, which is relatively recent in terms of prehistory.

Further discoveries caused this first conservative dating to be revised. At the even more celebrated site of Jarlshof in Shetland, Dr A. O. Curle was able to demonstrate that huts of the Skara Brae type were in fact earlier than the Bronze Age; this discovery suggested a date for Skara Brae of the order of a thousand years earlier than Professor Childe's. This much greater antiquity was confirmed in 1937, when Professor Childe himself excavated a second hut cluster of the Skara Brae type at Rinyo in Rousay. Here 'beaker' pottery was found for the first time in Orkney. This is known to date from the late Neolithic or early Bronze Age. Even more exciting was the further discovery at a deeper level, of coarse Skara Brae pottery in association with Onston ware. In other words, the inhabitants of Skara Brae were contemporary with the megalithic tomb-builders. Bearing in mind that at least three successive levels of occupation have been identified at Skara Brae, and that the building of ordinary dwellings almost certainly came long before the building of elaborate tombs, it seems reasonable to date the foundations of the hut cluster as far back as 2500–2000 BC, though the buildings we see today may be the descendants of those original foundations.

The appearance of 'beaker' pottery in the higher, more recent

D

levels at Rinyo and in a chambered cairn at Yarso, also in Rousay, indicates that the ideas had penetrated as far north as Orkney which had been brought to Britain by people who had some knowledge of metallurgy, for the Beaker Folk—so called from the distinctive shape of their pottery—belonged to the early Bronze Age. They were bowmen and practised a more pastoral kind of life than the neolithic folk already settled in Britain when they entered from the European mainland. It has to be remembered that there was a great deal of overlapping of cultures among the people classified by the archaeologists into periods, and that sometimes new incomers themselves would take their distinctive artifacts into a region; at other times, the inspiration would go ahead of them or quite independently, through trade or other opportunities for the interchange of ideas.

HENGE MONUMENTS

The Beaker people were not numerous enough to wipe out the inhabitants of southern Britain, even supposing they had wished to do so. They seem to have become, however, a ruling aristocracy and they introduced new religious ideas, the visible evidence of which remains in the form of great henge monuments, the construction of which bespeaks considerable mathematical and practical knowledge.

In Orkney the most striking signs of a bronze age presence are the henge monuments of west Mainland, namely the Stones of Stenness and the Ring of Brodgar. Both stand on the narrow nesses which almost separate the lochs of Stenness and Harray, and are within three miles of Maeshowe. There was formerly a third henge, the Ring of Bookan, now vanished.

The Stones of Stenness are four in number and stand in a circle 100ft in diameter surrounded by farmland. They are larger than the Brodgar stones. Beside them is a dolmen-like erection, much photographed, which was in fact built by the then Office of Works in 1902 on the basis of mistaken information. It should be removed.

The Ring of Brodgar consisted originally of about sixty large stones standing in a circle 120 yards in diameter. It is surrounded by a ditch which is always notably wet. Twenty-seven monoliths still stand erect, four more lie prone and about nine others can be discerned in the ground. The tallest stone is 15ft high and several more exceed 10ft, but it is clear from an examination of the stones that all were once much higher. It is difficult to tell now whether the effect of the monument when complete would have been that of an enclosure or a public forum.

Brodgar stands on the crest of a broad moorland ridge where farming reclamation has recently made much headway. There is a great sense of space and in every direction an uninterrupted view of the sky down to a very low angle. If indeed this was, as has been suggested, some kind of 'computer' designed to predict eclipses and make other astronomical calculations, then its position could hardly be bettered. It is however necessary to note that absolutely no evidence exists that such was the purpose of this henge monument, though highly ingenious cases have been made out suggesting that such predictions and calculations were theoretically possible from others, notably Stonehenge.

In the vicinity of both circles there are a number of isolated standing stones which seem to have formed part of a larger over-all plan, now impossible to decipher. Undoubtedly there were many more of these single stones, but farmers in the past hundred years have tended to remove them as obstructions to ploughing.

In addition to the great circles of stones, some important bronze age burials have been found in Orkney. The large mounds near the Ring of Brodgar date from this period as do most of the 'Burnt Mounds' marked on the Ordnance map. One burial, the Knowes (mounds) of Trotty, located in Harray parish, proved on excavation to be of outstanding richness, including sun-discs of gold, probably Irish, and amber beads.

It is impossible to say whether the Beaker Folk themselves pene-trated as far north as Orkney, or whether it was their religious ideas and their political and trading organisation which influenced peoples already inhabiting the islands. The Beaker people's pre-dominantly pastoral way of life must have been closely akin to that of the neolithic Orcadians, so that little economic change would have been produced. But, to see that the influence of the Beaker Folk was strong, one has to look no further than the great stone circles, built with incredible labour for a clearly understood purpose. That purpose we still have to discover. It was many hundreds of years before a new major influence added more to the Orcadian landscape.

The extraordinary richness of Orkney in neolithic and bronze age monuments is equalled by those of iron age date. The Iron Age was a time of climatic deterioration, when the warmer and less stormy sub-Boreal period gave place to a wetter stormier sub-Atlantic period. These conditions favoured a new development of peat on the low Orkney uplands, and settlement was forced to retire downhill from the higher levels it had reached in neolithic and bronze age times. As the climate worsened, fertile lowland tracts must have become more and more sought after. Throughout western Europe it is thought that a deteriorating climate led to a shortage of farmland, and that this tended to produce an age of movement and political turbulence. Groups of people crossed to Britain bringing with them a knowledge of working in iron and they spread from their original landing-places in the south-east to almost every part of the British islands. Relatively early in this period some of these incomers sailed up the coasts of Scotland to Orkney.

In Orkney, the Iron Age is most strikingly represented by 102 fortified towers or 'brochs', most of which seem to have been built during the first century AD. All the larger islands except Eday have examples, and the distribution extends from the southern point of South Ronaldsay to the northern point of North Ronaldsay. Most of the brochs are coastal, but there are also concentrations in the inland parishes of Birsay and Harray. Orkney farmers will say today that good land is always to be found near a broch, and the distribution of the towers in the islands is probably to be explained first in terms of good land, secondly of access to water for transporting the necessary stones, and thirdly of good defensive sites. Defensive sites in Orkney are hard to find except in coastal locations.

The brochs are the largest dry stone structures ever raised in Britain. In the world at large, only the mortarless walls of Zimbabwe are more splendid in scale. In plan, brochs were circular and 40–80ft in diameter. In elevation they were roughly bell-shaped, narrowing somewhat from a broad base, then straightening in their upper sections. The best-preserved example, the broch of Mousa in Shetland, stands 40ft high, and there are signs that higher parts of the structure once existed. The walls were double, enclosing a succession of low galleries which were connected by a spiral stair. The galleries would make the use of scaffolding unnecessary when the broch was being built, a useful device in a treeless country. There were no outside windows. Entrance was by a low doorway at the base of the tower, and the unwelcome visitor would have had to emerge into the interior in a practically prone position, an ideal arrangement from the defenders' point of view. The lower part of the broch interior was probably roofed and it may have been divided into family compartments by radial walls.

The broch was probably the unanswerable defensive invention of its days, the iron age equivalent of the 1914–18 trench system. Each broch had a central well, which assured a supply of drinking water. Hardly any wood was used in the construction, so that the defenders could not be incinerated into submission. Starvation would eventually have broken them, but the organisation of prolonged sieges in hostile territory must have been extremely difficult in iron age times, and the besiegers were just as likely to starve as the besieged. To all intents and purposes a broch must have been impregnable, provided that its defenders managed to get themselves inside in time.

It is not yet clearly established whether or not the Orkney broch people lived continuously inside their brochs, or only retreated into them for defence. What is certain is that the brochs were only used defensively for a comparatively short period. From about the beginning of the second century AD peaceful conditions appear to have been established, probably because of Roman intervention in the affairs of northern Scotland, and the brochs fell into partial decay. Large numbers of domestic buildings were then erected inside and around them, using stone pillaged from the broch walls. Many of these post-broch dwellings were roughly circular in plan, with their interiors divided by radial walls opening onto a central hearth space. Such circular structures are commonly termed 'wheelhouses'.

The broch people were farmers who grew grain, probably

bere, tended numerous flocks and herds, hunted the red deer and supplemented their diet by fishing. Some were expert at stranding whales in bays. Piracy and raiding, probably for slaves, seem also to have been favourite occupations. Presumably the raids were directed at other groups, rather than at neighbours, and the hillfort dwellers on the Caithness mainland seem to have been likely victims. Raids no doubt provoked reprisals, hence the need for a defensive tower in every settlement.

The number of brochs in Orkney might be used as a clue in estimating the size of the population during the first century AD. On the basis of an estimate that a broch could shelter about 50 people, then those in Orkney could accommodate about 5,000. Bearing in mind the deteriorating climate, the spread of peat and the enforced concentration of people upon limited pockets of lowland, this seems a not unreasonable estimate for the total iron age population of Orkney.

Much has been said and written about the origin and purpose of the brochs. It has been suggested that the brochs were built by a conquering group to hold down a hostile population. This may have been the case in certain areas, notably in Shetland and perhaps in parts of north-west Scotland, but their distribution and number in Orkney suggest that they were built by established communities for self-defence. Their distribution is undoubtedly significant, and points to an origin either in Orkney itself, or nearby in Caithness. Outside Orkney, brochs are most heavily concentrated in Shetland, where so far 95 have been identified. On the northern Scots mainland 239 are recorded; they are grouped in Caithness, in Strath Naver and along the north and east coasts; they extend along the eastern coast of Sutherland to Brora and follow the general line of the A897 road towards Kinbrace. In the north-west there are a small number near Kyle of Tongue, Loch Hope and Loch Eriboll. Further south again, one or two occur on the shores of Dornoch Firth and in the vicinity of Bonar Bridge. There are also groups in the Hebrides, notably Skye, Tiree and Mull. Occasional examples have even been identified far to the south in the Border counties and Wigtownshire.

The picture given by this distribution seems to be of a well-organised and warlike political entity based upon Orkney, Shetland and Caithness, with substantial outposts in the western isles. The southern frontier lay in the wild hill country between the Dornoch and Cromarty Firths, which is still a formidable barrier to road transport in a snowy winter. That this was a turbulent frontier may be deduced from the occurrence of numerous hillforts which have been destroyed by fire. These hillforts appear to be contemporaneous with the brochs, and their burning presumably represents incursions of brochmen southwards in search of slaves and loot.

The facts of physical geography strongly favoured the growth of political power in Orkney and Caithness in periods when there was no unity in Scotland. The Old Red Sandstone lowlands on the shores of Pentland Firth were fertile and could support considerable populations. Immediately to the south there lay a vast wilderness of mountain, bog and moor wherein there were almost no opportunities for groups of people to become established in any but the smallest numbers. The nearest possible area to the south where political and military power could be developed was the Moray Firth lowland, fifty roadless miles away. The natural boundary between this and a northern power thrusting towards the south would tend to be the hill country south of Dornoch Firth. At any given time, the exact position of the boundary would reflect the relative strength of the two opponents. This pattern of a power contest north of the site of modern Inverness seems first to have developed in the broch age. It was to persist in varying forms for at least ten centuries. In more subtle and less violent ways, perhaps it still does.

THE PICTS

Throughout the foregoing discussion the use of the word 'Pict' has been avoided; the brochs are sometimes thought to have had connections with this mysterious people, and until recently they were often termed, and even mapped, as 'Picts' castles'.

The Picts were a grouping of peoples already present in the north—of this we may be almost completely certain. It is not known how early this grouping came into existence, nor whether the peoples who built the brochs already formed part of the Pictish confederacy or empire. The first recorded reference to them comes from AD 297 when the Romans applied it to all people living north of the Clyde-Forth line who were neither 'Scots' nor 'Britons'. By this date the Orkney brochs had already fallen into partial decay and were becoming surrounded by secondary domestic buildings. As a recognisable political entity the Picts emerge from obscurity about the middle of the sixth century. Presumably they had begun to develop their organisation before this, and possibly they grew out of a defensive alliance provoked by the Roman incursions into Scotland in the second century. They came to exercise effective power over much of northern Scotland, including Orkney, and their power centres lay in the Old Red Sandstone lowlands of the east. They were never a Highland people.

The Roman view of the Picts, based mainly upon impressions gained from the opposite side of a battlefield, was of a horde of savages, and this view has persisted down to modern times. There is however a mass of archaeological evidence to show that they developed a relatively high level of culture, thus described by W. Douglas Simpson :

'We must imagine our Pictish predecessors in those early days as an energetic and intelligent agricultural population, tilling the soil and tending herds of oxen and swine and flocks of sheep. They were possessed of a high degree of practical and artistic knowledge. Their metallurgic skill is evidenced in the beautiful brooches, rings, pins, massive embossed armlets, and harness mountings all wrought in bronze, sometimes finely enamelled in various colours; and in the heavy double-linked silver chains which are a peculiar characteristic of this period. A similar degree of skill is exhibited in their iron tools of ordinary domestic use, and by their beads of variegated glass and their implements and ornaments in stone, bone and wood, sometimes beautifully carved. They wove cloth in bright colours and varied patterns. Their constructional skill, no less than their power of combined effort and capacity for organization, are revealed in the immense stone hill-forts, sometimes vitrified, and the crannogs or pile-dwellings which they built as refuges in time of war, and on a smaller scale in the earth-houses which they constructed as subterranean adjuncts to their hut-dwellings.'

Pictish power was extended to Orkney from the eastern Scots mainland; it waned in face of the Scandinavian raids and settlements which began in the eighth century and eventually over-whelmed these island outposts. On the Scots mainland it survived longer and made a contribution, though not the dominant one, to the development of the Scottish nation.

The limits of Pictish dominion may be defined by the distribution of symbol stones. These have a predominantly eastern distribution and extend north-south from Shetland to the Forth. An outstanding example was found in 1935 on the Brough of Birsay in Orkney. These stones carry the characteristic signs of 'mirror-case', 'crescent and v-rod' and 'rectangle', the meaning of which is unknown. The Birsay Stone also portrays three robed warriors carrying short swords, spears and square shields, and an eagle and what looks like an elephant. It is now preserved in the Museum of Antiquities in Edinburgh.

The language spoken by the Picts, including some at least of the peoples who preceded them in Orkney and elsewhere, has been much discussed. Fragments of Pictish writing survive in the form of an Ogam script. It certainly has Irish antecedents and can be shown to contain some Gaelic words. It seems possible that some Picts spoke a language which was not directly related to the other Celtic languages and which has now been entirely forgotten; but it is more likely that the majority spoke a dialect for which the term Celtic-Pictish has been proposed.

The final word about the Picts' language remains to be written. Meanwhile it may be noted that Hugh Marwick and others have claimed to demonstrate a faint though undeniable Celtic influence in the place-names of Orkney; but of any other language, place-names have given not the slightest hint.

CELTIC CHRISTIAN MISSIONARIES

Sometime during the long period of Pictish hegemony the first Christian missionaries arrived in Orkney, bringing with them the distinctive features of the Celtic church. These were intrepid men, great travellers by sea and land. From various bases in the south and west they penetrated to virtually every corner of what we call Scotland, and carried the gospel to far-off Shetland, Faeroe and Iceland.

It is hard to assign a precise date for their coming to Orkney, but the medieval chronicler Joceline of Furness, who is known to have used Celtic sources, states categorically that St Kentigern, following his great sixth-century evangelisation of the mainland Picts 'sent forth those of his own whom he knew to be strong in faith, fervent in love, lofty in religion, towards the Orchades, Noruuagia and Yslanda, to announce to the dwellers therein the Name of the Lord and the Faith of Christ, for that in those parts the harvest indeed was great, but there were no labourers'. Although Joceline wrote centuries after the events he describes, he may be echoing matters of real history and there is much topographical evidence to support him. It is just possible that there may have been an earlier penetration by followers of St Ninian, but modern opinion judges this unlikely.

Because of political rivalries sometimes amounting to open warfare between Picts and Scots, the followers of St Columba, whose connections were with the Scots, never had much to do with the northern isles. One Columban hermit, Cormac, did travel to Orkney, however, and the circumstances of his coming give eloquent testimony to the reality of Pictish power in the north. Columba went in the year 563 to the hillfort of King Brude Mac-Maelchon, High King of the Picts, located near Inverness, where he engaged in a famous duel of words with the druids. While there he asked King Brude to give safe conduct to one of his followers, Cormac, who wished to seek solitude in the northern isles. This request was granted, and what is more it was effective. Twice at least, Cormac was saved from death by its use. There is no doubt that the princeling of Orkney was subject to his king in Inverness.

Celtic Christianity was an affair of monasteries which were used as bases for evangelising the surrounding countryside, of preaching places marked first by crosses and later by tiny chapels, and of cells in remote places suitable for solitary contemplation. In Orkney there are two sites with Celtic remains of some substance, located at the north-western and extreme eastern tips of Mainland.

The westerly site stands on the Brough of Birsay, a small tidal island. Excavations were begun here in 1866 and have brought to light a complicated succession of remains dating from at least six centuries of occupation. At the base of the site stand the foundations of a Celtic church and probably a monastery, and a graveyard where the Birsay Stone was found.

The eastern site is on the Brough of Deerness, a small and precipitous fragment of the Deerness peninsula, from which it is separated by a narrow chasm. The Brough is a remote place, made more so in recent times by depopulation of the adjacent farms. Various walls are to be seen and the ground is obviously very full of fallen stone. There is a persistent tradition that here once stood a Celtic Christian monastery, but no systematic excavation has yet been attempted.

A visit to either of these sites will convey some impression of the remoteness and seclusion favoured by the *papae* of the Celtic church, but the visitor should not be disappointed to see almost nothing in the way of identifiable remains dating from this early period.

4   NORSEMEN AND SCOTS

IN the eighth century, perhaps earlier, sea-raiders and settlers from the western fjords of Norway began to appear in Orkney. Their coming was part of a great movement of peoples throughout Europe and beyond which followed the decay of Roman power in the west.

First from Norway, later from Denmark, viking longships set out each year to raid and pillage lands already populous and to found colonies in lands too empty or too poorly organised to resist their coming. Norse colonies were soon dotted around the margins of the North Atlantic from Orkney to Greenland; a few adventurers even reached North America. To the south of this predominantly Norwegian endeavour, Danish raiders and settlers threatened the very existence of an Anglo-Saxon England struggling towards unity. Further east, vikings from Sweden and Gotland opened up the great river route across Russia to the Black Sea and Byzantium.

THE NORSE SETTLEMENT

Because of their fertility and abundance of sheltered havens, the Orkneys seem to have been used by the Norsemen from a very early date as a base for raids to the south. The Norsemen who sacked Lindisfarne in 793 are thought to have come from Orkney, as are those who raided Dorset at about the same date. At this stage, Norse groups were in the habit of 'ness-taking' in the islands. Easily defended headlands or nesses were occupied and entrenched across their landward approaches, then used to dominate the surrounding countryside. The islands of Orkney, and especially the North Isles, had many suitable sites for this purpose. The most accessible example is that on the small headland on which stands Onston cairn, close to the Kirkwall-Stromness road.

Settlers, as opposed to raiders, also came to Orkney at a very early date and in relatively large numbers, probably before the ness-takers and certainly afterwards. These newcomers to the islands imparted a Norse imprint upon the entire culture, language and landscape of Orkney which persists to this day. The overwhelming character of the Norse settlement may be seen from the Ordnance survey map; virtually every place-name is of Norse origin. Most of the seeming exceptions are relatively recent, nineteenth-century introductions by Scots landlords, or else anglicisations of ancient Norse names.

The Settlement: Evidence and Problems

The story of Norse settlement in Orkney has been partly unravelled by workers in several associated fields. The evidence available consists of written sources, archaeological remains and place-names, supplemented to some degree by studies of the Norn, the variant of the Old Norse tongue once spoken in Orkney. The principal written source is the great Orkneyinga Saga, the story of the Norse Earldom of Orkney from the time of its foundation by King Harald Fairhair of Norway in the ninth century to its fading away in the face of Scots infiltration some three hundred years later. The Saga was a more or less contemporary account composed for recital by *skalds*, professional chroniclers in verse and song, in chieftains' halls and written down in Iceland very much later, probably in the thirteenth century.

Unfortunately, the various kinds of evidence sometimes fail to agree in most puzzling and intriguing ways. There are two major questions concerned with the settlement phase to which so far no satisfactory answers have been found. The first is, were the islands deserted when the Norsemen came? The second, when did they in fact come? In both cases the Saga story conflicts directly with other forms of evidence.

The 'empty islands' hypothesis

Did the Norsemen find Orkney empty? The Saga makes no reference whatsoever to a conquest of Orkney or to the presence of any other people. From the Saga one may infer that the viking longships came to an empty land where presumably the deserted and crumbling ruins of earlier times stood as inexplicable and mysterious as were the statues on Easter Island for modern explorers. This picture of Norse settlement has been accepted by some scholars, yet it stands in flat contradiction to the abundant evidences of pre-Norse archaeology.

The Saga is a special kind of story. It deals with the heroic deeds of Norwegian great men—the story was in fact originally called the Earls' Saga—and it was composed for those men themselves and for their contemporaries and descendants. It does not provide details of the background against which they acted out their parts unless that background presented obstacles to be heroically overcome. One feels that a skald who tried to include a discourse on pre-Norse social and economic history in his declamation would have had short shrift in an Icelandic drinking hall. His audience was simply not interested in peaceful invasions.

Archaeology, backed by common sense, suggests a quite different picture of the settlement. It seems inconceivable that the considerable populations whose forebears built over a hundred brochs in Orkney in the first century AD, and who continued to live around their ruins for generations afterwards could have utterly vanished by the time the Norsemen came. Of course, there might have been some kind of disaster, an epidemic possibly, which wiped out the population, but there is no sign or tradition of anything of the kind. Further, the well-attested activities of Celtic Christian missionaries in the pre-Norse period certainly indicates the existence of people there to be converted. In the words of Hugh Marwick, these intrepid men were 'not despatched to preach the gospel among Orcadian seals and seagulls'.

Such slight written sources as exist apart from the Saga do in fact refer to pre-Norse people in Orkney. Thus, the twelfth-century *Historia Norvegiae* categorically states that in the days of Harald Fairhair, King of Norway, pirates of the family of Rognvald of Møre 'destroyed' the people of Orkney, then called Pictland, and took the islands for themselves. The same history states that the island people were of two kinds, Picts and Papae (Christian fathers). The Picts were said to be very small and to hide themselves in underground dwellings during the day, emerging at morning and evening to perform prodigious feats of building. The Papae were said to have been white-robed. It is impossible now to determine what was meant exactly by the word 'destroyed'. It may indicate actual extermination or a more gradual process of expropriation followed by the inevitable starving to death of the expropriated. Whichever it was, the islands were certainly inhabited. In addition to this slight account there are brief references to Orkney in certain Irish annals which suggest that there was a population in the islands as late as 709.

Students of place-names have also suggested evidence that conflicts with the Saga story. The late Hugh Marwick and others have been able to demonstrate with a fair measure of certainty the existence of Celtic place-name elements embedded in the predominantly Norse names of Orkney. If this theory is correct, then there must have been Celtic-speaking peoples present from whom the Norse settlers learned these elements. Generally speaking, the Norsemen would name the natural features of the new land, and also their own farms, in their own tongue. However, when they expropriated a native farmer, they might just possibly adopt the native farm-name. The sound of this name would tend to be reproduced approximately in Old Norse; it might perhaps be altered slightly into a word with meaning, a different meaning, in the new language. Today, the problem is to recognise the native name through its Norse disguise. Marwick proposed thirteen farm-names, some of which are found in several places, in which he believed a pre-Norse element might be preserved. Every one of these has been challenged by other scholars, but no one has challenged all thirteen 'possibles' simultaneously.

In order to appreciate his argument, one of Marwick's suggested examples may be examined in the field and assessed in a hypothetical reconstruction of its early history. In the Mainland parish of Sandwick, Marwick proposes the farm Arion as a derivation from the Celtic *An Aireagh*, a shieling. To what extent does an examination of the site tend to support his view?

Assuming that the total pre-Norse population of Orkney was relatively small and that therefore there was plenty of land available, it seems reasonable to suppose that most pre-Norse farms would be in the most fertile areas. When the Norsemen came they would seize the best farms first and name them in their own language, usually after themselves. The pre-Norse farms which might expect to escape seizure longest would be those situated in relatively remote places on the margins of the waste. The longer they escaped seizure, the more opportunity would there be for the Norse settlers to learn something of the language of the conquered people and so to adopt a native farm-name when they eventually took possession of a farm.

Arion stands on a rising spur of ground above the Loch of Stenness on a ridge which was moorland until relatively recent times. Place-name study has shown that none of the Norse names in the vicinity belongs to the very first phase of settlement, except perhaps for Langskaill, over a mile away to the west and located in a small valley. It might be, therefore, that Arion was indeed a remote shieling when the Norsemen came to take it, and that they did not come until they had taken the more fertile lands of Langskaill and nearby Kirbister, by which time they could have learned to adopt the existing names of the farms they took over.

Dating the settlement

When did the Norse settlers arrive in Orkney? The Orkneyinga and several other sagas say that the islands came under the rule of Harald Fairhair after his unifying wars against his rebellious Norwegian chiefs, wars which culminated in the 'crowning mercy' of the battle of Hafrsfjord. King Harald's determination to establish one single authority in Norway drove many dissident chiefs to seek sanctuary in Orkney and Shetland, and from the relative security of these bases they returned each summer to harry King Harald's domains. Accordingly, after his great victory at Hafrsfjord, the king determined to bring these rebellious subjects to book.

According to the sagas Harald gathered an expedition together, sailed to Orkney and cleared the viking pirates out of their lairs, and conferred the islands upon a loyal supporter, Earl Rognvald of Møre, as compensation for the loss of his son Ivar in the campaign. Earl Rognvald was not able to take up this grant himself because of his responsibilities in Norway, and he therefore transferred it to his brother Sigurd, who became thereby the first Earl of Orkney. Thus was the 'Old Earldom' founded, to endure until

Page 71 (above) Quernstones, an old kiln-ended long-house near Rackwick, Hoy; (below) plan and sketch of an old Orkney long-house. Details from several examples have been combined in the drawing

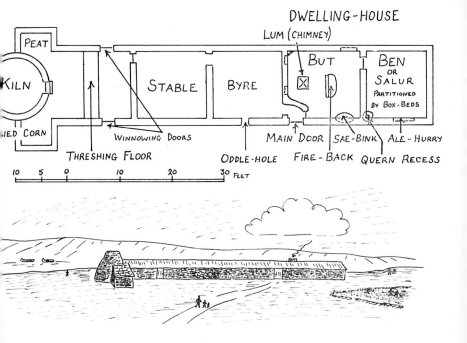

DWELLING-HOUSE

LUM (CHIMNEY)

PEAT

KILN

BUT

BEN OR SALUR
PARTITIONED BY BOX-BEDS

STABLE

BYRE

DRIED CORN

WINNOWING DOORS

THRESHING FLOOR

ODDLE-HOLE

MAIN DOOR

FIRE-BACK

SAE-BINK

QUERN RECESS

ALE-HURRY

10   5   0   10   20   30 FEET

Page 72 *(above)* Quern alcove in a ruined house in Firth, Mainland; *(below)* the flagstone cupboard, sae-bink and goosenest at floor level at Winksetter in Harray parish

1468. Unfortunately, this saga account is in clear conflict with the evidence of place-names in Orkney.

The dates of King Harald's reign are not precisely known, but a consensus of opinion places the battle of Hafrsfjord at AD 880–900. If the Norse settlement of Orkney, as opposed to the establishment of viking lairs, began after this time, as the sagas assert, then this settlement must be assigned to the late ninth and early tenth centuries. Yet place-name evidence suggests with overwhelming force that settlement in strength began in the eighth century, at least 150 years before Hafrsfjord.

The substance of the place-name argument is based on the division of Orkney place-names into several distinct categories, such as those which contain a personal name or those with certain kinds of ending; and on the arrangement of these categories, to some degree, in chronological order. In particular, it is thought possible to distinguish some names which were given before the earldom was founded from those which were given after this time. The argument, of which a brief summary follows here, is set out in detail in J. Storer Clouston's *History of Orkney* and Hugh Marwick's *Orkney Farm Names*.

It is known from a number of sources that the Earldom of Orkney was founded at about the time Iceland was being colonised, and also that in Iceland at this time colonists were naming their farms in a special way. A man would give his own name to his farm and add the ending *stadir* (steading or abode). It seems reasonable to think that, if Orkney were being settled simultaneously, similar names would be given. *Stadir* names do occur in Orkney, modified by time and isolation into the form *-ston*, but they are by no means common and they are also distributed in a particular way. The outer North Isles are nearest to Norway and so were probably settled first; some like Sanday and Westray are fertile and attractive. And yet, not one single -ston is to be found there. The inner North Isles have one only, in Rousay, and there is one in all the South Isles.

In contrast with this, the central plain of West Mainland has about a dozen examples. Here one finds Tormiston (twice), Corston, Knarston, Tonston, Germiston and several others. These -ston settlements lie in a belt of country between the two favourite residences of the Norse earls, Birsay and Orphir. This distribution of names may be interpreted as suggesting that the first earls, wanting to set up their followers on lands not previously inhabited, had to look inland to find such empty land, because the best coastal sites were already occupied by Norse settlers. The absence of any -ston elements in such a well-favoured North Isle as Sanday also suggests that it was fully populated when the earldom was established.

Further place-name evidence for Norse settlement in strength long before the founding of the earldom lies in the significance of two other names of special interest, *skaill* and *bu*. Skaill is derived from Old Norse *skali*, which in early times meant a hall, but later came to mean a hut, shack or any detached structure. There are about thirty skaills in Orkney; all those for which documentary evidence exists were principal farms in their districts. Today, the first house in Orkney, the home of the Lord Lieutenant, is Skaill in Sandwick. If the Orkney skaills were principal houses, they were originally halls not shacks, and therefore they must have been named very early. Can they be dated more precisely?

In Norway, *skali* was used for a wooden hall only as long as timber buildings were new fangled and therefore something in the nature of status symbols. This was the time when axes first came into use in these parts, long before the saga period. The occurrence of skaills in Orkney as the names of principal houses therefore suggests early settlement in the period when timber halls were still thought remarkable. Significantly, there are almost no skaills in Iceland which was, as we know, settled in saga times.

Equally informative is the distribution of the name *bu*. In this case the present-day distribution tends to give a partially incorrect picture, because only those early *bus* which were earldom properties are relevant to the present argument. Later, the name was often given to the principal or head-house in any district, whether an earldom property or not.

Starting again with the North Isles where -stons are absent, seven instances of bu are to be found in the fertile islands of Sanday and Westray. Six stand on headlands or nesses, some of which carry the marks of viking earthworks, and the remaining bu is very close to a ness. This highly characteristic location suggests very strongly that when Harald Fairhair smoked out the viking lairs on the headlands he took the vikings' land for his own. It further suggests that this was the only land he could properly take, because the rest of the land was already farmed by his own loyal subjects.

The spread of settlement

Marwick was able to develop his place-name argument with reference to more widely distributed names, and to demonstrate a clear chronology relating to successive stages of the Norse colonisation. He assembled a strong body of evidence to suggest that the earliest names of all are those with the ending -by, derived from Old Norse *byr*. The -by farms he regarded as family steadings founded by leading men, not necessarily chiefs. It must be noted that Marwick's reliance upon -by names as an almost infallible index of primary settlement has been questioned; such names were given at much later dates in other parts of north Britain.

Somewhat later, but still in the first phases of settlement, farms with the elements -land, -garth (or -scarth) and -bister (Old Norse *land*, *garthr*, *bolstathr*) were established. These like those with -by were usually large properties. At this stage in the evolution of settlement, King Harald arrived in Orkney and, in return for destroying the sea-pirates, perhaps, laid *skat* on all existing Orkney farms, except for those which he took for himself and which henceforth became earldom properties. Skat was a royal land tax, and so far as is known it was never subsequently laid upon Orkney, nor extended to properties which came into existence later. In the old rentals, of which Marwick makes much use, virtually all the -bys and most of the -lands, -garths and -bisters are shown as liable to skat.

Another class of farm-names seem to be very old; these are the -setters (Old Norse *setr*). Some of these were skatted, some not. Presumably some were already in existence when King Harald came, some are of more recent date.

Finally, names with the element quoy (Old Norse *kvi*) are almost never skatted. This word has been in use in Orkney until the present century to mean a field or enclosure. Originally it indicated a small farm broken from the waste on the margins of old-established farmlands. Generally speaking, settlement would not have developed to this stage by 880–900.

The generalised place-name chronology as outlined by Mar-

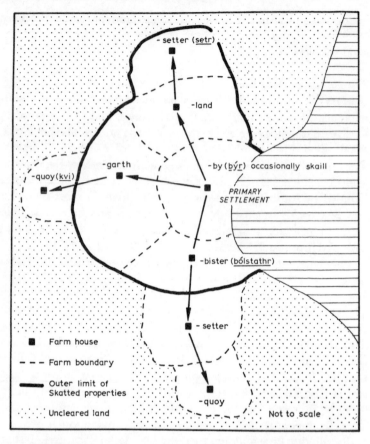

The spread of settlement as interpreted from place-name elements

wick may be represented in the form of a simple model or schematic map. It has to be emphasised that this presents an ideal picture and cannot be matched exactly against any one part of Orkney.

Origins of the settlers

Finally, from which part of Norway did the settlers come? The answer to this question can be given with a fair degree of precision by place-names and by analysis of the Orkney Norn, the language spoken in Orkney throughout the Norse period and long afterwards. Such archaeological evidence as exists tends to confirm the findings of the other two lines of inquiry.

The Norwegian farm-name element -*bolstathr*, which becomes -bister in Orkney, is concentrated in that part of south-west Norway north of the two counties (*fylke*) of East and West Agder. These two counties lie near the southernmost bulge of Norway. Further east towards Oslofjord, the *bolstathrs* disappear; their heaviest concentrations lie in Møre, whence came the Norse Earls of Orkney, and in Sogn og Fjordane. The farm-element *setr* has a similar distribution.

Linguistic studies of the Orkney Norn make use of the fact that the language spoken in different parts of Norway varies very considerably. It has been possible to demonstrate that Norn was derived from that version of Norwegian spoken along the fiord coast of the south-west, and especially in the district of Rogaland near modern Stavanger.

THE ORKNEYINGA SAGA

The story of the Orkneyinga Saga has often been retold, and the reader who wishes to follow it from beginning to end is recommended to consult A. B. Taylor's translation or J. Storer Clouston's learned rewriting, contained in his *History of Orkney*. Some of the incidents of the Saga throw light on the stormy days of these dark ages and on the character of the leading men of those times.

As soon as the earldom had been established, the Norsemen revived that ancient contest between northern and southern power which had been characteristic of earlier periods, a contest fought out along the eastern passes and lowland corridor between Caithness and the Moray Firth. So one reads that the first of all the earls, Sigurd the Mighty (the Norsemen were strongly addicted to nicknames) died violently, as was the Norse custom, while campaigning in eastern Scotland. He had arranged to meet a Scots chief Maelbrigd Buck-tooth for a decisive battle on the shores of Dornoch Firth, forty men a side. Fearing treachery, Sigurd brought double the number agreed, two men riding on each horse. Unexpectedly the Scots chief had abided by the agreement and was consequently slain. Riding away in his hour of triumph, Earl Sigurd was unwise enough to cut his leg on the protruding tooth of his dead rival, whose head was swinging from the victor's saddle. Blood poisoning resulted from this trivial wound, and shortly afterwards Sigurd was 'howe-laid' overlooking the waters of Dornoch.

Travellers to Orkney by the east coast road may observe the location of Sigurd's burial, now recorded in the farm-name Sydera (originally Sigurd's howe). This farm stands high on a gravelly plateau looking out to the Firth and the hills behind Bonar Bridge. A little distance from the farm there is an esker, a long ridge of gravel and sand deposited beneath the ice during the glacial period. The esker rises in a succession of humps which are brilliant with gorse in early summer. No one knows precisely where Sigurd lies, but the top of the highest esker mound would seem the obvious place.

From time to time the Saga relates incidents which cannot be supported by the findings of place-name study and archaeology. A striking instance comes from the year 995 when King Olav Tryggvason is stated to have converted Orkney to Christianity.

At this time, another Sigurd, styled 'the Stout', held the earldom. He was lying with three longships in the Bay of Osmundwall, in that part of Hoy now known as Walls (originally and literally, 'bays') when King Olav descended upon him with a superior force and fresh from baptism in England, and presented him with the choice either of immediate conversion and baptism in the waters of Scapa Flow, or instant death. This second alternative was to be supplemented by the destruction of Orkney by fire and sword.

To reinforce his arguments in favour of acceptance of the gentle creed of faith and love, the king seized Sigurd's young son and vowed to put him to death unless his father complied with the royal request. It is hardly surprising that Earl Sigurd saw fit to accept baptism immediately. Thereupon the king sailed for Norway, taking the earl's young son as hostage. The unfortunate lad soon died in his captivity, and the Saga says Earl Sigurd did his king no more honour. Soon afterwards he is found carrying fire and sword in a thoroughly pagan way through the realm of Brian Boru, the Christian king in Ireland. While so doing the earl died at Clontarf in the year 1014.

The difficulty with this story is that we can be reasonably sure that Orkney was to a large extent already Christian by 995. Place-name evidence assures us that Celtic Christian papae lived there through the Norse settlement though written sources are silent on the matter. The place-name *papa* is widespread. Many examples apply to remote islands such as the Christian fathers might have favoured for retreat and contemplation; the valley behind Kirkwall is also named Papdale, 'dale of the fathers'. This naming of places from the presence of Celtic clergy suggests that the Norsemen recognised them as men out of the ordinary; they may well have left them very much alone, for superstitious reasons if for no other.

Further evidence can be adduced to support the view that Christianity was established in the islands long before King Olav's time. It has already been noted that many -bister names were already in existence by 880–900; and yet several of them carry the prefix kirk-, eg Kirbister. The kirk referred to was presumably Celtic. It may of course be argued that kirk was added to the name at a later date, but Marwick judges this unlikely. Some indirect support for a later addition of the kirk- prefix might be gained from the absence of kirk- prefixes before the earliest names of all, those ending in -by; yet this may be pure chance; kirk- and -by occur together in Faeroe.

Archaeology also tends to contradict the Saga story. At the celebrated Jarlshof site in nearby Shetland it can be shown that the Norsemen came as pagans and built small pagan temples besides their houses, but that these were very soon abandoned presumably because their owners had become Christian. The small temple at Jarlshof was abandoned about 850, more than a century before King Olav's 'conversion' of Earl Sigurd of Orkney.

Acceptance of the Saga story at its face value is thus hedged about with difficulties. If however the story is factually true, which it may still be, it must indicate that the earls and Norse nobility were the last people in Orkney to be touched by Christian influences. Possibly they regarded themselves as the repositories of ancient pagan virtue and defenders of ancient faiths. Almost certainly they must have regarded the revolutionary creed of peace and love as a dangerous one for a man to adopt who had his life and dominions to defend in desperate times.

NORSEMEN AND SCOTS

In the year 1020 Thorfinn the Mighty became earl over one-third of Orkney. From this point the Saga narrative becomes more connected, and the scale of events increases so that one has the impression of reading about a kingdom of consequence rather than of a small colonial society set in a waste of northern seas. The story is of a medieval golden age, though we do not know how it appeared to the unprivileged majority of Orcadians.

Thorfinn demonstrated the considerable independence which a determined earl could exercise in this remote island domain. He quickly gained full control of the earldom by a combination of political skill and military and naval prowess, and held on to it for the rest of his long life by virtue of these same qualities, aided by a very full measure of good luck. His high-handed ways soon brought him into open conflict with King Duncan of Scotland, who was unaccountably called Karl in the Saga. The result was a series of naval actions and land campaigns which left Thorfinn master of north Scotland until he died. He was also soon in conflict with his liege lord on the throne of Norway. Norwegian kings, with great fleets at their disposal, had to be treated with more caution than the land-based kings of Scotland, and on several occasions it seemed inevitable that a Norwegian king would be provoked by the earl's doings to come to Orkney and settle accounts; but none ever did. By a mixture of sheer effrontery and well-timed statesmanship Thorfinn contrived to stave off the day of reckoning until either a king died, or lost his throne, or became involved in more pressing matters elsewhere. In his latter years the great earl lived mostly in his hall on the Brough of Birsay, next to which he had built a 'splendid minster', called Christ Church. Here he was eventually laid to rest in the year 1064.

The Saga is at its most eventful and stirring in the twelfth century. One reads of Magnus, Earl of Orkney, who was from time to time a conscientious objector to the violence of his day and who was murdered brutally on the isle of Egilsay in Easter week, 1116. One reads at great length of Rognvald, the young Norwegian nobleman who seized the earldom from Earl Paul with the help of the adventurer Sweyn Asleifsson of Gairsay and held it with greater distinction than any other earl before or after. He it was who caused St Magnus Cathedral to be built

80

in Kirkwall, the work being supervised by his astute and able father Kol.

During Rognvald's tenure of the earldom, which lasted until 1159, Norse society and culture reached their peak in Orkney. The times seem to have been relatively prosperous. A group of notable men were gathered around the earl and his father; the bishopric, a new and potent force in the land, was held for over sixty years by William 'the Old', a man of diverse talents. Earl Rognvald himself was a man of considerable culture, a skald and master of the runic art, a gay adventurer in his youth and a capable administrator when he grew older, invariably a man of his word and a great benefactor of the church. He was not, however, always the most alert of military commanders.

When the building of St Magnus Cathedral was well in hand, Rognvald led a crusade to the Holy Land. Few incidents in the sagas make one wish to have been there; times were hard for the majority of people and life was cheap, so that the view which is sometimes expressed that this was a romantic period cannot bear scrutiny. But the Orkney crusade was an exception. There was good company and high adventure and little of the brutality so characteristic of the age. The crusaders sailed their longships into the Mediterranean where they found that Moslems could be both cultured and humane; they encountered that wind Euroclydon which had once been the undoing of St Paul; they visited Jerusalem, and finally swam to the farther bank of Jordan, before returning to Norway via Constantinople and the overland route from Italy. One is impressed by their obvious grasp of European geography; one would dearly like to see the charts they used, and to know what navigational instruments they possessed.

NORSE SOCIETY IN ORKNEY

A highly structured society developed in Orkney during the Norse period, which differed in several respects both from the parent society in Norway and from other Norse colonial societies.

At the head of this Orkney society stood the earls. These men were hereditary rulers and as such were unique in Norse society as a whole. All the earls were descended from the great family of Rognvald of Møre, whence sprang a remarkable line of men who made their marks in European history. Perhaps the most notable of all was Rolf, first Duke of Normandy and ancestor to William the Conqueror.

The hereditary principle made the Orkney earls more like petty kings than subject nobles. They were absolute rulers, and in the first 150 years of the Saga period especially no subject, however wealthy and influential, could gainsay them. Those who tried, even for the best of reasons, often had to flee from Orkney.

Things or annual councils were indeed held, but these seem to have been less influential in Orkney than in the Norse world generally. The probable site for the principal Orkney *thing* was Tingwall (*thing* bay) in Rendall; Dingieshowe on the narrow *aith* or isthmus between Deerness and the rest of Mainland may have been another. Laws in Norse Orkney were made by the earls, so far as one can tell; one notable difference between the Orkneyinga and most other sagas is the complete absence of reference to lawsuits in the former, and the abundance of such references in most of the others.

Around the earls was a bodyguard of warriors of noble descent, the *hird*. Membership of this body was almost the only way to wealth and position. Below this small force of picked men, many of whom would normally be earls' kin, came the housecarls, and below these again the *thralls* or unfree servants. Earls were sometimes democratic enough to look to their thrall-women to mother their sons.

The earls had a considerable estate scattered throughout the islands; they also came to possess properties on the Scots mainland itself, notably in Caithness. Their income came from their *bus* and other farms and from taxes paid by their subjects, usually in kind. They were entitled to call upon their subjects to man ships for the defence of Orkney and for viking raids. Earls who made too heavy demands for service on ship board were naturally unpopular. The earls lived in two principal residences, on the Brough of Birsay and in Orphir, and from time to time they travelled round their properties, guesting at their *bu* farms.

Beneath this powerful, indeed all-powerful, upper crust of Norse society came the majority of Orkney folk. The backbone of rural society was the odal farmer. Odal families held their land on absolute freehold; they had, however, to pay a sum to each new earl at his accession for the regranting of their odal. Land became odal after passing from one generation of a family to the next, but it could not be used for such vital transactions as the payment of blood-money or a dowry until it had passed through six generations. Nothing could replace odal land in the payment of such debts, and this created a great difficulty in the early days of settlement. King Harald Fairhair in effect set aside the six-generation rule by a legal manipulation in order to disperse the accumulated debts. Somewhat later, Norse settlers in Iceland, foreseeing this difficulty, drew up a new code of law to meet it.

At his death, an odaller's land was divided among his sons, and at a later stage it became customary to give daughters half-shares. This system of repeated subdivision worked well as long as farms remained large and there was plenty of spare land from which a small heritor could supplement his share. But, when coupled with continued population growth and a limited supply of cultivable land, the system eventually produced a veritable mosaic of small plots, the farming of which became less economic after each subdivision.

An odaller's land extended from low water mark to the highest stone of the highest hill, a fact which is still of significance in that foreshores in Orkney are not Crown property and may be fenced. Theoretically, odal ownership extended downwards indefinitely, so that anything of value found in odal land was the odaller's property. Even today there could be doubt about the status of treasure-trove on proven odal land.

The odaller was a mixed farmer who at least in good years, probably lived at a standard somewhat above the standard of his time. The type of house he inhabited may be seen in outline on the Brough of Birsay, the tiny island off the north-west corner of Mainland. The best-preserved example there is 56ft long by 15ft wide. It had turf walls faced inside with drystone walling, and is aligned up and down the slope. The upper end of the house was occupied by the family, the lower by their animals. No pottery has been found, indicating that this house is of early date, for there was little Norse pottery in Orkney before the twelfth century. The house is similar to long-houses which were built in Orkney until very recent times.

The society so far described was characterised by the wide

gap between the earl and the people. The great Earl Thorfinn seems to have been responsible for establishing a new class of 'best men' or gødings, some sixteen in number, who filled this gap. The gødings were regional administrators and defenders of the earl's widely scattered dominions. They were placed on the earl's own *bu* farms and on other principal properties, also called *bus*, all of which were located at strategic points near the shore. Each gøding had oversight of a district large enough to man a warship in time of need.

In the twelfth century the 'best men' and their families developed into a powerful class, well able to influence an earl when they thought fit. The accounts of such powerful earls as Hakon who slew Magnus, Paul who was supplanted by Rognvald, and Rognvald himself all contain references to influential advisers and to counsel given by leading men. The existence of something like an Orkney nobility is implied by the Saga account of Rognvald's crusade, 1151–3. In the following century and probably earlier, some of these leading men were accepted into the *hird* of the king of Norway himself, where they received the finest education available in the north at that date. A detailed account of such an education is given in *The King's Mirror (Kongespejlet)*, written by a thirteenth-century Norwegian nobleman. Storer Clouston's *History* contains a long extract from this fascinating document.

Orkney's leading men undoubtedly lived in considerable style but they nevertheless remained farmers and fishermen who worked alongside their men. Norse gentlemen did not keep their hands clean. The style of their living was not based entirely upon their lands and fisheries; viking raids provided a useful supplementary source of income, and the Saga thus describes the annual cycle of work and raiding followed by Sweyn Asleifsson of Gairsay in Earl Rognvald's time : 'in the spring [he] worked hard, and made them lay down very much seed, and looked much after it himself. But when that toil was ended, he fared away every spring on a viking voyage and harried much about the Southern Isles and Ireland, and came home after midsummer. That he called his spring-viking. Then he was at home till the corn fields were reaped, and the grain seen to and stored. Then he fared away on a viking voyage and did not come home again till the winter was one month spent, and that he called his autumn-viking.'

Some of the wealthier gødings built themselves drinking halls, or even castles, on their properties. Sweyn of Gairsay had a large drinking-hall at Langskaill where he lived with what can only be described as a small court of eighty followers. This hall was 60ft long by 16ft wide, and before it was divided by cross-walls must have been a splendid example of its type, excelled only by those of the earl. Several castles are mentioned in the Saga. On Wyre, the excavated remains of that built by Kolbein Hruga are to be seen; there was a castle on the tiny isle of Damsay in the Bay of Firth (such island sites were favoured because they were difficult to take by surprise), and there was a third at Cairston, a mile east of Stromness near the farm Bu. At Westness on Rousay, home of Sigurd, Earl Paul's chief adviser, there was a strong tower. There were probably other strongholds on other gøding estates.

The church grew to power and influence in Norse Orkney, mainly after the time of Earl Thorfinn, whose Christ Church on the Brough of Birsay was probably the first major ecclesiastical building to be raised in the islands. For many years this was regarded as the senior church in Orkney; it may possibly have been the first seat of a bishop in the islands. Later, probably in the twelfth century, a small monastic community grew up around it. A second, which may also have had Celtic antecedents, was established on the tiny island of Eynhallow.

The bishopric was founded in either the first or second decade of the twelfth century, its first incumbent being William 'the Old'. William was bishop for about sixty years, and during this time the bishopric estates grew until they rivalled those of the earldom itself. The initial grants of land were almost certainly made to the bishopric by Earl Hakon, the slayer of Magnus, probably as a guilt offering. Hakon also made a pilgrimage to Jerusalem, and built the little round church in Orphir on his return, modelled upon the Church of the Holy Sepulchre. The estates grew through Bishop William's skill in extracting further grants from successive earls, by gifts from the pious, by the purchase of land as an investment and by the lending of money on wadsets which were never redeemed. Sometimes, gifts were made by those who wished to secure provision for themselves in old age. Fines were also levied in land for breaches of church law.

Another notable church is that dedicated in the name of St Magnus in Egilsay. Its round tower is visible from afar and betokens Irish connections. But, of the ecclesiastical monuments of Norse times, St Magnus Cathedral in Kirkwall is incomparably the finest. It was begun by Earl Rognvald in consequence of a vow he had made while striving to wrest the earldom from Earl

Round church in Orphir: a twelfth-century fragment

Paul; possibly the vow was suggested by Bishop William, who travelled to Norway at about that time. The canonisation of Magnus in 1136 was also the bishop's idea, almost certainly, and seems to have been a shrewd political move which rallied the support of a strong 'Magnus party' behind Rognvald. At all events, Rognvald provided the bishop with the cathedral he desired.

For the financing of the great building, it was announced that the odallers of Orkney would be excused the payments which they would be expected to make to all future earls at their accession by a once-for-all contribution to the cathedral. That many were able to do this and that the first part of the cathedral was built and consecrated before 1154 are clear evidences for the prosperity of Orkney at this time.

In addition to these notable church buildings, a great many small chapels were dotted about the countryside; these were distributed in a special way. Ever since King Harald Fairhair's day, the land had been divided into units worth 18d, called *eyrislands* or *urislands*; these units were used for the collection of skat. When Orkney became Christian, the urislands provided a readymade basis for church organisation, long before parishes were thought of. Urisland chapels and burial grounds became characteristic features of the Orkney landscape. In addition, some leading men built private chapels of their own, which remained their own personal property. When parishes were eventually laid out (the date of this is unknown) it was customary for the chapel of the principal family in that parish to become the parish church. Sometimes it was enlarged for the purpose. The remains of many urisland chapels lingered on for centuries, certainly down to the time of the first Statistical Account, 1795–8. Today, the parish church tends to be located near to what was, and often still is, the principal property in its parish.

The twelfth century saw the founding of two schools in Kirkwall. One was the Song School attached to St Magnus Cathedral, whose revenue came from three *bu* farms in Sanday. Only an earl could make such an endowment, and the connection with the cathedral points to Earl Rognvald as the benefactor. Kirkwall Grammar School drew its revenue from land in Wyre, the home of the Saga chief Kolbein Hruga. Kolbein's son was Bishop Bjarni, one of the most learned of all Orkney churchmen, and almost certainly he was the founder of this ancient school, among the oldest in Britain.

THE FADING OF NORSE POWER

Seen in retrospect, the events of twelfth-century Orkney remind one of a Halloween or Guy Fawkes fire. In the early evening the flames burn brightly and their warmth is a focus for excitement and jollity. Later the fire burns low, the visiting children go home and the night closes in, wet and smoky. The high quality of a few leading men and membership of an empire based upon mastery of the northern seas kept the night at bay for a while; but as this empire faded into history Orkney lapsed into the darkness of an isolation which was inevitable as soon as the northern sea lanes ceased to be important. The odal system of dividing the land helped; in only a few generations from the great saga days Orkney became a country of smallholders, and smallholders cannot afford high adventure. Most of those who were not smallholders were tenants on the growing earldom and bishopric estates.

Gradually the Norwegian crown lost the power to influence events in the northern isles of Scotland, while at the same time Scots influence grew apace. From the year 1230 all the earls of Orkney were Scots, though they still held their earldom from the crown of Norway. Scots settlement in the islands seems to have been gathering momentum at this period.

From time to time the Norwegians made a show of strength. It is significant that when King Hakon came across the sea to exert his power in 1230, half his expeditionary force for the onward voyage to the Hebrides and Man were drawn from Orkney; but when he came again in 1263, the Earl of Orkney, a Scot, though professing loyalty, stayed at home with his followers. Hakon's expedition met with disaster and the king returned to Kirkwall a broken man. He died in the long-vanished upper hall of the Bishop's Palace ten days before Christmas 1263, and his death marked the end of an age. Henceforth the earldom was administered directly from Norway by royal sysselmen, because no Scot could be trusted in effective occupation of it; and yet there was no legal alternative.

TRANSFER TO SCOTLAND

The Orkney earldom was restored to effectiveness and a degree of independence when Henry Lord Sinclair acceded to its dignity and properties in 1397, with the express approval of the Norwegian crown. Probably he was an Orkneyman and therefore more acceptable to the Norwegians than a mainland Scot. Very detailed instructions were drawn up by the crown to govern the new earl's behaviour, presumably a sign that the Norwegians were not very sure what he would do.

Page 89   A calm sea and sunlight on the perpendicular cliffs of western
Mainland, near North Gaulton Castle

Page 90 (above) Click mill of the early nineteenth century, on the remote moorland of Harray, Mainland; (below) Barony mills, Birsay, Mainland. The left-hand mill, built 1873, is the last working mill in Orkney

Henry Sinclair seems to have been an able and, except in one respect, loyal subject of his king. The exception was the great castle he built in Kirkwall, in defiance of the instructions given to him at his accession. Symbolically the castle stood between the town and the Bishop's Palace, dominating both. The strength of this castle was graphically attested two centuries later when an Earl of Caithness had the unenviable task of subduing it. 'I protest to God', he wrote, 'the house has never been biggit without the consent of the devil, for it is one of the strongest holds in Britain, without fellow.'

The Pledging

In 1468 the reality of Orkney's political situation was finally acknowledged by the transfer of the islands, together with Shetland, to the Scots crown. Yet even at this late date an open and final transfer of ownership does not appear to have been politically practical. The odd arrangements made presumably reflected the exact stage reached in the delicate power-shift from Norwegian to Scot in the northern isles of Scotland.

Norway and Denmark had now been united under a single crown for half a century, and at this point in time the crown was worn by Christian I, King of Denmark and Norway. The order of precedence within the union is revealed by this title. King Christian was a Dane who found himself saddled with irksome problems deriving from former Norwegian colonial enterprises. To him fell the thankless task of making new arrangements with Scotland which recognised the facts of political life in the mid-fifteenth century. The time was ripe for change; the problem was how best to make it.

The solution took the form of a marriage settlement between King Christian and James III of Scotland. Christian's only daughter Margaret was contracted to marry James before the latter ascended the throne, and it was then agreed that she should bring with her a dowry of 60,000 florins of the Rhine. Of this sum, 10,000 were to be paid immediately, the rest guaranteed by the pledging of Danish royal rights in Orkney to King James.

It seems almost certain that Christian never intended to raise this very large sum. What he did was to pay 2,000 florins and to pledge his rights in Shetland for the remaining 8,000. It is

F

interesting to note the great difference between the valuations of the two island groups at this time. No further payments have ever been made, and in theory both island groups remain 'in pawn', capable of being redeemed by Denmark on payment of the agreed sum. King James's subsequent actions strongly suggest that he and Christian had agreed privately that the transfer, alleged to be temporary, was to be permanent.

James now had in his personal possession all Norse royal lands in Orkney; he also gained the allegiance of the earl, but not the earl's estates. His first move entrenched his position so firmly that any reversal of the transfer became virtually impossible. He made himself Earl of Orkney in person by requiring Earl William Sinclair to exchange his Orkney estates for a royal estate in Fife. After this, only the bishopric lands and the lands of surviving odal farmers lay outside James' personal jurisdiction. There can have been no doubt in the mind of James or of any Scotsman that henceforth Orkney was to be a Scottish province. Nevertheless, the history of Orkney remained somewhat separate from that of Scotland for another century and a half.

King James had of course no intention of living in his new earldom. He therefore appointed tacksmen who paid an annual sum for their privileges and were left to conduct themselves in Orkney as profitably as they saw fit. The first tacksmen recognised the ancient laws and customs of Orkney and life proceeded much as before, though more and more Scotsmen settled in the islands. In 1489 the tack was granted to Henry, Lord Sinclair, who was grandson to the last earl and of an ancient Orcadian family. Unhappily this just man fell at Flodden in 1513 and henceforth the tack passed to lesser men who showed neither understanding nor compassion in their charge.

Misrule sparked off a rebellion in Orkney in 1528, led by another representative of the Sinclair line. A Scots army was sent from Caithness to restore order and was trounced at Summerdale (the name means 'south boundary dale') near the parish boundary of Stenness and Orphir. The Ordnance map marks the place and date but not the name. Significantly the Scots took no reprisals. It was thought prudent not to press the Orcadians too hard in case they appealed to Denmark for help. The leader of the rebels, James Sinclair, was later knighted, given extensive personal properties in the North Isles, and made tacksman of Orkney. In 1540 King James V demonstrated his interest in the political health of the northern isles by paying a state visit to Orkney, while the ancient Norse laws were formally confirmed by the parliament of Scotland in 1567.

THE STEWART EARLS

King James V, following the fashion of monarchs of his day, had several illegitimate sons, and one of these, Lord Robert Stewart, obtained a heritable grant of the earldom of Orkney and the office of sheriff from Mary Queen of Scots in 1564. His appointment ushered in what is always regarded as the darkest period of Orkney history.

It would appear that Earl Robert, (he was granted this title in 1581) and his son Patrick were tyrants who exploited Orkney for purely personal gain. Details of Robert's principal depredations were set out in a Complaint presented by leading men in Orkney to the Crown in 1575, while a similarly comprehensive list of Patrick's misdemeanours was later contained in a letter from Bishop James Law to James VI. Bishop Law was appointed Bishop of Orkney in 1603 and was mainly instrumental in the final removal of the Stewarts from power.

Relatively little is known about the Stewarts apart from these two damaging documents, and certain events of the time suggest that they had other sides to their characters than those presented by their accusers. In the present state of knowledge, final judgement must be suspended for lack of proper information. A reassessment of the traditional view of Earl Patrick Stewart is certainly a possibility.

In the Orkney landscape, the Stewart phase is represented by two fine palaces: Earl Robert's palace in Birsay, which looks out to the Brough where Earl Thorfinn had his residence, and Earl Patrick's in Kirkwall. The second is an architectural gem; it has in fact been described as the finest renaissance building ever raised in Scotland, and is a great asset to the town.

The difficulty of deciding what the Stewarts were really like is illustrated by the desperate events which brought their rule to an end. In 1609 Earl Patrick was arrested for treason and taken to Edinburgh for examination. Instead of waiting quietly for his case to be forgotten, as it might well have been in those days of uncertain justice, he sent his young son Robert to Orkney to recover his lands by force of arms. This extraordinary action has never been explained satisfactorily. King James VI (James I of England) ruled Scotland with a firmness never seen before, and a rebellion in Orkney was no more likely to succeed than one in the Isle of Wight today.

Young Robert Stewart landed in Orkney in May 1614. Immediately a strong force of Orkneymen gathered around him, mainly drawn from West Mainland. This ready support after so great an alleged tyranny has never been properly explained either. It has been suggested that Robert's mother came from this district, and that through her influence as the earl's favourite mistress his oppressions there had been less severe. The tenants on Earl Patrick's former estates also rallied to Robert's support. Robert established himself in the earl's palace in Birsay, built up a force armed with 'hagbutis, muscattis, pouder, lead and other warlike provisioun' and in July marched to Kirkwall 'with sounding of trumpettis, touking of drummis, ensignes displayit' and captured the Sinclair castle and the two palaces without serious opposition. Their coming does not seem to have been entirely unwelcome to the people of Kirkwall. Preparations were immediately put in hand to repel the inevitable counter-attack from Scotland, and a ship was sent to Bergen for more 'pouder and bullet'.

In Edinburgh there was some consternation at this turn of events; but the only real question to be decided was, who could conduct the punitive expedition most economically? A willing leader was ready to hand in the person of George, Earl of Caithness, whose forebear had been defeated by the Orkneymen at Summerdale. So keen was he to go to Orkney that he even offered to bear the expenses of the campaign himself. One can imagine the relief with which his offer was accepted. Earl George sailed for Orkney with two warships, taking with him a small force of soldiers and cannon from Edinburgh Castle, prepared to pound the Sinclair castle into rubble if necessary.

The conduct of the campaign suggests Earl George to have been a soldier of considerable incompetence who was fortunate enough to be faced by one even more incompetent and with less experience. If the earl knew that Robert Stewart had mobilised a force of 500 well-armed men in Kirkwall, then his plan of operations was an absurdity—unless he knew that Robert would never be able to lead such a force effectively. He sailed through the String and landed his men just to the south of Carness only two miles from his adversary's base. Robert Stewart had a splendid opportunity to strike a crippling blow while the Caithness men were getting their guns ashore and so to repeat the triumph of Summerdale in even more spectacular fashion. In fact he marched his men out from Kirkwall, fired a few desultory shots in the general direction of the invaders, and then retired. When the invaders were safely ashore he came out again, but thinking the opposition now too strong he retreated for good. This display of military ineptitude caused most of Robert's supporters to leave hastily for home, hoping not to be recognised when the day of reckoning came.

Robert now established himself in the cathedral tower, the Earl's Palace and the Sinclair castle with his mother and a band of devoted followers. Earl George had his cannon dragged to Weyland just north of Kirkwall and on 27 August began his bombardment. Two days later the guns were brought closer and a monster called 'thrawn-mouth', firing at point-blank range, soon made the palace and cathedral tower untenable. The rebels took final refuge in the castle. They now numbered only sixteen men; and yet, so strong was this building, that the besiegers still thought a frontal assault too hazardous.

The bombardment continued with little result for several weeks until the besiegers were short of ammunition. 'This castle is one of the strongest houses in Britain', wrote Earl George, 'for I will bring with me . . . cannon bullets broken like golf balls upon the castle, and clovin in twa haffs.' Bishop Law watched the progress of the siege, or rather the lack of it, and wrote that at long last a breach had been made in the wall, but that 'the haill pouder, except ane half barrell' was used up. Had not treachery delivered the fortress into Earl George's hand the siege might have been a very long one indeed. As it was Robert Stewart's chief adviser Patrick Halcro turned traitor and betrayed the garrison into the besiegers' power. Young Robert was taken to Edinburgh and executed for treason.

Five weeks later his father Patrick was also executed. Right at the end it was discovered that he did not know, or at least would not say, the Lord's Prayer, and his execution was postponed 'till he were better informed, and received the Lord's Supper . . . So he communicate upon the Lord's Day, the 5th of Februare, and was beheadit at the Mercate Cross of Edinburgh upon Monday the 6th of Februare.' The year was 1615.

Bishop Law performed a further notable service to Orkney. Earl George was determined to wreak an indiscriminate vengeance upon Orkney for being involved in the Stewart rebellion. The tower of St Magnus had sheltered rebels, therefore he proposed to blow it up, and the rest of the cathedral with it. The bishop forbade any such thing, and the quality of the man was such that he, and not Earl George, had his way. So St Magnus Cathedral was saved for posterity, and the earl had to content himself with rampaging through the islands, slaying, banishing and levying fines.

The last puffs of sulphurous smoke from Earl George's cannon marked the end of a separate history for Orkney. Henceforth the islands formed an integral part of Scotland and later of the United Kingdom. There were occasional hints of a continuing Danish interest in the theoretically redeemable pledge, but in terms of practical politics such interest had no significance. Orkney had become a county of Scotland.

5　FROM THE STEWARTS TO VICTORIA

J AMES VI's suppression of the Stewart earls in Orkney was
part of a wider policy whereby this strong and capable,
though inevitably poor king strove to exert effective authority
beyond the Scottish Lowlands. In the Highlands, his determined
moves to impose the will of central government were actuated
in part by roseate views of riches waiting to be exploited there,
notably in fisheries. There was a widespread opinion at court
that disloyal clan chiefs were obstructing the legitimate development of Highland resources to the loss of the royal treasury. It
may be that similar considerations helped to move the king to
action in Orkney. The earls had built two fine palaces for themselves in two generations and may therefore have been suspected
of withholding substantial revenue from the crown. Whether
this was so or not, it is clear from observation of the king's own
methods in the Highlands that the oppression of Earls Robert and
Patrick and other outrages were fairly normal practice in the
Scotland of their day. It was the suspicion of treason rather than
any moral objection to their behaviour which led to their removal.
Henceforth, despite the county's remoteness, the future of Orkney's people was bound up closely with political and economic
events in Scotland.

In the early seventeenth century Scotland was still a medieval
country—in modern terms it was a classic example of an under-
developed country. The lot of most Scots was grinding poverty
and famine was a constant threat over large areas, especially in
the Highlands. Farming, primitive at that, was the economic
mainstay of the people. Industry was practically non-existent.
Communications were extremely rudimentary and large parts
of the country were inaccessible at certain times of the year because of snow or flooding.

Government was conducted on feudal principles, but in the Highlands the distinctive clan organisation sometimes clashed with both the theory and practice of a central government which was Lowland based. Such trade as existed was monopolised absolutely by a few tiny Royal Burghs, and outside these centres there were neither villages nor towns. Crafts were also monopolised by the Burghs, and none could be practised outside their limits. Kirkwall was a Royal Burgh and therefore under Scots law possessed complete monopoly over trade and crafts throughout Orkney. The next Royal Burgh along the eastern side of Scotland was Inverness, which held the monopoly for Caithness, Sutherland and its own county. On the west coast, the nearest Burgh to Kirkwall was Dumbarton.

In international trade Scotland was a primary producer, selling such items as cattle driven south from the Highlands for fattening, hides and skins, wool, furs, fish and timber. Manufactures and luxury goods all had to be imported, and there was a constant deficiency in the balance of trade which resulted in Scots currency falling from parity with English in the thirteenth century to one-twelfth its value in the eighteenth.

When at last Scotland began to modernise its economy and institutions, most of the reforming ideas and practices took root first in the Lowlands, so that Orkney became more remote and backward rather than less so. Improved farming methods were applied first in such counties as the Lothians and Berwickshire. Many of the new practices were not in any case appropriate to contemporary conditions in Orkney. Industry when it came needed coal and Orkney, being devoid of mineral resources, could take no part in the new developments.

On the credit side, the religious and political fanaticism of the times were moderated by the time they reached Orkney. The islands' leading men were determined to avoid trouble. For instance, when the Marquis of Montrose landed in Orkney in 1650 on his way to lead a Stewart rising in the south, he was received courteously enough by Orkney's chief citizens. They did not prevent his enrolling 2,000 of their tenants, but when he left not one of the chief citizens went with him. Montrose suffered utter rout at Carbisdale near the head of Dornoch Firth, almost within sight of the place where Earl Sigurd the Mighty lay buried; and Orkney's men of property no doubt congratulated themselves on their discretion.

During the Cromwellian occupation of Scotland and the Dutch war, an English garrison came to Kirkwall and a fort was built on the shore near the place where the Earl of Caithness had set up his cannon. The English soldiery were no great nuisance to the Orcadians, and legend has it that they taught local people better methods of gardening. Part of the Cromwellian interest in the north isles of Scotland related to the valuable fisheries which for generations had been a mainstay of Dutch prosperity. Successive Scottish and British governments tried to stop the Dutch fishing in north isles waters, or to tax them when they did, and also to encourage Scotsmen to compete with them; but the Dutch retained a strong position until the Napoleonic wars, and indeed their stern-sailed drifters were to be seen each season in large numbers in harbours from Lerwick southwards until 1939.

The Jacobite troubles of the eighteenth century all but passed Orkney by. There were a good many 'ale-house Jacobites' among the islands' leading men and copious healths were drunk with due ceremony to the king over the water; but nobody actually took any action on his behalf. Nevertheless this indiscreet toping came to the ears of a nervous government and there was a little unpleasantness in Orkney after 1745, so that Westray to this day has a 'gentlemen's cave' where certain citizens prudently took refuge for a while.

TRADING ACTIVITIES

Orkney was remote from the centres of development in Scotland, but it was still well placed to benefit from any commercial activity involving use of the northabout route through Pentland. It was also suitable as an advanced base for voyages into high latitudes.

This advantage of position was apparent in the period before the American War of Independence when the British government strove through Navigation Acts to control and tax all shipping using American colonial ports. This onerous arrangement required all such ships to call at a British customs port on every voyage to or from North America. It became usual for American ships bound to and from such ports as Archangel, Riga, St Petersburg, Gothenburg, Bergen, Hamburg and Amsterdam to call at Kirkwall to pay their dues. A British customs station was established in the town and proved very lucrative. Between 1745 and 1774 American vessels paid at least 84 per cent of the customs collected each year in Kirkwall. Then came the quarrel with the North American colonies, and in 1775 the figure dropped to zero. While it lasted the American trade brought much profit to Orkney, but it had of course no natural basis and there was no lasting benefit to the islands' economy.

Kirkwall also exported quantities of grain, mainly bere and oatmeal. Most of this was carried in smacks owned either in Kirkwall itself or in Leith (the modern link with Aberdeen had not yet been forged). Usual destinations were the west Highlands and Norway, where grain shortages were common, also the Netherlands, Ireland, Spain and Portugal. The cargoes carried back to Orkney included Norwegian timber, Dutch utensils and Spanish salt. Ships went to the Baltic for flax and to central Scotland for coal. As yet, there were no regular shipping services between Orkney and mainland Scotland.

Profits from the grain trade and its complementary import business led to the rise of a merchant class in Orkney who invested their capital in land. In consequence several large estates' were built up by an entirely new class of landowner. The Baikies were merchant-landowners of this kind; they seem to have originated in Beaquoy, Birsay. In the Kirkwall of Stewart days they built up a business founded in part on the earl's extravagances. In 1650 they bought the property of Tankerness on Deer Sound and shortly afterwards they appear in the records as among the largest landowners in Orkney. Being first and foremost merchants, the Baikies like many others in their class bought a town house in Kirkwall; this was Tankerness House, opposite St Magnus Cathedral.

Among other families who made their money in Kirkwall trade and later branched out as landowners were the Traills, whose founder-member in Kirkwall business was George Traill, Earl Patrick's chamberlain, the Craigies, Richans, Youngs, Moncrieffs and some others. Their presence shows Kirkwall to have been something of a growth point in an otherwise static rural economy, and this was to be important when the time came for estate improvement in the nineteenth century. Working as it were in the opposite direction, a number of landowners who managed to accumulate a small amount of capital from grain sales invested their gains in the trading ventures of Kirkwall merchants, and when these proved successful, they put out their money to would-be landowners on mortgage. The general picture is of a close connection between many landowners and the merchant community based mainly, though not exclusively in Kirkwall. During the eighteenth century and up to the Napoleonic wars, a similar connection between landowners and merchants developed in Stromness, once that town had broken Kirkwall's trade and craft monopoly.

RURAL LIFE

Conditions in the Orkney countryside in the three centuries following the fall of the Stewart earls were primitive and change was so slow as to appear non-existent within the lifetime of an individual. For most Orcadians living on the land, whether tenant or landlord, life was poor and uneventful. The Orkney countryside of today owes many of its aspects to the developments, both social and economic, of these centuries.

The tunships

Ever since Norse times, and probably long before, the country people of Orkney have lived in small, distinct communities, called by the Norsemen *tuns*. The Orkney tun, tunship or town (spellings vary) has persisted into modern times. Their distribution was well shown on Murdoch Mackenzie's maps of the 1750s. They then had the appearance of islands of settlement and cultivation set among the moorlands which occupied the greater part of Orkney. Many tunships were coastal, fertile enclaves set between sea and hill.

Originally the Norse founding family of a tunship lived at its head-house or bu and most other members of the tunship community were related to it. Many would have the name of the tunship as their surname. Later, this simple pattern of ownership was disrupted by the incoming of Scots settlers and even more effectively by the expropriations of Stewart times. The Scots

101

changed the character of the old tunship community in a fundamental way, by transforming the independent odaller into a tenant, who held his land on short lease or no lease at all from a proprietor, small or great. Thus, the group of houses and fields which constituted a tunship in the eighteenth century probably looked much as it had done in the twelfth, but its social structure was quite different. Proprietors lived much as their tenants for the most part; only one, Gilbert Balfour of Westray, tried to build himself a great house, the grim castle of Noltland. About 1750 a typical tunship consisted of several properties, perhaps two or three, which in turn were split between several farms. Each farm held a compact block of the *toomal*, the best land in the tunship and anciently cultivated. Outside these toomals were arable fields called sheads which were divided into a great number of strips or rigs. Because the quality of soil in these fields was variable, the rigs were allocated in turn to the farms, beginning in the north or east and proceeding to south and west. Thus the head-house would hold the north—or easternmost rig, the next senior farm the next rig, and so on. Rigs remained the permanent property of their farms. The whole arrangement of intermingled strips was termed runrig.

Strips of grass, called merkesters, were interspersed with the arable rigs; there were also larger areas of grass or meadows. In addition there was unimproved land on which stock grazed. Both grass and rough grazings were as intricately divided between the farms as the arable.

The tunship was enclosed by a dyke of turf and stones about 3ft high. This separated it from the moor, which was used in common by the whole tunship community. Here a man might dig peats and graze an agreed number of animals. Inside the tunship the cultivated land was totally unenclosed, partly because of the inordinate length of walling which would have been needed to go around all the small plots. In consequence growing crops were at the mercy of wandering stock. There was also a strong prejudice against any kind of enclosure, which was looked upon as an infringement of the natural liberties of man and beast.

About 1760 the first attempt was made to rearrange the tunship lands into more convenient units. This first 'planking' of the land removed the ancient runrig system over much of Orkney but failed to replace it with anything better. Every farmer in the tunship insisted on having his fair share of all qualities of land, and the result was a patchwork arrangement much like the old, though intended to be very different. This new-old state of affairs was described by the minister of Evie and Rendall in 1797. 'Above 30 years ago, a division took place, but so injudicious, that even where there are large and compact fields belonging to a single proprietor, and divided into nine or a dozen farms, each farmer possesses perhaps twelve patches of ground, of a plank each, scattered over the whole.'

Real improvement had to wait until the middle of the next century, when a second planking was carried out and the land divided into compact and viable farm units. The modern landscape of rectilinear fields mainly derives from this second planking, which was to be a major foundation for all subsequent agricultural advance in the islands. The second planking was carried out by owners of estates who had been influenced by reforming ideas from the south and who had greater financial capacity, at least in many cases, for making their wishes effective.

Farming practices

In the tunships, agricultural practices were extremely primitive and relied upon the use of large numbers of low-paid workers. Two crops were grown almost exclusively, oats and bere. There was no proper crop rotation, though there was some alternation. In winter the toomal was manured by trampling stock. More systematic manuring was rare, though as far back as Jacobite times some more enlightened estate owners did put animal and household manure and also seaweed on their crops. Crop yields were very low though difficult to compute exactly because of the great confusion about common weights and measures, deliberately engineered by the Stewart earls. Because of these low yields, every scrap of grain was meticulously cut and counted on the well-run farms. There was no drainage; fields were full of weeds; and the quality of grain crops had not been improved since neolithic times.

The chief instrument of cultivation was the single-stilt plough, an example of which may be examined in Tankerness House museum. This ineffectual contraption was thus described by Daniel Gorrie, writing about 1860; he never saw one in actual use. 'The old Orkney plough was single-stilted and wanted a mould-board. It was drawn by three and sometimes four ponies or oxen, which were yoked abreast and had their heads fastened to a beam of wood. The driver, grasping this piece of wood with one hand and his whip with the other, walked backwards in front of the animals; and the ploughman, following up in the rear, leant his weight against one side of the instrument, occasionally using a pattle-tree to clear away clods, or hasten the pace of his refractory team. All this expenditure of energy was quite superfluous, as the plough only scratched the surface of the fields, and the trampling of so many feet and hoofs poached the soil when soft, and hardened it when dry . . . Notwithstanding the imperfection of the instrument, there must have been a delightful picturesqueness in the rural scenes of springtime, when the teams of oxen, rigged out in homespun harness, toiled slowly up and down the infield patches of ground, dragging at their indignant heels the ancient plough of Egypt and Rome.'

This plough was followed by a harrow with wooden teeth, often dragged by the womenfolk. Again to quote Gorrie, this instrument 'served only to comb the ground that had been previously scratched'.

Livestock were of low quality, and the shortage of winter feed such as turnips made it impossible to keep more than a minimum of beasts through the winter. Orkney cattle were very small, black, white, brown and brindled, and have now entirely vanished. When fully grown they were about the size of a modern bullock, though much less plump. They produced tough meat and a minimum of milk. Together with the native short-tailed sheep, now preserved only on the beaches of North Ronaldsay, the cattle were driven out to the commons in spring and left very much to their own devices until the autumn. Gorrie describes the hazards of their return when the common grazings had become exhausted. 'The *infield*, or land under cultivation, was almost entirely destitute of enclosures, and when the autumn stampede of livestock occurred, late crops inevitably disappeared before the hunger and hoofs of the invaders. During the winter and spring months the infields became a commonty, crowded with cattle, horses, sheep, swine and geese.' At least the manure must have been beneficial.

Living conditions

The houses of both landlord and tenant in the seventeenth and eighteenth centuries were of the same general type, with very few exceptions. This old Orkney house was long and low in proportion, built of drystone with a roof of thatch supported on a frame of imported timber or driftwood. In some areas such as Rackwick in Hoy and Stromness, thin flagstones could be obtained locally and these replaced thatch as the roofing material. The house was divided into a 'but' and a 'ben' end by a free-standing fire 'back', against which a peat fire perpetually burned filling the whole house with acrid smoke. There was a chimney, or more accurately a hole in the roof framed by rough boards, called a lum, which drew out some of the smoke, but the general effect was to fill the house with smoke without either warming or drying it effectively. Roofs were not waterproof, and in heavy rain a mixture of cold water and soot dripped down the necks and into the food of the unwary.

But and ben were really a single room, and between them they fulfilled all the functions of living, which included not only working and resting, cooking, eating and sleeping but also the care of a variety of livestock. Calves would customarily be raised indoors, hens roosted on the rafters and geese nested in recesses at floor level. There would be dogs and cats, often a sow and her piglets. There were no windows, the only light coming through the lum or sometimes skylights. Furniture was of the most rudimentary kind and some of it was made of stone, rather in the manner of Skara Brae. Stone 'fitted furniture' included shelves and cupboards, a quern recess where meal was prepared, and a water-jar shelf. The floor was sometimes flagged but more often of trodden earth, which was seldom dry in winter. In early times the beds consisted of stone recesses set into the wall; later wooden box-beds became fairly general, except in the poorer houses. These were placed cross-ways to partition the room, since there were no internal walls, and clothes were stored on top. In the ben end, really the best room, the master and mistress of the house slept in some degree of privacy. Here was to be found the ale-hurry or cupboard, often a large recess, which was under the master's personal jurisdiction.

The opposite end or but led straight into the byre. Entrance to the whole building was usually through the house to the byre, so that man and beast shared the same door and the same roof and of course certain other characteristics. The ever-present smoke must have been invaluable as a disinfectant. Sometimes a barn was added to the byre making a very long house indeed, but often barn and byre were separate, standing alongside the house with a narrow sheltered close between them and it. In appearance the two long buildings were almost indistinguishable, but the barn might have a round tower-like kiln at the end, used to dry grain. These round kilns were a highly characteristic feature of old Orkney houses. Doors in opposite walls of the barn created a cross draught during threshing, to blow away the chaff. Threshing was done with a flail, a simple but effective instrument.

Inside, the byre looked like a larger version of the stalled burial cairn of megalithic times. Thin flagstone slabs were placed vertically along one wall to make stalls where cattle were tethered. A flagged culvert ran along the floor in the centre of the building leading to an oddle-hole by which liquid manure was drained off. In winter the floor level rose inexorably as dung and the peat-mould and ashes used for bedding accumulated, until the animals' heads were near the roof. To postpone the unpleasant job of cleaning out as long as possible, a second row of tethering places (lithies) was set high in the wall. When a horse was kept in the byre his feed was placed high in the corner so that it would be at the right height when the floor level rose. At cleaning-out time a small platform of waste was left for him to stand on.

The diet of the islanders was monotonous rather than inadequate. There were of course bad years when grain had to be imported to prevent famine, but in normal years Orkney landlords exported a certain amount of grain. Oatmeal and bere-meal were the staples of diet. Both were made into a porridge, while bere was made into a dark bread. Bere-meal was eaten with cabbage, a patch of which grew at almost every house; turnips and potatoes were also important. Finely ground bere-meal was roasted to make burstin, a flavouring for buttermilk and other foods. Its preparation required much skill, and a miller

Page 107 (above) Interior of an old Orkney house about 1890, showing fire-back and, in the background, a box-bed; (below) harvest time in Birsay, late nineteenth century

Page 108 *(above)* Air view looking south-east over Kirkwall. The Peerie Sea lies at the bottom right, with built-over reclaimed land between it and the old town; *(below)* Kirkwall in 1766, from *Estate of Grain* map—a single street leading to the houses on the ayre, a cathedral and crumbling palaces beside the Peerie Sea

who made burstin well was highly regarded. Bere was also made into Orkney 'home-brew', which was drunk by all members of the family, and replaced milk in winter-time.

Every householder tried to keep at least one cow, whose milk provided an essential balancing element in the diet. A pig was kept, to be killed and salted in autumn. There were usually a few hens, and a goose, whose fate was to be smoked at a time of celebration. Fish supplemented the diet of those who lived near sea or loch.

The way a man and his family lived depended very much upon the rent his landlord charged. Some indication of the living standard about 1790 may be gathered from the fact that a plough-man received from £2 10s to £3 10s with full board for a year's work, while a manservant was paid from 12s to £1 with board for harvest; and that oatmeal cost 1s 3d–2s 6d a stone, beef 2d a pound, eggs 2d a dozen, butter 6d a pound and a whole goose 1s–1s 3d.

Parish and tunship

The tunships lay in parishes, of which at the present day there are twenty-one in Orkney. Originally there may have been more, but the exact number in early times is unclear. It is not known when these parishes were laid out, but it is interesting to note that evidence exists for their being pre-Christian administrative units of some kind. The parishes in Mainland, for example, correspond so well with what must have been obvious and visible subdivisions in terms of streams, ridges and other features in the days before farm improvements made everywhere look much alike, that it seems very likely that they formed the administrative units of Norse pagan times, and the Norsemen may well have adopted them from the Picts. On this last point we have no certain information.

Since the Reformation, each parish has had its parish church; these replaced the many chapels formerly dotted over the country-side. Parish churches usually stand on the site of chapels that dated from Norse times and on land which had then belonged to the principal landowner of the district. Some Norse chapels are known to have been built on Celtic Christian chapel sites. Thus, although most Orkney parish churches as we see them today are of nineteenth-century date, their sites are usually very ancient indeed. Continuity of occupation through many successive periods is a recurring theme in Orkney.

THE OLD STATISTICAL ACCOUNT

Before leaving this account of life and conditions in post-Stewart Orkney, it is necessary to refer to that monumental work of Sir John Sinclair of Ulbster, the *Old Statistical Account of Scotland*. This distinguished Caithness baronet, who invented the very word 'statistics', caused every minister in Scotland to write an account of his parish, based upon a questionnaire of 166 items. The results were published in twenty-one volumes in 1791–9. The Orkney parish accounts were published as they came in and are therefore inconveniently scattered through the volumes. They give us a unique picture of conditions in the islands immediately before the processes of modernisation began to take effect.

Churches and ministers

The men who answered Sir John Sinclair's formidable list of questions were men of high quality for the most part who were working under considerable difficulties. Reading their reports, one gets the impression that their cultural isolation was very great, rather like that of teachers in African bush schools today, and also that they were well able to bear it from the strength of their own characters. They reported that the Orkney people were generally speaking industrious, peaceable and hospitable and that there were virtually no class distinctions. Thus the minister of Rousay and Egilsay noted, under Sir John's heading 'Manners', that 'there is no difference in manners and habits between the cottager and the master of the farm. The master often turns to the cottager, and the cottager sometimes becomes the master. They all take social snuff together. Their houses and their furniture are exactly the same.'

Sometimes there were difficulties occasioned by superstition. The minister of South Ronaldsay and Burray noted that twice in the past seven years he had been interrupted in administering baptism to a small girl, before a boy who was also to be baptised. The parishioners feared that, if the girl were baptised first, she would certainly grow up with a strong beard and the boy would have none. Marriage dates were fixed after close study of the state of the moon and sometimes of the tide. On the whole, however, the Orcadians do not appear to have been unduly superstitious; or perhaps they did not tell their beliefs to their ministers.

The greatest difficulties were perhaps those occasioned by disintegrating buildings, for the repair of which no money could, or would, be found by the principal landowners of the parishes. The minister of Rendall and Evie was particularly scathing in his remarks, saying that he continued to officiate on alternate Sundays in his two condemned church buildings 'till the year 1788, when the danger became so conspicuous, that he fortunately deserted that of Evie, as the walls soon afterwards tumbled down on a Sunday, and the materials were set up to auction. The minister then travelled every Sunday to Rendall, and officiated in that ruinous house . . . till October 1794, when having lost his health officiating there, and that house also becoming very hazardous, he was obliged, by the injunctions of his physician, to desert it; so that, since that period, there has been no public worship in this charge, except in the open air, in the churchyard.' The minister of Hoy, who wrote cryptically that his parish 'does not furnish much room for Statistical investigation' and whose family at one time numbered twenty-two, said that his church had fallen down 'of itself before the heritors would offer to make any reparation of it, and at last they rebuilt it, and that in a very slight manner, so that it is not above half finished'. On the other hand, the state of many churches is not mentioned at all and may be assumed therefore to have been satisfactory. The condition of manses aroused much comment. The minister of Hoy was afraid to walk on his floors because they were so wormeaten, the incumbent of Westray complained of the extremely inconvenient location of his manse in relation to the churches he had to serve, while he of Evie had to live in a new manse without plaster or floors for two years, and the new building, though commodious, was 'exceedingly insufficient, receiving water at almost every part of the walls and roof'. The minister of Walls also had a new manse, built a long way from the old so as to be near the peat diggings. After careful consideration, he concluded that it was preferable to carry peat a short distance and to have a long walk to church than vice versa. 'In a country where there are few days, even in summer, that a fire can be dispensed with, the article of fuel comes to be a matter of material consequence.'

Most churches and manses in Orkney were either built, or rebuilt, between 1680 and 1730. If they received no further attention, which often seems to have been the case, they must have been in a poor condition by the time the first Statistical Account was compiled.

Agricultural improvements

Although most ministers deplore the backward state of agriculture, and support their conclusion with some knowledgeable observation, there are a few reports of improvement even at this early date. Enclosures had already begun here and there, as in Orphir, where Patrick Honeyman of Graemsay had also introduced two Scots ploughs on his property; the rest of Orphir was worked by 100 single-stilted ploughs. In Stronsay, some enclosure had been done and grain was growing on land which from time immemorial had been waste. On Eday the landlord Robert Baikie of Tankerness, a member of the old Kirkwall merchant family, granted his tenant a nineteen-year lease, and merely by giving him this degree of security encouraged him to enclose his land, introduce Scots ploughs, improve his cattle and mend his buildings.

The most striking improvements were those made by Major Balfour on the island of Shapinsay. He obtained the estate in the west of the island in 1782; his achievement was thus described by Rev George Barry :

'Previous to his purchase, nothing was to be seen over its whole extent, but a dreary waste, interspersed with arable land ill cultivated, a few miserable hovels thinly scattered over its surface, under the name of farm houses or cottages, which were not fit to shelter from the rigours of the climate a few ragged inhabitants, dirty through indolence, lean with hunger, and torpid by despair. Every thing on this estate now happily wears a very different and more pleasant aspect. An elegant house has been built, and an extensive garden laid out; the lands are substantially enclosed, and judiciously cultivated with the English plough; many barren fields are, by cultivation, made fertile; summer fallowing, with a change of seed and rotation of crops, is introduced with good effect; and the soil which formerly bore with reluctance coarse grass, and scanty heather, and puny oats and bear [bere], now cheerfully produces oats, rye, barley, pease, wheat, potatoes, clover, and turnips, in considerable quantity and of a good quality. Together with these improvements, the same gentleman has erected a little village by the side of the harbour of Elwick, in which he has placed joiners, carpenters. weavers, tailors, shoemakers, coopers, and labourers of various sorts, furnished them with work sufficient to employ them; and thus enabled them from the fruits of their industry to marry early, and to produce numerous families. In short, Cliffdale, which is the name of this gentleman's seat, taken in conjunction with its appendages, exhibits to the eye of a stranger coming from the sea, or from Kirkwall, rather the appearance of a neat little villa in the vicinity of some opulent city, than of a gentleman's house recently raised in a remote sequestered part of the kingdom.'

Major Balfour was resident on his estate, something most unusual on the larger Orkney properties of his time. At the end of his report on his parish, the minister underlines the advantages accruing from this fact.

'Among the people in a country parish, whose farms are small and whose tacks [leases] are only verbal, the residence of heritors, if they be men of sense and virtue, is of the greatest advantage. They silence disputes, and terminate any differences which may arise, by their authority; they set an example of industry, and by their smiles or their frowns, not only distinguish the deserving from the worthless, but reward the one, while they punish the other.'

The Rev Barry was much concerned that population should increase, regarding this as an index of progress, and he notes that it had done so under the Balfour administration in a most satisfactory manner. In 1755 the population of the island was 642, in 1790 it was 730. His final comment: 'The cause of this increased population, we are able to trace to the residence of a single proprietor.'

The kelp industry

A number of reports on the coastal parishes in Orkney carry

references to kelp making. This was in fact one of the only ways by which a landlord, in the economic conditions of the times, might extract some profit from his island estate.

Kelp was the ash produced when certain kinds of seaweed were burned. It was an essential material in bleaching, soap and glassmaking and the production of alum. Most Orkney kelp was shipped to Tyneside for use in riverside glassworks. Four species of seaweed were used, the tangle itself, sea-oak or black tang, bell-wrack or yellow tang, and serrated seaweed or prickly tang. The weed was cut with billhooks from November onwards and taken in barrows to a convenient beach to dry. About March burning began, the dried weed being placed in burning kilns which would be built or dug on the shore, depending upon local circumstances. Eventually a liquid was produced, which it was essential to keep free of sand and other impurities, a difficult task in Orkney winds. When this liquid cooled, which took about two days, a solid substance resulted, which was cut out and stacked under cover to await transhipment.

The first Orkney landlord to develop the kelp industry was James Fea of Whitehall in Stronsay in 1722. He brought an expert from Fraserburgh to instruct his tenants in the appropriate methods. This man, by name Meldrum, believed the Orcadians were simpler than they were, and tried to persuade them that certain incantations, which he alone knew and for which he charged, were necessary for success. The Orcadians were not persuaded, but shortly afterwards they were busy adulterating their kelp with sand and small stones in order to increase their profits. When the adulteration was discovered by the purchaser in Newcastle, the price of Orkney kelp fell but the industry still remained profitable. Landlords encouraged their tenants to participate in the industry by such devices as subdividing properties to such an extent that they were too small to support a man and his family, driving him to the kelp making. Foreshores were carefully divided into short sections for kelp gathering, a process made possible by the persistence of the old Norse odal law with respect to the coastal limits of properties.

When the *Old Statistical Account* was compiled, kelp making was in its heyday, and the minister of Stronsay calculated that his parishioners had earned, for their landlords and themselves, no less than £29,000 in 71 years, a sum equal to 41 years' rent for all properties in the islands; and that the rest of Orkney had earned nine times as much. No wonder he styled kelp as 'this valuable, and, as it may now be considered, staple commodity of Orkney'.

Kelp produced a useful income for Orkney estate owners for about a century but, except on the estates of such farsighted proprietors as Balfour of Shapinsay, the laborious collection and preparation of the seaweed led, so it was said, to a neglect of the land and of agricultural improvement. In 1832 the industry collapsed, as a result of the removal of the import duty on barilla, the cheaper alternative to the home-produced substance. It at once became unprofitable to gather kelp on Orkney beaches. The price fell from £15–20 per ton to a mere £5—about the cost of production and shipping. Estate owners now had to choose between going into bankruptcy, after their golden years of high income, and making their land yield profits by some other means —as it turned out, through agriculture.

While it lasted the kelp industry undoubtedly promoted some growth of population in Orkney and there was a certain amount of new coastal settlement of tenants who obtained most of their livelihood from kelp gathering. When the industry collapsed many such tenants found themselves unable to make even the barest living and were forced to leave Orkney in search of work. The remains of their primitive cabins, overgrown with nettles, may be seen here and there.

Transport and travel

The society portrayed by the *Old Statistical Account* was a predominantly static one. Neither people nor goods moved very far or very often. There was an annual Lammas Fair in Kirkwall to which all came who could, but otherwise only the relatively wealthy, the merchants and the seamen did any travelling.

Horses were the principal means of conveyance for persons of quality and for goods. There were a few carts, but not enough to create a demand for roads. A small number of roads had in fact been built in Mainland about 1760 through the efforts of certain landowners, but they were ill constructed, tended to serve as main drains for the land along certain parts of their route, and had fallen into grave disrepair by 1790. The main road from Kirkwall to Stromness followed a somewhat meandering course south of Wideford Hill, the line of the present-day 'old road', to the Binscarth Gap, then wound through Stenness a little to the south of the modern road to the Bridge of Waith. Crossing this structure was a notoriously hazardous operation at high tide, in bad weather or at night. It was not so much a bridge as a causeway about 150yd long built of logs laid upon stone pillars. 'It has never been properly finished,' wrote the minister of Firth and Stenness in 1793, 'and having no railings at the sides, young children and weakly people run no small risk of being blown over, and drowned.' At this date no regular coach ran between Kirkwall and Stromness, and there were no turnpike roads.

A weekly mail was despatched south from Kirkwall by way of the post-road through Holm to the ferry at the tip of South Ronaldsay. In these days before the Churchill Barriers were built, this was a laborious journey in itself involving two ferries, from Holm to Burray and Burray to South Ronaldsay. The mail was rowed across to Huna near Duncansby Head and from this point the postman had to walk across Caithness and Sutherland. The minister of Kirkwall and St Ola noted this slow postal connection as a major drawback to Kirkwall business. At least, he thought, the postman might have a horse for the Caithness and Sutherland section of his journey.

Travel between the various islands of Orkney was entirely at the mercy of bad weather and was quite unorganised. There were few if any piers on the outer islands. The minister of Eday and Stronsay summed up the situation thus :

> 'The ferries in this district, and throughout all Orkney, except on the post road from Caithness to Kirkwall, are not under proper regulations. There are no stated ferry-men, the freights are accordingly imposed at the pleasure of the boatmen who cross over with passengers, which renders the expence and trouble of travelling through these islands very great, and difficult to be ascertained.'

6 MAKINGS OF MODERN ORKNEY

CONSIDERING the primitive conditions and slow change of earlier centuries it is somewhat remarkable to find that by the end of the nineteenth century Orkney was counted among the leading, indeed the exemplary farming counties of Scotland. As far back as the 1860s Daniel Gorrie had been able to write that Orkney, until recently so backward, might now be regarded as 'well abreast of the sister Northern counties in point of agricultural development'. Improvement had thus been both fundamental and rapid.

One immediate cause of agricultural improvement was the collapse of the kelp industry which had diverted both labour and attention from the farms. The estate owners now had to find alternative ways of making their properties pay and many opted for agricultural improvement.

A second stimulus to improvement came from the steady percolation of new ideas from the south. Orkney was far distant from those parts of England and Scotland where the methods of the agricultural revolution, associated with such names as Coke of Holkham, had first taken root, but it was not wholly insulated from them. Orkney's soils are naturally fertile and even under the deplorable agricultural regime to which it had been subjected the county had managed to produce a surplus for export. In due time therefore the techniques of modern farming were likely to be adopted. The introduction of such techniques was helped by a movement of men with capital into the islands, and also by the establishment of regular steamer communication between Kirkwall and Leith in the late 1830s. In 1766 it had taken Patrick Fea of Sanday five full days' sailing in the month of June to make this same journey, which by steamer took only 34–40 hours. Henceforth men, goods and ideas could move more rapidly than ever before between islands and mainland.

117

It has been said, rather sourly, that the only benefit Orkney ever obtained from its union with Scotland was the privilege of eventual membership of the United Kingdom. However, that national relationship proved to be most beneficial to Orkney in the nineteenth century. The unprecedented increase in size, wealth and purchasing power of town populations in England and southern Scotland in the nineteenth century gave Orkney a market for farm produce which never existed before. It has been customary to criticise Orkney landlords in centuries before the nineteenth for being backward, but in fact no one could make an estate in Orkney pay until there was an effective market for its products. There was no such outlet until the day of the southern industrial towns and the steamer.

THE NEW STATISTICAL ACCOUNT

In the 1840s a second *Statistical Account of Scotland* was compiled, and ministers' reports on the Orkney parishes show a society in which modernisation and improvement were everywhere in the air.

The enclosure of the land into fields, which had begun late in the seventeenth century, was gathering momentum, though it still affected only a minority of the parishes. The Pollexfen estate at Cairston, just north of Stromness, was by 1839 an oasis of good husbandry in an area where farming had long been neglected in favour of seafaring. Good crops of potatoes, oats, bere and hay were growing there, and Mr Pollexfen's grass and turnip seed had attracted attention outside Orkney and was much in demand. In nearby Sandwick three principal proprietors had begun improvements, though the rest of the parish was still farmed in small plots by seventy tenants, many without leases. In Walls, Mr Heddle of Melsetter was demonstrating that the wastes of southern Hoy could be farmed. Shapinsay was still divided into a reformed and prosperous Balfour estate and two others which were unimproved. On Sanday improvements were in hand at Stove near the south of the island. On Stronsay, 100 acres of waste had recently been broken by the plough by Mr Laing of Papdale. Notes of improvement and good husbandry came also from the estates of Baikie of Tankerness and Traill of Woodwick.

There may have been others not mentioned in the Account, since several ministers do not seem to have had much interest in these matters.

Most of Orkney was still farmed by a multitude of small tenants, who had no security of tenure, who had to work unpaid on the masters' estates when required, and whose rents had to be paid in kind instead of money. Sometimes the rents were fixed so high that the tenants had perforce to take part in the herring fishery that was developing—an echo of the landlords' action when they wanted their tenants to work kelp. Tenancy conditions like these were widespread in South Ronaldsay and Burray and were responsible for a neglect of farming and placed the livelihood of families at the mercy of bad weather and the vagaries of herring shoals.

The problem of the miserable tenant-at-will, the man with no lease and no security, was already being tackled by a few estate owners. The minister of Sanday reported that the proprietor of Stove had allocated plots of six acres to his tenants for their own cultivation and grazing, in return for a fixed annual rent of £5 5s. They were offered paid employment on their landlord's farm and a proper payment for kelp gathered. 'Such was the effect of this free system.' wrote Rev George Ritchie, 'that men considered notoriously slothful were converted into willing and industrious labourers . . .' Help was given on this estate towards the improvement of tenants' houses and buildings and also to the marketing of their produce. Another innovation which became more common as the century advanced was the placing of tenants under carefully thought out 'regulations', governing such things as manuring, crop rotation and the proper care of livestock. Lord Dundas, holder of the earldom estate, led the way in this particular reform.

DIVIDING THE COMMONS AND PLANKING THE FARMS

Each parish possessed an area of common land or commonty, compounded from the common lands attached to each component tunship. These commons were mostly moorland where peat was cut and the wild native sheep ran free. In order to secure a more equitable use of the commons, division was begun in 1816. Elaborate surveys were carried out, and the resulting maps were triumphs of that almost maniacal regard for absolute fairness which had characterised the old runrig system and the first attempt to reform it. A section of common was henceforth attached to each farm in the parish, and every effort made to secure equal division of all qualities of rough ground available. The most ingenious and impractical patterns of allotment imaginable were laid out, and the maps lodged with Kirkwall solicitors. There they remain, still the ultimate authority in disputes over the ownership of peat rights.

Divisions of the commonties began in Stenness, and by 1859, when the commons of Harray were divided, the task was in large measure completed; there were some later, lesser divisions. In the parish of Stromness no division ever seems to have been made, possibly because the land was early stripped of peat and the common was hardly worth dividing. The divisions regularised the use of peats, the only fuel available to the bulk of the population, and was therefore beneficial; but it did inhibit the use of the moors for grazing.

On the farms themselves, the second planking was carried out in the 1830s. The process took nearly thirty years to complete but this time the job was done properly. The whole countryside was at last divided up into compact farms. Most of the old groupings of houses were broken up and new houses built on the consolidated farm units. Many Orkney houses date from this period. On some estates the total number of farms was reduced, the land being made into larger units, so that some tenants were displaced and had either to break in new farms for themselves from the commons, or leave Orkney. Which they did often depended upon the date of division of the commons for, once divided, these became private property and new settlement on them became almost impossible.

THE NEW FARMING IN ORKNEY

There was a spectacular increase in output from the land in Orkney as a result of planking, enclosure, drainage, crop rotation, reseeding of grassland, the production of winter feed and generally

120

improved management. It is always said that arable acreage increased two and a half times in the second half of the nineteenth century, and this may well have been so. In Shapinsay for example there were 700 acres under the plough in 1848 and 6,000 by 1863, but this was exceptional.

Livestock were the basis of this new prosperity. Early in the century some landlords realised that Orkney could never make its living from grain sales. Grain requires a drier and sunnier climate than the north isles can provide. On the other hand conditions for growing grass were seen to be ideal. The improvements in grass management that Thomas Pollexfen and others developed paved the way for the large-scale beef exports that relied on the new regular steamer service.

Note was made in the *New Statistical Account* of a few cattle of improved breeds but dramatic changes came after mid-century. The new breeds were Shorthorn crosses, ideally suited to Orkney conditions and giving excellent beef. By the late 1860s about 10,000 head of cattle a year were being shipped out of Orkney and by 1900 there were 28,000 cattle on the islands. This was only a beginning..

Sheep breeds were also improved and the export of sheep became important. It is thought that at the beginning of the nineteenth century about 50,000 native short-tailed sheep roamed the Orkney commons; sheep farming at this period partook more of the nature of hunting than of animal husbandry. The first improvement came when Malcolm Laing of Papdale built up a flock of Merinos, Southdowns and Merino-Orkney and Merino-Southdown crosses, a thousand strong by 1813. Some time later an English proprietor introduced Cheviots to Orphir and showed that these hardy animals could be wintered on the hill. Experiments in crossing native sheep with Southdowns, renowned for their lambing performance, were made on the Balfour estate in Shapinsay. By 1900 there were about 36,000 sheep in Orkney— far fewer than a century earlier, but their quality and usefulness were incomparably superior.

On the other hand the growth in poultry numbers was remarkable. It had been the custom from time immemorial for Orkney families to keep a few hens for domestic use and rents were often partly paid in eggs. The care of the hens was by ancient practice left to the womenfolk, who might keep any small profit that accrued. Early in the nineteenth century it was realised that Orkney eggs could be profitably exported, and by about 1830 a hundred thousand dozen were being shipped out annually. This number grew enormously as the century advanced, so that by the 1890s the export amounted to over a million dozen and became a crucial source of extra income to all Orcadians, rich and poor. As in earlier times, the housewife raised and tended the hens and kept the profits, while her husband provided their feed and accommodation and other overheads.

THE FIRST TRANSPORT REVOLUTION

In July 1836 the first regular steamer service (summer only) between Orkney and the mainland of Scotland came into operation, the ports of call being Leith (Newhaven), Aberdeen, Wick and Kirkwall. The ship used was the *Sovereign*, a paddle steamer of 378 tons. A regular winter service began with the introduction of the first screw steamer in 1861.

This steamer service, whatever may have been its irregularities and other defects, was the most potent force for change in Orkney, in that it gave the island farmers reliable trade connections with southern markets and allowed the rapid and certain transfer of mails, newspapers and other sources of information from the south. At first it developed only slowly, and sailing vessels remained in service alongside the new steamers for several decades. In addition to the Kirkwall-Leith route, Stromness had regular sailings to Liverpool. There were also two ferries to the Caithness mainland across the Pentland Firth, from South Ronaldsay and Walls.

In Orkney itself, the building of serviceable roads was a notable improvement. There was a certain amount of rather sporadic improvement of roads in the twenties and thirties, but real progress began with the passing of the 1857 Orkney Roads Act; this was reinforced by a number of other acts, and then by the comprehensive Roads and Bridges (Scotland) Act of 1874. The present-day roads of Orkney date largely from this period. Because there were still large expanses of common land it was possible in many areas for roads to be built very straight, as in West

Mainland; elsewhere the co-operation of major proprietors helped to produce straight roads, as in Shapinsay. Late in the century the Congested Districts Board made funds available for road construction and improvement, and by 1914 every populous island had adequate roads. The first motor bus ran on the new Kirkwall-Stromness road in 1905; the first Orkney-owned motor car made its appearance two years earlier.

The rapid increase in the number of wheeled vehicles was noted by minister after minister in the *Second Statistical Account*. Gigs and phaetons could now be hired in Kirkwall, while a regular mail-coach ran daily between Kirkwall and Stromness from June 1838. 'It was an interesting as well as novel scene, to see a regular mail-coach in *ultima Thule*' wrote the minister. From 1839 a daily postal connection was opened between Kirkwall and the Scottish mainland, winter and summer. About mid-century the notorious Bridge of Waith, at the point where the Kirkwall-Stromness road crosses the tidal exit from the Loch of Stenness, was rebuilt and its approaches improved so that it was no longer necessary to walk or ride along the shore to its eastern end. The remains of this hazardous stretch of the old road are still to be seen from the modern road. Better roads encouraged another innovation, the travelling shop, which carried the town to the country and, as it turned out, encouraged the country to come more often to the town.

It is not entirely clear why the population of Orkney began to grow as rapidly as it did about the turn of the century, though smallpox vaccination had a good deal to do with it; the major increase came before new improvements had time to affect the standard of living of most people. The peak year was 1861 when the census recorded 32,225 people in the islands. A gradual decline then set in which has continued ever since. This decline mainly resulted from emigration and was part of the great movement of people from marginal areas throughout Britain, and indeed western Europe. Orcadians went south to the growing industrial towns and also overseas in large numbers. The far-flung character of this movement is recorded today by the existence of many Orkney societies and by the occasional Orkney name on the map of a faraway land, like Melsetter in Rhodesia. Some believe this emigration left the necessary elbow room for those

123

who stayed behind to make a decent living from the land; but many of the most enterprising and able left their homes, which cannot really have benefited Orkney. There was also some migration of people into the islands; in the 1880s something of an influx of farmers from Aberdeenshire occurred, who brought with them capital and ideas for improvements; certainly their coming coincided with a spurt of agricultural development.

THE CROFTERS COMMISSION

The plight of tenants without rights eventually became a parliamentary matter. The problem in Orkney was part of that which affected all the northern Scottish counties and islands where there were estates with tenants-at-will, though it was in general less serious for the Orcadians. In 1886 the Crofters Holdings (Scotland) Act became law and a commission under Lord Napier was sent north to ascertain the situation of tenants and bring matters into line with the requirements of the Act.

In August 1888 the Napier Commission held its first sitting in Orkney, at the town hall in Stromness. Its arrival was greeted by an explosion of excitement among the tenantry though landlords were rather less enthusiastic. A great crowd assembled in the town hoping to get into the building. Eventually the windows had to be opened so that those outside could hear what was happening, as evidence was given by man after man about the conditions under which he and his family lived. The Commission moved through the Mainland parishes and then to the islands, taking evidence at it went. Its report makes it clear that much needed to be set right but also that landlords were not, in general, unprincipled grinders of the poor. As a result of the enquiry many tenants had their rents reduced and arrears cancelled, some rents being reduced by as much as a third, as at Rackwick in Hoy. To this day the sheets of paper on which the judgements of the commissioners were given are treasured possessions of many Orkney families.

The Act has rightly been called the 'crofters' magna carta'. Its main provisions were to ensure security of tenure to a crofter, as a tenant on a property worth not more than £30 annual rent was called; to make his tenancy heritable, or assignable to another,

Page 125 Kirkwall: *(above)* the present-day Street and the Big Tree; *(below)* the old Lammas Fair on Kirk Green in front of St. Magnus Cathedral

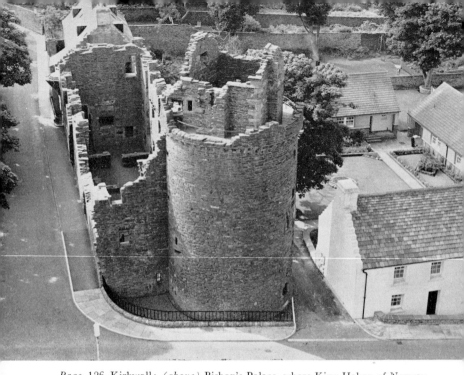

Page 126 Kirkwall: *(above)* Bishop's Palace, where King Hakon of Norway died in 1263. Mainly sixteenth-century reconstruction of the twelfth-century original; *(below)* Earl Patrick's Palace, built by a Stewart in the late sixteenth century and described as the finest renaissance building ever raised in Scotland

very much as the tenant wished; and to ensure that rents were fair, with right of appeal to an independent panel. Henceforth the landlord had almost no means of dislodging a tenant or of raising his rent, but he still retained considerable responsibilities for the condition of the property.

In Orkney the terms of the Act were implemented rapidly. A secure and increasingly responsible class of tenant set about improving properties, and because of the fixed rents a higher proportion of the increased income thus achieved went into tenants' pockets instead of landlords'. It was not the intention of most of the promoters of the Act that estates should be broken up by its agency; their objective was to ameliorate the lot of an oppressed group of people. But, in the course of events in the next forty years, the Act laid an axe to the very foundations of estates in Orkney. In 1911 the maximum rental qualification for crofters was raised to £50 per year, a recognition of the legitimate rise in fair rents on improved properties.

THE FIRST WORLD WAR

In the opening years of the twentieth century the British Admiralty turned its attention to Orkney, for reasons not unlike those of Norse sea-kings centuries before. Orkney harbours command the northabout route from ports in continental Europe into the Atlantic, and the merchant ships bringing food and raw materials to Britain and taking away British exports converge upon that part of the Atlantic known to seafarers as the western approaches. In case of war, which the Kaiser evidently intended, German cruisers might be expected to slip out from bases such as Kiel and the Elbe to harry British shipping. The English Channel would be closed by British and French shore batteries and ships; the passages needing to be watched every day of the year would be the Pentland Firth, Sumburgh Roost and the waters between Shetland and Faeroe. The ideal base from which such a watch could be mounted was Scapa Flow and preliminary steps were taken to prepare it as a naval base.

Because of the scanty population and entirely rural nature of the surrounding islands, most of the installations in the Flow were seaborne rather than shore-based. Most were concentrated in the southern end of the Flow near Longhope and Lyness on the east coast of Hoy. In July 1914, with the outbreak of war imminent, Winston Churchill ordered the Home and Atlantic Fleets to Scapa. Though physically ideal as a base, Scapa Flow was in fact quite unprotected and blockships were hastily sunk in the vulnerable approach channels to discourage German submarines. Some shore batteries were installed, manned by Orkney Territorials. Minefields and booms were later added to the sea defences and the anchored ships were made secure from underwater attack.

Scapa was emphatically not a popular posting for naval officers and men, except for a tiny minority who, despite the discomforts of war, perceived something of the islands' unique character and grew to appreciate it. In the minds of most men Scapa was an endless wait, 'swinging round the buoy' in chilly northern waters. Leave meant a very long boat and rail journey across the whole of Scotland and most of England to a home in London or Plymouth. The ships might have been anchored off Greenland for all the town amusements there were on shore and duty periods were filled with seemingly pointless activities. An on-shore activity—gardening—was encouraged in order to provide fresh vegetables for the fleet.

When in 1916 the navy put to sea from Scapa it engaged the German High Seas Fleet in the last battle ever to be fought by surface ships in the style of Nelson's day, off Jutland, a battle both sides believed they had won. This same year saw the departure of the British Commander-in-Chief Lord Kitchener of Khartoum, from Scapa Flow on a mission to encourage Britain's hard-pressed Russian allies. His ship, the cruiser HMS *Hampshire*, struck a mine off Birsay and sank with only a handful of survivors. The Orkney people raised a memorial to Kitchener on Marwick Head which is visible from afar and commands splendid views of the west Mainland cliffs. Recent research has cast much doubt upon the character and capacity of the benign father-figure that public sentiment saw in Kitchener and it is perhaps appropriate, though unintended at the time, that the memorial was large, ponderous and completely faceless, and that the entrance is now blocked up, making it impossible to penetrate within.

One of the conditions of the armistice was that the German

HMS *Hampshire*, lost off Birsay 5 June 1916

navy was to be interned in an allied or neutral port to await the peace treaty. Scapa Flow was considered ideal for this purpose—at least by the British government—and the first units of this fleet entered the Flow on Saturday, 23 November 1918. Soon a truly formidable array of sea power lay off Lyness. As soon as they dropped anchor the crews began to fish, which some observers thought remarkable, even improper, on a great historic occasion, but the German sailors were no doubt hungry. Shortly liners took off all but skeleton crews. During the long wait that followed while the victorious allies tried to agree among themselves as to the ultimate disposal of the German navy, the skeleton crews at Scapa reached a state of near-mutiny. The large capital ships were hardest hit by this breakdown of discipline. On the German flagship *Friedrich der Grosse* men roller-skated thunderously on the iron decks over the heads of the officers, and the admiral had eventually to transfer his command to a cruiser where things were quieter. But despite this chaotic situation, plans were made by the German naval officers to destroy the ships should the peace terms prove unacceptable.

The isolation of each ship was almost complete. Food supplies were brought direct from Germany, and the crews existed on a diet of black bread, potatoes and turnip jam. All winter the ships lay at anchor, while their crews were gradually brought back into order and plans for the scuttle completed. On 31 May 1919 the crews celebrated the 'German victory of Jutland' to the annoyance of British naval persons present. From then on, events moved to a climax. The peace terms were published and were staggeringly severe; the German government hesitated about signing, and were told that they must do so before 21 June. The German admiral at Scapa saw a copy of *The Times* giving this deadline, which was in fact extended almost immediately afterwards though he was never told. He decided that the time had come to put his ships once and for all beyond the victors' reach.

21 June 1919 was a fine afternoon, and the motor vessel *Flying Kestrel* took a school party from Stromness out to see the German fleet. As things turned out, this must have been the most exciting school outing of all time. Suddenly men were observed running on one of the battle-cruisers; then the whole fleet began to sink. One ship turned bottom-up while the pupils and their teachers watched amazed. The children were hustled below for safety, but there was no danger. Either by accident or by design, the British fleet was at sea on exercises, so that little could be done to stop the scuttle. Such naval personnel as were present tried to run as many as possible of the sinking German craft ashore or into shallow water. Some destroyers were beached, but only one capital ship was saved, the battleship *Baden*. A German sailor danced a hornpipe on her deck as she settled in the water. All told, seventy-four German ships went to the bottom before the little *Flying Kestrel* got her passengers home for tea.

The sunken ships in due time served as a reserve of scrap and the firm of Cox & Danks raised all the large and many of the smaller vessels between the two wars, towing them south to be broken up. The last battleship had just been raised when war restarted in 1939.

BETWEEN THE WARS: THE OWNER-FARMER

After the first World War Orkney became very rapidly a country of independent farmers, tenants no longer but owners of their own land. The estates, large and small, between which almost the whole of Orkney had long been divided, now broke up with astonishing speed and lack of trouble. This change was unique to Orkney, and gives the islands much of their present distinctive character. No comparable development took place in Shetland, for example, where the estates and the old crofting system still survive.

The Crofters Act had fixed rents at a low level, thereby making it possible for the tenants in Orkney to keep a large part of the profits gained from sales to the forces during the war. Since these profits had been considerable, the tenants for the first time had a little capital at their disposal.

With the post-war fall in food prices, estate owners found it almost impossible to make any profit from their lands in Orkney and moreover many were burdened with death duties, now at a higher rate, which could only be paid by selling their property. Most decided to sell before they went bankrupt, but the only possible purchasers were the sitting tenants. Most farms were sold for the equivalent of twenty-three years' rent, often less than £100. This sounds a small sum today to pay for a farm and indeed it would not buy an acre of good land in modern Orkney; but it was beyond the immediate means of most tenants, who therefore had to raise mortgages. The break-up of estates was so complete that today only Hoy and North Ronaldsay are estate islands; there are one or two estates in Mainland, in Orphir for example, where one is in the hands of a trust and therefore cannot be disposed of to its tenants. Otherwise Orkney is now a country of owner-farmers.

The newly independent Orkneymen had a very hard struggle through the twenties and thirties—mortgages had to be paid off in the teeth of world economic depression—and there were no government subsidies to help. The modest prosperity of today was achieved only by hard graft and hard saving.

Several factors favoured the Orkneymen. First, their farms were of a size that could be worked by family labour. There were no wage bills to pay and it was never customary to cost the labour of the farmer and his family. Secondly, there was a ready market for Orkney beef-cattle, sheep and eggs. Prices were low, but all cattle fodder was home grown and it was possible to show a profit. Poultry food had to be imported but the cost of this was bearable in an era of undervalued grain. Thirdly, each farm was practically self-sufficient in terms of food supplies. Therefore the farmer was to an unusual degree insulated from the economic blizzard that raged in the inter-war period.

Clear indication of the success of Orkney farmers in these years is to be seen in the increasing numbers of cattle and sheep in the islands. In 1920 Orkney had 31,500 cattle and 29,700 sheep. By 1930 the totals were 36,000 and 63,000 respectively; and by 1939 they had reached 39,700 and 88,300, which marked a rare achievement for those times.

Nevertheless, housing conditions and the provision of amenities in general remained poor. Even as late as 1961 the legacy of the hard years was revealed by the census, which reported Orkney at the bottom of the table of all Scottish counties for household sanitation. On the smaller islands, conditions were much worse than on Mainland; on one island seventy-eight per cent of all inhabited houses lacked modern sanitary arrangements. There has been very marked progress since that date as a result of improvement grants. The growth of the tourist trade has also been a stimulus to modernisation of domestic facilities.

THE SECOND WAR AND AFTER

The outbreak of war in 1939 saw the British fleet once more based in Scapa, for strategic purposes similar to those of 1914–18, namely the defence of shipping and the enforcement of a blockade against Germany. Now however there was an added threat from air attack which made the Flow much less secure than it had once been. In October 1939 German bombers raided the base and holed the obsolete battleship *Iron Duke*, which had to be beached. Raiders came again in March 1940; British fighters appeared, whereupon the Germans fled, jettisoning their bombs at the Bridge of Waith, an incident in which an Orkneyman became the first British civilian to die by enemy action.

On 14 October 1939, in the early hours of the morning, a heavy blow was struck at the Royal Navy by a German submarine, which slipped into the Flow through a supposedly blocked channel and sank the battleship HMS *Royal Oak*. On 17 October the First Sea Lord gave an account of this disaster to the Commons. 'When we consider that during the whole course of the last war this anchorage was found to be immune from such attacks on account of the obstacles imposed by the currents and net barrages, this entry by a U-boat must be considered a remarkable exploit of professional skill and daring,' said Mr Churchill. 'It appears probable that the U-boat fired a salvo of torpedoes at the *Royal Oak*, of which only one hit the bow. This muffled explosion was at the time attributed to internal causes . . . Twenty minutes later the U-boat fired three or four torpedoes, and these,

HMS *Royal Oak*, torpedoed in Scapa Flow 14 October 1939

striking in quick succession, caused the ship to capsize and sink. She was lying at the extreme end of the harbour, and therefore many officers and men were drowned before rescue craft could be organized from other vessels.' All told about 800 men went down that night under the cliffs of Gaitnip.

In April 1940 the fleet sailed from Scapa to try to intercept the Nazi invasion armada bound for west Norwegian ports. It proved impossible to use surface ships against shore-based German aircraft and so Norway fell. This brought German forces within 300 miles of Orkney, the distance away of Newcastle, and a good deal closer to Shetland. Further invasion attempts seemed likely, directed at Faeroe and Iceland perhaps, or even at the

133

northern isles of Scotland. The two former were occupied by British forces, and in support a very powerful garrison was concentrated in Orkney. At its peak this numbered 60,000 men, three times the total civilian population of the islands.

After the early alarms the events of the Second World War passed Orkney by. The islands were the base for ceaseless patrols by sea and air over the northern sea approaches. From time to time a ship was mined or torpedoed somewhere around the islands, like the tanker *Inverlain* whose rusty bows still lie in the channel between Hoy and Graemsay, a familiar landmark on the boat run from Stromness to Hoy. She was mined early in 1940 east of Orkney and broken in two; her stern is now on the bottom of Inganess Bay. Now and then, a small boat would appear out of the seas to eastward, bringing Norwegians to join their compatriot forces in Britain. Visitors to Westness in Rousay may observe a small boat of ancient Norse design lying in the farm-yard. This once carried two young Norwegians across the North Sea, a voyage which showed the old viking spirit no whit abated.

Among the great concourse of people who came to Orkney in the second war were 550 Italians, captured during General Wavell's victory in the Western Desert of North Africa. They helped to build the Churchill Barriers across the eastern entrances to Scapa Flow. Sometimes the part they played has been exaggerated; much of the heavy work was done by Orcadians and Scots under civilian contract. Quite understandably the Italians saw no reason for over-exerting themselves and were much concerned to devise shelters from the weather. They lived in a camp on Lamb Holm where in 1943 they turned a nissen hut into a Roman Catholic chapel, using scrap materials and a great amount of skill. Today this chapel is all that remains of Camp 60. It is visited by most organised tours of Orkney and some years ago was re-painted by the artist who had done the work originally as a prisoner. It must be judged a work of ingenuity rather than of art.

The Churchill Barriers turned out to be much more than a defence of Scapa Flow. By linking the islands of South Ronaldsay and Burray to Mainland they undoubtedly prevented the serious depopulation which has been the fate of most outer isles. They also provided the road connection for a new short ferry route across the Pentland Firth. Today, a drive across the Barriers is a favourite jaunt for Orcadians on a fine Sunday afternoon.

World War II was as great a turning point in the development of Orkney as had been the Norse settlement or the annexation by Scotland. The presence of the garrison of 60,000 acted as a kind of social and economic forcing-house upon Orkney society. Personal contacts between Orcadians and southerners on such a scale could never have been arranged by any other means. By the time the war ended Orkney people had found out more than they had ever known before about how other British people lived and the things they regarded as normal. They looked at their own islands with fresh eyes. What was equally important, the hard cash the garrison paid for its food provided the means to make the changes they desired.

Thus Orkney farmers entered the post-war period with many of their mortgages paid off, genuinely independent in a way none of their predecessors had ever been.

Relics of war

Orkney is still littered with the steel and concrete bric-à-brac of two world wars. Most of it is unsightly, some is dangerous, and all needs to be cleared away. One of the most beautiful sections of cliff coast in west Mainland is marred by the shattered remains of an anti-aircraft battery. The Bay of Howton in Orphir is a very lovely place; it is not improved by the relics of a RNAS seaplane base of 1914–18 vintage. The old airfields in west Mainland have unsightly weed-covered runways, bunkers which rival Maeshowe and wrecked control towers. In Harray there are the remains of a camp which once housed the Gordon Highlanders, where the hut chimneys stand up like grotesque standing-stones from a jungle of willow-herb. More remarkable and less well-known is the 'Burma Road' across the moors of Deerness. This road was built by troops in the second war as an exercise in employment without purpose: the stones were set individually by hand in order to delay completion as long as possible. It is just possible, perhaps, that this road may be used one day when the wastes of Deerness are cultivated.

7   ORKNEY TODAY

T ODAY, Orkney is first and foremost a farming community, a traditional role that is likely to continue. It is also an island community; no improvements in the means of communication can alter the fact that it costs time and money to transfer people, goods and information across the Pentland Firth. These two considerations are fundamental to any discussion of present-day conditions and future prospects.

FARMING

Of Orkney's total area of about 240,000 acres roughly 46,000 acres were arable and another 66,000 acres were under permanent grass in the late 1960s. On the arable fields, rotation grasses and oats are about equal in importance, but the acreage of oats is falling and that of grass increasing; by the mid-1970s grass may be the only significant crop grown. There are about 1,400 acres of barley and a small acreage of potatoes, mainly in garden plots. Livestock numbers are approximately 70,000 beef cattle, 6,000 dairy cattle, 78,000 sheep and a small number of pigs.

Exports from Orkney in 1969, a representative year, were 20,000 beef cattle, sold off the farm at £90 per head, giving a total gross return to Orkney farmers of £1,800,000, and 30,000 sheep at £7 per head, worth £210,000 gross. Beef cattle thus provided the major source of income for Orkney farmers, and for the islands as a whole. Most cattle went for slaughter, but a considerable number went for breeding purposes. Orkney beasts are notably disease-free, and after the foot-and-mouth disaster in England and Wales in 1967–8 they were much in demand for restocking.

Other exports included about 25 million eggs, worth £28,600 gross, and a large quantity of milk products, including Orkney

136

cheeses. During the year, the sale of 3 million gallons of milk earned Orkney dairy farmers £58,500. About 2,000 pigs were also sold off Orkney farms at an average of £18 per head, but only a small number were exported.

Imports consisted of fertilisers and feedingstuffs, agricultural machinery, vehicles, petroleum products and other consumer goods which cannot be produced in Orkney. A small number of lowland sheep and cattle of non-traditional breeds were brought in. The broad picture is therefore of a community making its living from livestock sales, using its land mainly to feed its animals, and paying its bills from the profits gained from these operations.

The average size of Orkney farms is, in statistical terms, around 42 acres but the majority of genuine farms are in the range 50–150 acres. Almost all are worked as family farms. The average conceals the existence of many very small properties which are in no sense economic units, most of which belong either to retired people or to those with jobs outside farming. Many still come under crofting regulations, though they are not crofts in the Shetland or Hebridean sense. There is also a considerable number of large and, in terms of production, very important properties of 600–2,000 acres; some of these are in fact several farms worked as a unit.

There is great variation in farm sizes between different parts of Mainland and between Mainland and the islands. For instance, in Sandwick parish in west Mainland, there are ninety-seven farms, one of which, Skaill, is exceptionally large, about 900 acres. This has been the principal house in Sandwick since Norse times and was more recently the nucleus of a large estate. Today it is the first house in Orkney, home of the Lord-Lieutenant, Col Scarth of Breckness. Excluding this exceptional property, the average size of Sandwick farms is 98 acres; but this figure includes thirty-one units of 100–650 acres and a few very small properties. In Orphir parish the average farm size is 51 acres, in Harray 65 acres and in the island of Shapinsay 80 acres, excluding exceptionally large properties in each case.

A typical family farm of between 50 and 150 acres has from one-half to two-thirds of its arable under rotation grass and the rest under fodder crops, usually oats and perhaps turnips. There may be a field or two of barley, grown for the Kirkwall whisky

137

distilleries, and even a field of bere, grown for milling and export to the Hebrides. In addition to this improved land, the farm will probably have some permanent grazing, but this will very likely have been ploughed and reseeded at some time in the recent past. The rotation grasses are mown for hay, sometimes for silage. In a dry year, some of the rough grazing will also be cut for hay.

The numbers of livestock kept depend somewhat on the policy and circumstances of a particular farm, but one of about 70 acres is likely to have about 50 beef cattle, ranging from calves to three-year-olds and over. Aberdeen Angus and Ayrshires are the most popular breeds; some others have recently been tried. Only large farms have a bull and artificial insemination is generally practised. Cattle have to be wintered indoors, and this gives Orkney a strange and deserted air between October and May. Winter feed is partly grown on the farm, partly imported. Firms in Orkney bring in barley, maize and concentrates in bulk for processing and distribution within the islands.

A variant on this beef-cattle pattern is the dairy farm, of which there are about 100, in Mainland only. Dairy farms are a legacy of the second World War, when the needs of the garrison for fresh milk caused many farmers to turn over from beef to dairy animals. When the garrison went the milk market collapsed, and to absorb the large surplus two creameries were built, in Birsay and Kirkwall. These produce cheese and other milk products for export, and the total number of dairy farms and size of herds are regulated by their capacity.

In addition to cattle, a large and increasing number of sheep are kept, on the improved farmland rather than on the moorland. There has always been plenty of lowland grazing for sheep in Orkney, in marked contrast with Shetland. Flocks of prosperous-looking Cheviots, Southdowns and Leicesters may be seen on many farms. Flock size varies greatly, but on a 70 acre farm 40 breeding ewes, 1 ram and 58 lambs would not be untypical.

Orkney farms are mechanised—some would say over-mechanised—but agricultural machinery has proved a boon where the weather at harvest is as uncertain as it is in Orkney. In the 1950s there was a spectacular increase in tractor numbers; there are now about 1,600 in the islands. In the 1960s grass harvesting machines were imported in large numbers and these now give an unprecedented security to the crucial hay harvest. Less frequently used machinery such as combines and ditch-diggers tend to be hired, though large farms sometimes have their own. So far there is little co-operative ownership of expensive machines, and it is difficult to see how this could be developed when most machines are needed at the same time by all farmers. Virtually every farm possesses a car or van of which there were in 1969 about 4,800 in the islands. A car is not a luxury in rural Orkney but an absolute necessity of life, because there is almost no public transport. It was significant that car purchases rose steadily throughout the 1960s irrespective of farm-price fluctuations and the virtual collapse of the egg business; many purchases were second-hand.

Houses and farm buildings are of several kinds. On most farms there are buildings which date from at least two distinct periods of development, often more. For example, there may be the remains of a long-house, probably two hundred years old and possibly much older. The farmhouse may be a two-storey stone structure of nineteenth or early twentieth-century date, solid and well proportioned. There may also be a post-war house or bungalow. The many new houses and farm buildings which dot the Orkney countryside and the numerous improvements which may be seen in older structures result from the post-war decades of government subsidy. A grant is available towards almost any improvement which tends to bring a house up to national minimum standards or to enhance the efficiency and cleanliness of farm buildings.

Empty hen-houses stand on many farms. These date from the halcyon years when eggs were a richly profitable sideline and the egg cheque paid most of the housewives' bills. After World War II the profit to be made in egg production increased enormously and exports rose to such quantities that the normal steamer services were unable to handle them. A local company converted a drifter specially to take eggs from Orkney to Glasgow through the Caledonian Canal. 1960 was the peak year when 72 million eggs were produced, to earn over £1,000,000. Thereafter the basis of the egg subsidy was changed, and henceforth the operation of a free market price and increasing competition from very large-scale producers in the south made small-scale production less and less profitable. By 1967 output was down to 42 million eggs, worth less than half the 1960 figure, and the steep fall has continued. Egg production in the island of Westray shows this strikingly—in 1950 there were 60,000 birds, in 1964 15,000 and by 1968 only 3,700. No substantial recovery of the egg business is to be anticipated, but the position may be stabilised if Orkney were to join an all-Scottish consortium of egg producers. A large and widespread organisation of this kind could overcome the serious disadvantage under which Orkney producers labour of having their exports interrupted by bad weather. Interruptions in supplies are very much disliked by large-scale egg buyers, such as supermarket chains.

Most Orkney farms own an area of peat land on the former parish commons. This land may be adjacent to the farm, as in parts of Orphir, Stenness or Harray, or some distance away, or even on the far side of a sea channel. Farms in Sandwick have their peat land in Harray, while those on Sanday have always had to bring peats from Eday and Calf of Eday. Peat is still a principal fuel in rural Orkney, because both alternatives, coal and electricity, are much more expensive. Peats are cut in May and June with the traditional tools of ritting-knife, moor spade and tusker, the first being used to prepare the ground and the last to cut out the peats, which are then placed on top of the cutting to dry. In July they are carted home and stacked, crisp and sweet-smelling, beside the house. The modern style, which would have surprised Turf-Einar the Norse earl who is said to have taught Orkney folk the uses of peat, is to go peat-cutting by motor-car. On a fine cutting day parked cars and vans line the moorland roads of Orkney.

Most farm lands are compact as a result of the nineteenth-century plankings, but not invariably so. In Harray particularly there is much fragmentation of farms, which can be extremely inconvenient for working. This fragmentation results from the survival of independent farmers throughout the Scots period, holding their lands under ancient odal law, which required equal subdivision between heirs. Nineteenth-century rearrangements were only partially effective because all the small proprietors or 'peerie lairds' insisted, quite understandably, upon fair shares of

140

all qualities of land, especially the best. The fragmentation of farms has led to fencing problems. Harray is the parish of innumerable wire fences, often enclosing very small parcels of ground. Because of the tremendous total length of property boundaries, this parish lacks the drystone walls which are so pleasing a feature of nearby Sandwick, a parish of compact farms.

Though the land of Orkney has been farmed for a thousand years and more, few specific farm properties can be shown with certainty to be more than 100–150 years old. Most were in fact created out of older units by the nineteenth-century plankings. The only farms which are likely to be older than this are those which, like Skaill in Sandwick, have remained principal properties throughout history. Of these, only those which escaped the expropriations of Stewart days are now in the hands of the families who founded them in Norse times. There are nevertheless farms which have been in the possession of one family for a very long time indeed. The *New Statistical Account* noted that 'The Hall of Rendall is at present possessed by Mr John Halcro, whose small remaining property has escaped the waste of eight centuries'. The Halcros are said to descend from a Norwegian king and are connected by marriage with the Scottish royal house. They still live at Hall of Rendall today. Other examples of long occupation include the Linklater family of Upper Housgarth, who have held their lands for about 900 years. In Birsay there are twenty-four families who claim occupation of their lands for upwards of 400 years.

The present time is one of farm amalgamation. When an elderly farmer retires it is very common for his farm to be combined with one adjoining. This process has gathered momentum since 1946 and in the decade 1958–68 over 1,000 farms passed out of separate existence in this way, thereby reducing the total number of farms in Orkney by a third.

In 1968 the government took positive steps to aid amalgamation. A farmer who wishes to retire and sell his farm for amalgamation with one adjoining may claim either a pension or a lump sum, the choice partly depending upon his age. Both payments are calculated on the acreage of the farm. The incoming farmer can claim a grant of half the expenditure necessary to

141

make amalgamation effective. This arrangement, known as the 'copper handshake', will if it continues in force help to produce a county of large farms by the end of the century—in which case many Orcadians will need to find jobs off the land.

SOCIAL CONDITIONS

Throughout Mainland and on several of the outer islands, most houses now have piped water and mains electricity. Piped water has replaced the many wells which provided Orkney households with water from time immemorial, the remains of which are to be seen everywhere. Some farmers still prefer to rely on their wells. Extension of mains water to small islands can be very expensive. The cost of a submarine pipeline, begun in 1970, to bring water from Hoy to Flotta was estimated at £13,000. It may be noted in passing that the famous Well of Kildinguie in Stronsay, whose waters when taken with dulse (seaweed) gathered from the nearby shore were said to cure all ills but the black death, still exists and has even brought a pilgrim to Orkney in very recent times—though the water does not look too inviting.

Electricity supply

The mains electricity supply is always called 'the Hydro' in Orkney. It is generated by a post-war diesel power station belonging to the North of Scotland Hydro Electric Board located on the shore of the Peerie Sea at Kirkwall.

The extension of electrification since 1946 has been spectacular. In that year about 1,200 consumers were connected to the old, small power station near St Magnus Cathedral, and a mere 10 miles of underground and overhead cable were installed. In the next decade power lines reached out into Mainland, parish by parish, and also into the South Isles of Burray and South Ronaldsay. In the 1960s submarine cables were laid from Mainland to the islands of Shapinsay and Rousay. The total number of consumers increased from 3,500 in 1951 to 6,350 in 1970, a figure which represents a connection of 99 per cent of all Mainland households and a slightly lower percentage in the islands. Length of power line increased steadily to 375 miles in 1962, then more rapidly as lines were taken out to the islands. Thus, the connection

142

Page 143
Stromness: an air view looking south over Hamnavoe and Hoy Sound to the glacially shaped valleys of north Hoy. On the right is the arm-chair shaped Kame of Hoy

Page 144 Stromness: the town's long connection with the Hudson's Bay Company is reflected in the signs offering lodgings and refreshment to seamen in Dundas Street. This photograph was taken about 1890; the street is little changed today

of 650 new consumers from 1962 to 1968 required 185 miles of additional line, whereas the previous 650 consumers, all in Mainland, required only 60 miles.

About 1,500 potential consumers exist in the outer North Isles and in Hoy and the small islands south of Scapa Flow. To connect these with Mainland would be very expensive indeed—the cost per connection is estimated at a minimum of £1,500—and so further extension of the mains service seems unlikely. It is worth noting that the North of Scotland Board receives no government subsidy but must make a fair profit on its operations.

Mains electricity has revolutionised life in rural Orkney. For instance, in 1946 there were just 70 electric cookers in the islands, but by 1951 there were 880 and in 1970 about 3,150. There has been a very high rate of installation of new electrical appliances, and annual demand has risen slightly faster in Orkney than in Britain as a whole. The recent increase in demand has been 8–10 per cent per annum, and this has made extensions to Kirkwall power station necessary every 2–3 years. In 1970 its installed capacity was approaching four times the 1951 figure of 4,275kW.

With electrification in rural areas have come the refrigerator and, more recently, the deep-freeze cabinet. These allow families to enjoy a more varied diet than ever before, especially in winter when foods containing vitamins have always been scarce. However, the deep-freeze has joined forces with the motor car to put out of business that most characteristic Orkney institution, the travelling shop.

Travelling shops, at first horse-drawn then motorised, have been an important part of Orkney country life for over half a century. As recently as the 1950s every house in Mainland was visited by at least two every day. Since then, operating costs have risen steeply, while at the same time housewives have started travelling to and from Kirkwall and Stromness by car. As deep-freeze refrigerators enable them to store their perishable food almost indefinitely, they are using the travelling shops less. There were always too many of these shops and it was customary to buy a little from all of them, so that none made a really satisfactory profit. Their disappearance is a hard blow to those without a car, and will encourage people to retire to the town rather than to the country.

I

With the spread of electricity television has been brought to many homes and to judge from its effects upon rural life in the Highlands this will accelerate the breakdown of the distinctive Orcadian way of life. Thus, when electricity came to Rousay in 1966–7 people started to stay at home to view television and social life in the island, already hard-hit by depopulation, almost ceased for the time being.

Telephones

Rural isolation is much reduced by a widespread telephone connection. Orkney falls within the Aberdeen Telephone area, an arrangement which reflects the close links between the islands and that city.

The first telephones in Orkney were installed sometime before 1914, and the first GPO exchange opened in Kirkwall in 1923, but extension of the service was slow until after World War II. Since then, progress has been rapid and there are now over 2,800 subscribers in the islands. About 950 of these are linked with the central exchange in Kirkwall, which is manually operated; the rest are served by 16 local automatic exchanges and 6 small manual exchanges, some of which are located at sub-post offices or in private homes. Kirkwall handles about 20,000 trunk calls annually and there has been an annual growth of traffic of 8 per cent in recent years.

It is expected that all parts of Orkney will have Subscriber Trunk Dialling facilities by 1972. A building to house the new equipment was erected in Kirkwall in 1969, and the installation of an extremely up-to-date automatic cross-bar exchange with associated cordless switchboard began shortly afterwards. The automatic system handles all dialled calls, the switchboard deals with calls requiring the services of an operator. This is one of the first installations of its kind in Scotland. Local automatic exchanges will then receive STD facilities, and the small manual exchanges will be replaced by automatic units linked to Kirkwall by radio. Unfortunately, there have been cases where a family that was responsible for working a manual exchange has had to leave an island to seek fresh employment; this happened in Rousay in 1968.

For telephone charging purposes Orkney is divided into a

northern and a southern zone, based on Kirkwall and Sanday respectively. This follows the national system of charging which was introduced with STD in 1958. Untimed 'local' calls can be made inside each zone, but calls across the boundary are charged at the 'up to 35 miles' rate. This subdivision into zones places the North Isles at a disadvantage compared with Mainland, Rousay, Shapinsay and the South Isles and has been the cause of much complaint by North Isles people. In recognition of the special conditions which obtain in an island community such as Orkney, it is proposed to allow all calls within the islands to be charged at the 'local' rate as soon as modernisation is complete. This of course represents a considerable subsidy to the North Isles by the general body of telephone users.

THE TOURIST INDUSTRY

The beginnings of the tourist trade may be regarded as going back to 1822, the year in which Walter Scott published his novel *The Pirate*. The story, which is now rarely read, is set in Shetland and Orkney. Scott himself visited Orkney in 1814, staying at Papdale House, Kirkwall, then the home of Malcolm Laing, the Scots historian. About the same time the artist William Daniell visited the islands and made such scenes as the Ring of Brodgar, the Hoy cliffs and St Magnus Cathedral familiar to people in the south through his aquatints, now collectors' pieces.

Later in the century the North Company was a pioneer in bringing visitors to Orkney on round-trip tickets and cruises. All-inclusive round trips on the company's regular steamers began in the mid-1880s. Shetland benefited from these more than Orkney until after the second World War, when great efforts were made to expand this side of the business and the Standing Stones Hotel in Stenness was brought into the tours organisation. The first cruise to the northern isles of Scotland took place in 1894, when Kirkwall was visited as part of a tour which included Fair Isle, Foula and Lerwick. The fare was £5.

Nowadays accommodation for visitors is provided by hotels and private households, and recently holiday cottages have been offered for letting in increasing numbers. A register of accommodation (all of which is carefully inspected) is compiled each

147

year by the Orkney Tourist Organisation. Most hotels are in Kirkwall or Stromness, but there are also some country hotels in Mainland which are good centres for fishing; accommodation is available on most of the outer islands. Hotel standards are quite good, in some cases excellent, but many establishments would be improved by the employment of properly trained staff, and they could also profit by providing more locally produced foods in their restaurants.

It is easy to exaggerate the benefits likely to accrue from a substantial increase in the number of summer visitors to Orkney and to underestimate the problems which such an increase would bring in its train. The tourist trade is a notorious breeder of seasonal unemployment, and Orkney would be well advised to develop the holiday trade as a complement to the islands' basic economic activities of farming, fishing and light industry. This could be done by relying heavily upon the employment, during summer vacations, of Orkney university and college students as a matter of policy. Apart from its other advantages, visitors would thereby be brought into contact with local people who are likely to be well informed.

The provision of a drive-on ferry and more frequent air services will greatly improve travel facilities for holiday visitors to Orkney. At present, upwards of 36,000 visitors come to the islands each year, mainly in a short summer season (June–September), and the income from their spending on the islands is second only to the profits from farming. Some 3,500 cars belonging to holiday-makers are ferried over in a summer. Both visitors and cars are steadily increasing in number.

The number of car-borne visitors likely to visit Orkney in, say, 1980 cannot be forecast accurately, but it could be much larger than is commonly supposed—in other parts of the world, most estimates of tourist traffic growth have turned out to be underestimates. Taking into account the growth of Britain's urban population and of the number of cars it owns, as well as the growing popularity of car-camping and of longer holidays, it could well be that as many as 100,000 visitors, with 15,000 cars, will visit the islands in 1980.

How to contain and guide such an influx of visitors so that Orkney's own society survives its impact and how to conserve the natural environments of coast and country as major attractions are questions that must be considered. A first need is a precise, quantitative survey of the capacity of sites likely to attract visitors. The capacity of an attractive site, the Bay of Skaill for example, may be defined under four heads. Its physical capacity could be assessed in terms of the total space available and the proportion which could be developed for car parking, camping and other essential services without spoiling the attractiveness of the site. Its ecological capacity requires an assessment of the number of people the site could absorb at one time and in one season without harm to the natural environment. A psychological aspect of the area concerns the number of people who could enjoy the site together without spoiling it for each other. Lastly, an administrative survey would estimate the number of persons that could be handled at one time by such necessary services as archaeological site guides, restaurant and camp staff and cleaning-up services.

A survey of this type can alone provide information for a rational development of available resources. Experience in North American tourism strongly suggests that the provision of parking facilities appropriate to the capacity of a holiday site, coupled with a reasonable prohibition of roadside parking, will effectively regulate the numbers of visitors using a site at any one time, as long as alternative sites are provided and their existence made known.

There are many places in Orkney which could be developed as holiday sites; Skaill Bay, the Birsay and Yesnaby coasts, the Ness Battery area of Stromness and the Churchill Barriers spring immediately to mind. At one site, an Orkney Countryside Centre should be built, to include a countryside museum, a restaurant and information centre and with a car park and properly managed camp site attached. The design of the buildings might be based on the theme of the traditional Orkney long-house; an actual example of such a house might be rebuilt and furnished as part of the museum. Important archaeological finds from Orkney should be brought from Edinburgh and lodged in the museum during the summer. From the Centre, countryside trails could be laid out, involving in some cases the use of cars. Such trails would introduce visitors to all aspects of the countryside, from geology and ornithology to modern farming. A guide book on the lines of that already available, an Orkney Countryside Map showing the location and resources of sites available to visitors, and countryside trail guides would help visitors make the most of their stay in Orkney. Concise 'show yourself' guides to Kirkwall and Stromness would also be much appreciated by visitors. The *In Orkney* leaflets on natural history, archaeology and fishing are a start in the right direction.

It is desirable, of course, that the profits from a growing tourist trade should be spread beyond the confines of Mainland. At present only about seven per cent of all visitors go to the outer islands. Loganair services now bring the North Isles within 20 minutes' flying of Kirkwall, and the provision of air-car tours to places of interest in these islands would be a most useful service, both to visitors and to the islands.

INDUSTRIES

Visitors to the north isle of Sanday are surprised to find a small electronics firm in business there, Sykes Robertson (Electronics) Ltd. This firm was established in 1967 with a capital of £5,000 and entirely without government backing. Its connections are now world-wide. It prospers not because of any advantage of location in Sanday but because of the international reputation of its founder as a technical expert and inventor, and because it exploits niches left in the electronics business by the major companies.

Early successes included the sale of language laboratories in Stromness and Hong Kong, and a contract from the North of Scotland Hydro Electric Board to design and build equipment for the location of faults in unmanned substations. An early problem was shortage of capital. As the founder pointed out at the firm's first AGM, a long period of time can elapse between an inquiry, the placing of a firm order and final payment. Accordingly the authorised capital was raised to £15,000 in 1969, at which stage the Highlands and Islands Development Board offered help in the form of a grant of £2,000, repayment of which was to begin after two years.

While there may be some other opportunities to establish small businesses of a highly specialist type in Orkney, it would be unrealistic to suppose that they will make much contribution to the islands' economy and employment situation.

Generally speaking, Orkney industry is concerned with processing raw materials provided by farms and the sea. The two creameries in Birsay and Kirkwall have already been mentioned. In Kirkwall there are two large whisky distilleries, the Highland Park and the Scapa. In the days when jobs off the land were well-nigh unobtainable, a job at the Highland Park, which is the older distillery, was considered the ultimate in worldly security. A former proprietor of this distillery was Mr W. G. Grant, whose unique contribution to Orkney archaeology is to be noted.

Boat-building is a long-established Orkney industry, and there has been strong development since 1945. At present some fifty men are employed, working in four yards in Mainland and Burray. The largest yard is J. T. Anderson's, recently relocated on the former herring quay at Stromness. This is the largest yard in the Highland counties and employs thirty men. It was the first yard to build a boat under the Highlands Board's Fisheries Development Scheme, the 50ft stern trawler *Kildinguie*, for a Stronsay owner. This yard has become celebrated for its striking transom-sterned design first seen in 1967. Yards in Australia and France now build boats of this design under licence. Sinclair's yard in Stromness builds fishing boats, dinghies and cabin cruisers. Duncans' yard in Burray is the fifth generation of a father-and-son business and has built over 400 boats since the second war, ranging in size from dinghies to 36-footers. Sales of boats to the Western Isles have been a recent feature of this yard's business. 1969 was the boat-building industry's most profitable year to date, earning at least £120,000. Continued expansion is anticipated.

Fishing has recently made great progress. Although herring fishery was important last century, Orkney is not by tradition an important fishing centre, but a few fishermen have always worked the inshore waters for crab, lobster, clam and scallop. This side of the fishing business has recently developed very strongly, mainly through the enterprise of the Orkney Fishermen's Society, a co-operative organisation based in Stromness. This society was reconstituted out of an earlier body in 1961. Crab and lobster are processed for export, and live lobster is exported in large quantities, mainly by air from Kirkwall to London, Paris, Amsterdam, Copenhagen, Oslo and other destinations. Crab at first presented a special problem because it cannot travel live, as can lobster. The answer was found in blast-freezing, and crab exports have grown enormously. About 30 boats now fish for the society.

A second crab processing factory was opened by local enterprise in Westray in 1968. In 1969, its first full year of operation, 4–5 tons were processed weekly at the height of the season, giving employment to about 20 boats and 30 people, mainly women, on shore. Most of the output is shipped in the refrigerated compartments of MV *St Rognvald*. Lobster is sold through the Orkney Fishermen's Society organisation. In 1970 the Highlands and Islands Development Board made a combined grant and loan of £11,000 available for a fish and shellfish processing plant in Rousay. The clam and scallop fishery, which had always remained of local importance, showed signs in 1969 of becoming an export industry. Further developments in the fishing industry appear likely.

Other kinds of fishing are not yet much developed, and at present Orkney ports lack the on-shore facilities to support a more broadly based fishery. There are however signs that a big expansion will occur. The 1960s witnessed a fishing revival in Stronsay, which last century was an important base for the northern isles herring fleets. It is possible that a fish-meal factory may be established in Orkney; fish processing, if established, could well lead to the processing of a wider variety of foodstuffs, as has been the case at Thurso, just across the Pentland Firth.

A change in the beef export trade could stimulate new employment in food processing. At present only half the value eventually realised be exported live beef finds its way back to the Orkney farmer. Moreover the prices for live animals are subject to much greater variation than those for carcase meat. Orkney farmers are therefore engaged in the less profitable and more erratic aspect of the beef trade, and the provision of slaughterhouses on the island, with the necessary plant for processing or packing meat for export, might well be considered an economically desirable innovation.

Orkney is trying to diversify its economy in a time of great change. Above all, new industry is needed to take up the many people who will shortly be released from the land by farm amalgamation and increased mechanisation. There has already been considerable progress in this direction. The domestic knitwear industry has been expanded, and three knitwear firms are now engaged in the commercial manufacture of knitwear in the islands. It is hoped that further expansion may result in the establishment of at least one knitwear factory to supplement what is at present a cottage industry. Orkney tweed is a traditional product which has an excellent reputation for quality. An Orkney jewellery industry, using both local and imported materials and adapting designs from the islands' archaeological treasury, has become a highly successful sideline; in Shapinsay, fishing lures are made in large numbers for export to the USA, and in Holm half a dozen men are engaged in the manufacture of scallop dredges for home use and export. A new bacon factory and associated bone-offal reduction plant has opened in the wartime buildings at Haston, Kirkwall.

There are many hopeful signs that Orkney will adapt to changing conditions as successfully as it has done in the past. But so far the fundamental question remains unanswered, how will Orkney find work for all its people in the decades immediately ahead?

THE prosperity of island life depends in large measure upon the social well-being of the islanders. The conditions of such services as education and communications very closely concern the quality of their lives, and that quality is reflected in turn in their cultural expression—their newspapers, their creative arts.

EDUCATION

The quality of education in Orkney has been good for a long time. The importance attached to it may be judged from the large and growing complex of school buildings in the Papdale valley at Kirkwall, where what is in effect an educational precinct has been established since the mid-1950s. Good education has also allowed Orkney to send well-qualified men and women overseas for many years past.

Junior schooling is given in local schools, of which there are thirteen in Mainland and one on each inhabited island with children to be taught. Some of these island schools are very small; those on Flotta, Graemsay, Egilsay and Wyre have less than a dozen pupils apiece.

Secondary schooling was until recently provided in a number of district junior-secondary schools and by the two burgh schools of Kirkwall and Stromness. These two, Kirkwall Grammar School and Stromness Academy, were open to all pupils of secondary age in the two burghs, and also took pupils for academic courses from the countryside and islands, using an 11-plus selection procedure. Under the comprehensive reorganisation the secondary departments in former junior-secondary schools were closed, and all pupils now go to the enlarged burgh schools. The only exceptions are children in Westray and Sanday who can take the first two secondary years at their island schools. This reduces the need for boarding in Kirkwall.

Boarding has long been a feature of secondary education in Orkney. It has been provided in private lodgings and in a hostel at Kirkwall. The introduction of comprehensive education, together with the growth of sixth forms have greatly increased the demand for boarding facilities, and in 1970 a large new hostel for 200 boarders was opened on the Papdale site.

There are at present some 2,900 pupils in the thirty schools of Orkney, taught by about 190 teachers. Many teachers are Orcadians, especially in the primary division, but Orkney has never followed a near-sighted policy of automatically appointing the local candidate for a post. About 20 teachers are mobile ('itinerant' in Scotland, 'peripatetic' in England); some travel out to the islands to take classes in such practical subjects as needlework, art and craft.

The total number of schools has been much reduced in postwar years by the closing of one-teacher units, and the present total is about two-thirds of that for 1960. Closures began between the two wars, as outlying communities lost their young people. Sometimes closure of the community school was a key factor in speeding depopulation. This was the case at Rackwick on the Atlantic coast of Hoy where visitors may now stay in the school building, now a hostel; it closed in 1937. Nearby is a small stone building, really no more than a hut. This was the first school, within whose walls over 40 children were being taught a century ago by a single teacher. The teaching of those days must have been good, for an extraordinarily large number of boys became sea-captains. The development of education in Orkney has been a saga which deserves to be recorded at some time.

Kirkwall Grammar School merits very special mention as being not only the senior school in Orkney but one of the oldest schools in Britain. Its probable foundation by Bishop Bjarni of Wyre in the late twelfth or early thirteenth centuries has already been referred to. His foundation seems to have survived all the vicissitudes of subsequent centuries; probably the close connection with St Magnus Cathedral helped to ensure this. It would appear that all teachers in the early years were cathedral clergy, and in 1544 Bishop Reid, builder of the Moosie Tower on the Bishop's

Palace, linked the mastership of the school with the Prebendary of St Peter in the cathedral, and appointed one of his own staff, a graduate in the arts, to the post. The school was then located somewhere near the foot of Palace Road. The church controlled the school until 1700, after which time the town council gradually increased its influence, taking the school over completely in 1790.

The *Old Statistical Account* of 1795–8 gives us a glimpse of the condition of the school at this time: 'Here we have an excellent school, under the direction of two regularly bred, and well qualified masters, who with much fidelity teach the learned languages, writing, arithmetic, book-keeping, and the various branches of mathematics.' The school was then for boys only, but it was noted that a girls' school was about to open in the town, and that there was a Charity School.

Bishop Reid's school building was found inadequate, and in 1764 the school moved to another, which was also found unsuitable. In 1818 the town council determined to erect a 'more suitable and commodious edifice', and this was opened in 1820. It is said that every member of the council appointed himself clerk of works and personally supervised the building operations. The new site, which lay immediately east of St Magnus Cathedral, was to be occupied for more than 150 years. The 1872 Education Act, which made general school attendance compulsory, caused the Grammar School to be combined with a Subscription and infant school to form the Burgh School of Kirkwall; but the old name of Kirkwall Grammar School was restored early this century.

The Grammar School now has 1,250 pupils on its books, divided between infant, junior and secondary departments, all under one head. There are about 40 staff. In the secondary department, internal organisation is fully comprehensive, and there is no selection whatever until the age of thirteen, after which about three-quarters of the pupils take Certificate courses. The 1960s saw a marked growth in sixth form numbers, following the national trend. In recent years an average of 14 pupils a year have gone on to universities, 9 to technical colleges, 8 to colleges of education and 5 to art, design and other types of college. Aberdeen and Edinburgh are the favourite universities.

The school is gradually being moved from its site near St Magnus to the educational precinct at Papdale. The infant department moved out in 1955 and the junior in 1962. It is hoped to build a purpose-designed comprehensive secondary department at Papdale as soon as possible, associated with a Further Education centre.

Stromness Academy is a much newer and smaller school. It was established as a direct consequence of the 1872 Act, and the first building opened in 1874. An infant department was added in 1896. Further extensions were made to house the increase produced by the 1901 Education Act, which raised the school leaving age to fourteen and again to provide the new technical subjects introduced by the 1908 Act. Between the wars there was a fairly substantial reconstruction; and in 1969 a new primary block housing 280 pupils was opened; this now dominates the Stromness skyline.

As at Kirkwall, the internal organisation is entirely comprehensive, with no selection in the first two years of secondary schooling, after which all subjects are taught in sets.

A very interesting development at this school is the establishment of a Nautical Department in the former premises of a Stromness boat-builder. This provides 'O' level courses for boys in Navigation and Seamanship and Nautical Knowledge, also courses for merchant navy and fishing certificates at the Further Education level. The department is equipped with a variety of small craft. It is seen as part of the plan to encourage young Orcadians to think of careers in Orkney outside farming.

LIBRARY SERVICES

Library services are exceptionally good. The County Library situated in Laing Street, Kirkwall, has recently been thoroughly modernised. An Orkney Room is provided in which is housed a unique collection of books, maps and other documents of local importance, to which a study room is attached. Another collection of Orkney books is housed in Stromness public library. The provision of a library service to an island community presents special problems; Mainland is served by library vans, while books are sent in special family boxes to the outer isles. This family system has two pleasing results: Orcadians read more books each year than most other British people; and in this library service a book is almost never lost.

A recent development of the library service has been the creation of a sound archive. This is a collection of magnetic tapes on which are recorded specimens of Orcadian speech, which varies considerably from island to island and between one district and another in Mainland; sections of the Orkneyinga Saga read in Old Norse by an Icelandic scholar; and eye-witness accounts of events in that part of Orkney's history which is still within living memory. The collection has grown very fast since its inception in 1968, and will become a rich resource for future students of the twentieth century in Orkney, a time of unprecedented change.

Long before the days of modern public libraries there was a library in Kirkwall, the founding of which goes back to the time of the episcopacy; but real progress in providing a library on modern lines began in 1814 through the enterprise of Malcolm Laing and other leading men in Orkney. The *Orkney and Zetland Chronicle* of January 1825 notes that there were already 798 books in this 'respectable' library, and the balance of the subjects is interesting. Theology held first place with 261 books, followed by philosophy with 148 and novels and romances with 84 (the *Chronicle* places these at the end of its list). History, voyages and travel had 68 and 65 titles respectively, poetry and drama 60; while the law had only 11, medicine 5 and natural history 3. This library continued in existence until the end of the nineteenth century, when its books were auctioned.

In December 1851 the Kirkwall Newsroom was founded by a group of Kirkwall citizens. An entrance fee of 1s was charged and an annual subscription of 5s, payable in advance. The first newspapers to be ordered were *The Times, Examiner, Punch, Edinburgh Evening Courant, London Illustrated News, Glasgow Daily Mail* and *John O'Groat Journal. The Orcadian* was added in 1856 and the *Orkney Herald* in 1860. One of the rules of the room was 'that no member shall be allowed, within 24 hours of the arrival of a newspaper, to retain it longer than a quarter of an hour if applied for by another member'. The Newsroom remained in existence until 1871.

MEDICAL SERVICES

Medical care in Orkney is based first and foremost upon the devoted and very personal service of country and island doctors, supported by two hospitals in Kirkwall. Mainland is served by nine general practitioners, and there is one on each of the following islands: Shapinsay, Stronsay, Sanday, North Ronaldsay, Eday, Westray, Papa Westray, Rousay, Hoy and the eastern South Isles.

It is obviously very expensive to maintain a health service in a scattered island community. The average number of patients per doctor in Orkney is about 1,000, but in fact some island doctors have only 350 people on their books; this compares with up to 3,500 patients per doctor in the large conurbations of the south.

Inevitably the question of economies has been raised, and one recent suggestion has been for a flying doctor service. This scheme would base all the island doctors in Kirkwall; they would visit the islands regularly to hold surgeries, and it would be possible to pool the varied expertise of all the doctors to make this the most efficient possible service. A plane would be kept on day-and-night stand-by for emergency cases.

This suggestion did not commend itself to Orkney people, who greatly value personal contact with their own island doctors. More important than this, families with young children and aged persons are apprehensive of an arrangement which would make it necessary to call for help from a doctor in Kirkwall instead of just along the road. It is thought that people might well hesitate to make what could be a vital call. Moreover, there are many nights in winter when it would be impossible for the doctor to come until daylight, even if a call were made. The flying doctor service was developed in central Australia where the climate favours flying and the days, even in winter, are long. It is not appropriate to physical conditions in Orkney.

The two Orkney hospitals are the Balfour and the Eastbank, the latter being reserved for geriatric and chronically sick patients only. There are in addition two eventide homes, in Kirkwall and Stromness. The Balfour Hospital has 67 beds, including 44 for surgical cases, and there is a modern operating theatre in the charge of a consultant surgeon, a 12-bed maternity unit and an outpatients department, all post-war developments. Specialists in such branches of medicine as gynaecology and obstetrics, ophthalmology, dermatology, orthopaedics and psychiatry visit the hospital from Aberdeen. Patients who need specialist treatment are sent south to the mainland; BEA have for many years operated an air-ambulance service from Glasgow, and Loganair now fly ambulance missions within Orkney itself, and occasionally to Aberdeen. The hospital has a staff of 36 trained nurses under a matron and assistant, and 14 nurses in training. The Medical Superintendent, who is also Medical Officer of Health for the County of Orkney, has a staff of 21 district nurses and 3 health visitors. A Health Centre, with accommodation for 4–5 doctors and the Public Health Department, is the next projected development on the Balfour Hospital site.

The history of the Balfour Hospital goes back to 1836, when John Balfour of Trenaby, representative of a notable Westray family, conveyed Mexican Government bonds to the face-value of £20,000 to certain trustees for the purpose of building, furnishing and endowing a hospital in Orkney. Unfortunately the bonds proved not to be worth very much; half were sold in 1839 for £2,337 10s and the rest in 1845 for £3,711 18s. 1d, which sums were invested. In 1845 the trustees bought a house in the main street of Kirkwall for £450 and opened it as a hospital in November that year. This building remained in use, with various improvements, until 1926. The first matron was a Mrs Mary Peace; her salary was the princely sum of £4 per annum, with coal, gas and as many vegetables as she required from the hospital garden.

In 1914 the widow and family of Bailie Robert Garden of Kirkwall offered to build a new hospital in his memory for the Balfour Hospital trustees. The offer had to remain in abeyance until after the first World War, when work was at last begun and the Garden Memorial Building was opened on the present Balfour Hospital site in 1926. This new building included an operating theatre and X-ray unit, and was in the charge of a surgeon-superintendent. Part of the Garden building is still in use. During the second war, further extensions were made by the service authorities.

ENTERTAINMENTS AND COMMUNITY LIFE

Apart from the cinema, Orkney has always had rather limited facilities for public entertainment, a consequence of its small and dispersed population. However, in 1968 a new Orkney Arts Theatre was opened in Kirkwall in the reconstructed Temperance Hall. The reconstruction was outstandingly thorough, and the new building, which is very well appointed indeed, opened up entirely new possibilities for entertainment and cultural activities in the islands. It is now used with increasing regularity for stage productions and dramatic festivals and competitions, and its facilities make it possible for professional touring companies and musical groups to be invited to Orkney.

One of the first functions to be held in the new theatre was a conference of scholars from universities in Scotland, Iceland and the Scandinavian countries which was organised to commemorate the five-hundredth anniversary of the transfer of Orkney from the Dano-Norwegian to the Scottish crown. Lectures and discussions were held on such topics as the geography of Orkney, aspects of the history of the time of transfer, the characteristics of odal law in Orkney and other Scandinavian countries, and other related subjects.

Since that time, the theatre has accommodated several conferences, and it seems likely that Kirkwall will become something of a centre for international meetings of those interested in the history and archaeology of lands of Norse settlement.

There is a vigorous social life in Orkney despite the lack of facilities such as concert halls and theatres. The churches are in many instances the centres of thriving social activity, and many have youth clubs attached. Women's Institutes are very active throughout the islands, as are Ladies Lifeboat Guilds. There are Community Associations in many districts, often with their own halls, and these organise functions such as whist drives, dances and Spring Queen contests. Burns Suppers are held throughout Orkney in January each year.

The Orkney Field Club, which has about 100 members in most years, arranges a programme of winter lectures and summer study excursions, often using the expertise of visitors to the islands. The club also promotes the study of natural history in Orkney

K

schools. There is an Orkney Agricultural Society and several branches of the Young Farmers Club, and activities such as boys' ploughing matches are held annually. The Orkney Heritage Society is concerned with the preservation of historic buildings and other items of value from Orkney's past.

On the sporting side, Orcadians belong in considerable numbers to rugby and football clubs, which play in competitions within the islands and against clubs from outside. There are also squash, volleyball, badminton, darts, bowling and motorcycle scrambling clubs, and golf clubs at Kirkwall and Stromness.

Most of these activities tend to attract the slightly older and more settled parts of the population. Young people in their 'teens tend to find they have not enough to do in their spare time, especially if they have visited the towns of the south. This feeling of dissatisfaction is not in any way peculiar to Orkney, but it does encourage the drift of young people towards the town jobs and town entertainments which the islands cannot provide. It is very difficult to see what can be done about it.

'THE ORCADIAN' NEWSPAPER

The Orcadian, a weekly, is the senior of two newspapers published in Orkney during the past hundred years, also the senior of four published in the northern isles of Scotland in the same period. Today it is Orkney's only newspaper, the second *The Orkney Herald,* founded only six years after *The Orcadian,* having failed to survive into the 1960s. *The Orcadian* is independent of political affiliation and by tradition takes a carefully reasoned, middle-of-the-road point of view; the *Herald* was somewhat more radical in its views.

About 9,000 copies of *The Orcadian* are sold weekly, but because practically every copy sold in the islands is read by several people the paper reaches almost the entire adult population. Many copies are posted to subscribers in the south, especially in the Aberdeen, Glasgow and Edinburgh areas, and there is a substantial subscription circulation to Canada, the USA and other far-off places where Orkney exiles have made their homes. News of Orkney Societies in such places is regularly reported. The paper is produced at premises in Victoria Street, Kirkwall by a staff of about a dozen, including editorial, printing and front office personnel. The editorial staff consists of the editor and a reporter.

The paper concentrates mainly, though not exclusively, upon local news, which it reports in great detail. Most of the rather numerous official Reports which appeared in the 1960s on the social and economic health of Orkney were either reprinted in full, or lengthy abstracts were given. Controversial issues—such as whether or not a freight subsidy should come out of the rates, the advisability of a so-called short sea route across the Pentland Firth—received very full reporting and comment. In consequence, Orcadians tend to be exceptionally well informed about matters which concern their islands. The paper contains a miscellany of personal news and accounts of the doings of local organisations; there are regular natural history notes, frequent contributions of a literary and historical nature, photographs, also tide tables and shipping and bus timetables and a lively advertisement section. The paper gives a fascinating insight into the workings of a close-knit and highly personal island society.

The Orcadian is a family concern and has been so since its inception in 1854, with one rather mysterious gap (1863–81) when it was a limited company. It was founded by James Urquhart Anderson, son of one Magnus Anderson who set up a bookbinding business in Kirkwall in 1798. James served his apprenticeship in bookbinding in Leith, where he also developed an interest in printing and learned the rudiments of the craft. He returned to Kirkwall to enter his father's business, but brought with him an urge to print books as well as bind them, and also to found an Orkney newspaper. A hand-press was brought to Orkney by some local gentry, and for a time James Anderson, who was the only man in Orkney who knew how to work it, seems to have given lessons in printing at Kirkwall Grammar School. In the 1820s he acquired this machine himself and became, in a very small way, a printer. So the Kirkwall Press was born.

James Anderson's eldest son, also James, served his time as a printer in Edinburgh, and later took a post on the *Newcastle Chronicle*. Meanwhile James Anderson senior obtained a better press, with more type, and in 1854 the younger James came north to join his father in founding *The Orcadian*. The first issue appeared on Saturday 14 November in that year and cost 2d; it was subtitled *A Literary and Commercial Advertiser for Orkney and Zetland*. The father wrote the leading article and most of the news items; the son set the type with his own hands.

This first issue contained mainly national news, principally a long account of the battle of Alma in the Crimea. There was a lengthy article on 'The Rationale of the Austrian Alliance'. There were some local items; the erection of new lighthouses on North Ronaldsay and Kirkwall east pier was noted, and the first-ever Stromness notes appeared. Some interesting sidelights on the prices of the day at Kirkwall and Stromness were given: flour $2\frac{1}{4}$d a lb, butter 8d a lb, eggs 6d a dozen, cheese 3d a lb, geese (alive) 2s to 2s 6d each. There was a note on the dangers of smoking and a moral anecdote in favour of sobriety.

To found a newspaper in the 1850s anywhere in Great Britain was difficult enough because of the stamp duty on newspapers and a tax on newsprint; until 1853 there was also an advertisement tax. To found one in a place as remote as Orkney was a truly remarkable achievement. At first the paper appeared monthly, thereby escaping the stamp duty. When this was removed the year following *The Orcadian* became a weekly, which it has remained ever since. Its original four pages were soon enlarged by the addition of inside pages of national news printed first in London and later in Edinburgh. In 1860 communications were good enough for the entire paper to be made up in Kirkwall, and by 1870 one reads of news coming by the electric telegraph.

James Urquhart Anderson died in 1874 and James junior took charge of the paper. For a short while, printing was done in what is today The Leonards bookshop in Queen Street while a new steam press was installed in the Victoria Street premises. In 1877 W. H. Mackintosh, a talented journalist and editor from Ayrshire, joined the paper, married James Anderson's daughter and took over the business on his father-in-law's retirement in 1895. The paper has been in the Anderson-Mackintosh family ever since. W. H. Mackintosh's son James was in charge from World War I until 1938; he was followed by his widow, then by their two daughters. One of these, Mrs Robert Miller, has been in sole charge since 1949. It was fitting that she should press the button which started the printing of the special centenary issue in 1954.

Between the two wars James Anderson Mackintosh installed an ultra-modern Cossar flatbed press, capable of printing 4,000 copies per hour. This is still the finest press north of Inverness. Circulation gradually rose from 3,600 in 1914 to 6,000 in 1931 and almost 8,000 in the centenary year. On 3 November 1966 the paper, following the national trend, first put its main news on the front page.

During the second World War *The Orcadian* office published the troops' newspaper *Orkney Blast*, an appropriate title. This was founded by the Orkney writer Eric Linklater. The present editor of *The Orcadian* itself, Mr Gerald Meyer, edited the *Blast* jointly with Dr Linklater. Mr Meyer came to Orkney with experience on the London *Daily Sketch* (now *Daily Graphic*) and several forces' newspapers.

ORKNEY WRITERS

In recent times Orkney has produced two writers of national, indeed international, reputation, the poet Edwin Muir (1887–1959) and the novelist, essayist, playwright and historian Eric Linklater. Muir was born in Deerness but grew up on his father's farm Bu of Wyre. In his *Autobiography* he described how the bare Orkney landscape, with its clarity and sense of vast distances was the background against which his poetic insight and imagination developed. Eric Linklater is a native of Dounby, where he was born in 1899. Commander of the Orkney Fortress Engineers in World War II, he founded the forces' newspaper *Orkney Blast*. In the first war he served with the Black Watch and was severely wounded. After taking his degree at Aberdeen University he had a spell of journalism in India, then returned to university teaching at Aberdeen and in the USA. He began writing in 1929 and his *White Maa's Saga* was an immediate success. Since then he has produced many books, some of which are rooted deep in his native Orkney.

Muir and Linklater belong to a much wider canvas than Orkney, and their work is important quite apart from its reference to their native islands. There are however three Orcadian writers whose work during the past half-century or so has been concentrated mainly upon aspects of Orkney life and history, and whose writings have greatly enriched that life; these are Joseph Storer Clouston, John Mooney and Hugh Marwick.

Clouston was a novelist by profession, but his historical works are likely to be his enduring monument. His first substantial essay in this field was *Records of the Earldom of Orkney*, published by the Scottish Historical Society in 1914. This made available for the first time virtually every surviving medieval document on Orkney and was an essential foundation for future research. Clouston next wrote a series of papers based on documents held in the Sherriff Court House in Kirkwall which illuminated events in the Orkney countryside after the transfer of the islands to Scotland. In 1922 he was instrumental in founding the Orkney Antiquarian Society, was its president for many years and contributed many articles to its *Proceedings*.

In 1927 he produced a monumental work, *The Orkney Parishes*. This was a reprinting of the sections in the Old Statistical Account relating to Orkney, together with learned introductions to each parish report and to the work as a whole. Nothing like this has yet been attempted for any other Scottish county. Five years later Clouston published his *History of Orkney*. This relates in great detail, and with the most intimate local knowledge, the development of Orcadian society in the Norse and early Scots periods; later centuries are treated much less fully. Despite its great length and rather dull format Clouston's *History* is a very readable book indeed. Parts of it will almost certainly be superseded as new information comes to light, but the work as a whole is likely to stand for many years to come as the cornerstone of modern Orcadian historical scholarship.

A historian who worked within narrower limits than Storer Clouston was John Mooney. Mooney was a businessman and only in later life did he find time to set down the results of his detailed researches. His *Eynhallow*, which appeared in 1923, was a thorough study of the tradition, history and remains of the small 'holy isle' which lies between Rousay and Mainland, an island now uninhabited and rarely visited. He followed this in 1935 with *St Magnus Earl of Orkney*, a definitive study of Orkney's best remembered saint. His most notable and original work appeared in 1943, *The Cathedral and Royal Burgh of Kirkwall*, a scholarly account of the development of the two and of the relations between them. A second edition of this book is still in print.

Hugh Marwick was a more prolific writer than Mooney, and much better known outside Orkney; for many years his book in the Robert Hale series was the standard general account of the islands. Like both Clouston and Mooney, Marwick was a researcher and writer in his spare time; he was a schoolmaster by profession who became first a distinguished head of Kirkwall Grammar School and later Director of Education for Orkney. His knowledge of Orkney past and present was profound, and this gives special weight to certain of his historical opinions.

His book on *The Orkney Norn*, a highly technical work, appeared in 1929. It was ten years before *Merchant Lairds of Long Ago* followed it, describing some of the Orkney families who made their money in trade and invested it in land. In 1947 came *The Place-Names of Rousay*, lucid and closely reasoned, to be followed by the comprehensive, parish-by-parish study *Orkney Farm Names* in 1952. Meanwhile the more popular but nevertheless very learned book *Orkney* had been published, and almost simultaneously came the *Official Guide to the Ancient Monuments of Orkney*. This short booklet not only described the various archaeological remains in the Ministry's charge but set them against a comprehensive account of Orkney prehistory. Despite later discoveries, Marwick's account was deemed worthy of re-issue, with minor revisions, in 1969. In 1970 the text of Marwick's *Place-Names of Birsay*, which had been completed nine years earlier, was published by Aberdeen University Press, under the editorship of W. F. H. Nicolaisen. The book is the most exhaustive place-name study yet made of a single parish, and is a fitting monument to a great Orcadian scholar.

Today the line of authorship continues in Orkney, most notably in the person of George Mackay Brown. Mr Brown was born in 1921 in Stromness and lives and works there; his notes on 'Letter from Hamnavoe' are a familiar feature of *The Orcadian*. He was educated at Newbattle Abbey, Dalkeith, while Edwin Muir was Warden, and later at Edinburgh University. His poetry is rooted deeply in Orkney's past, as is the prose writing which has lately engaged more and more of his attention. *The Storm and Other Poems* appeared in 1954, *Loaves and Fishes* in 1959, *The Year of the Whale* in 1965.

Although George Mackay Brown writes about Orkney people and the Orkney scene with a profound understanding of the life of past times, his message concerns the universal state of man. In consequence he cannot be regarded as a purely local writer. The general appeal of his work was especially evident in his second volume of Orkney stories, *A Time to Keep* (1968) and in *Orkney Tapestry* (1969).

THE ORKNEY VOLUNTEERS

Weyland Park camp at Kirkwall, almost on the site of Cromwell's fort, is the headquarters of an Orkney territorial infantry unit, the 1st (Lovat Scouts) Company of the 51st Highland Volunteers. This is the latest in a succession of volunteer units to be raised in Orkney. The modern history of volunteering began with the expansion of the Territorial Army in 1937; it has continued since with only one short break in 1945–7 when the whole TA was stood down preparatory to reorganisation for peacetime. The infantry role of the Orkney volunteers is a new one. Traditionally they have been gunners, engaged either in anti-aircraft or coast defence.

In 1937, part of 226 Heavy Anti-aircraft Battery Royal Artillery (TA) was formed in Orkney. This was soon followed by the Orkney Heavy Regiment RA (TA), supported by the Orkney Fortress Engineers, commanded by Major Eric Linklater. 226 Battery fired some of the first shots in the war against German aircraft raiding Scapa Flow before being moved to positions in the south. The Heavy Regiment and Fortress Engineers manned coastal guns at Ness Battery, Stromness and Flotta. After *Royal Oak* had been sunk coastal defences were strengthened, and altogether nineteen batteries were brought into being. In 1944, when the German threat to Scapa Flow had become negligible, many Orkney artillerymen were transferred to the infantry ready for the D-day landings.

The early history of volunteering in Orkney goes back a very long way indeed, but details of the earliest period of all, that of

168

the Seven Years and Napoleonic Wars, are sketchy in the extreme. In 1793 Thomas Balfour of Shapinsay was busy raising a Fencible Regiment in Orkney, but this was difficult because so many men had already been taken for service in the navy. Nevertheless a regiment was formed; it appears in the Army List as The Orkney and Shetland Fencibles, and was the eighth regiment of its kind to be raised in Scotland. Most of the men were Orcadians. The pay-roll of this force survives and shows that privates received 1s a day, corporals 1s 2d and sergeants 1s 6d. These Fencible units, unlike the later Volunteers, came under full military law. Their uniform consisted of black cocked hat, scarlet coat faced with yellow cloth, white cross belt, white pantaloons and black gaiters. They had a march of their own, composed by Major Balfour, a copy of which survives. The Orkney Fencibles served not only at home but also at Berwick on Tweed—where their officers consumed an inordinate quantity of liquor—and in Ireland. They were disbanded in 1797.

The 1803 Volunteer Act authorised the formation of non-regular bodies of men trained to support the regular forces. Little is known about this period; there does appear to have been a company of gunners in Kirkwall. After the Napoleonic Wars, most units were disbanded. The government had never been enthusiastic about the existence of armed forces not directly under the control of parliament.

Activity in the volunteer field next developed in the 1860s, when there was general alarm about the low state of the country's defences. So in 1859 the government again authorised the formation of volunteer units. In December that year a meeting in Kirkwall agreed to form a unit in Orkney, and a subscription list was opened to finance it, the government being unable to give financial support. In January 1860 it was further decided that the Orkney force should be artillery. By May about 80 men had been enrolled and the construction of a battery at Cromwell's Fort began. Two cannon were installed, nick-named *St Magnus* and *St Ola*. A second company was formed in Shapinsay, and guns were mounted at a site named Fort Eleanor in 1863. A Stromness company was formed in 1862. After this early effort, further companies were later formed in several Mainland parishes and on the larger islands. In 1880 all companies were grouped together to form 1st Orkney Artillery Volunteers, based in Kirkwall. Their headquarters were now at Weyland Park, the present-day TA headquarters in Orkney; their weekend camp was near the Ness Battery at Stromness.

Many volunteer units served in the Boer War, and the Lovat Scouts, with whom the Orkney TA unit is now closely associated, achieved great fame for their ability to out-hunt the elusive Boer commandos. In 1908 the government determined to integrate volunteer units more closely with the regular army, and funds were at long last made available to ensure minimum standards of efficiency throughout the force. At this point the Orkney unit became the Orkney Royal Garrison Artillery (Territorial), and took over the defences of Scapa Flow and Fair Isle on the outbreak of war. In 1915 the Orkneymen were summarily dismissed from their posts, on the grounds that, because the defence of Scapa was a naval matter, all batteries ought to be manned by Royal Marines. For the rest of the war there were no Orkney units, and afterwards little enthusiasm for re-forming. An attempt to re-establish two artillery companies in 1920 had to be abandoned. Only the threat of a new war in 1937 awakened the old volunteer spirit in Orkney.

THE FARTHEST ISLAND

North Ronaldsay is the farthest north and most remote of the inhabited isles of Orkney. It is a full 30 miles from Kirkwall and is separated from its nearest neighbour, the large North Isle of Sanday, by North Ronaldsay Firth, two-and-a-half miles wide. This terminal position at the very end of Orkney has made North Ronaldsay in many ways the most Orcadian of all the islands; here the distinctive character of island life and landscape are most clearly developed, and the problems which affect the whole of Orkney made most explicit.

The island is small, only 2,300 acres in area and two miles wide in its southern part. It is so low-lying that visitors sometimes wonder whether the Atlantic will break right over it one winter day; salt spray does in fact impregnate the whole island in stormy weather, the west side suffering most severely. The island is not quite as flat as it seems; the ground rises by an almost imperceptible slope to a height of 54ft in the south, near the farm Holland (literally 'high land'). It is built in gently dipping, somewhat faulted Old Red Sandstone sediments of the Rousay group, considerably overlaid by glacial clays and other deposits, and by blown sand, as in parts of Sanday.

As in the rest of Orkney, the landscape of North Ronaldsay bears the marks of a very long occupation by man. A number of prehistoric burial cists, probably Bronze Age, have been unearthed, and there is a fine standing stone in the south-west of the island. In the south-east, on the shore of Strom Ness, stands the Iron Age broch of Burrian, a massive structure partly demolished by the waves. Its wall stands 15ft high on the landward side, there are signs of an entrance to seaward, as at Midhowe in Rousay, and there is a well slightly off-centre inside. Partitioning of the interior at a later date is evident. When excavated in 1870–1 Burrian yielded not only Iron Age domestic items but also signs of Celtic Christian connections, and it has been suggested that a Celtic religious community was at some time located nearby. The Burrian Cross, found inscribed on a flat piece of stone, has been adopted as a motif in modern Orkney jewellery. Just along the south shore from Burrian at Howmae, a group of interconnected huts were excavated between 1884 and 1890. These are believed to be Iron Age in date but to antedate the broch. Both excavations were carried out by members of the Traill family, then lairds of North Ronaldsay, a typically Orcadian arrangement.

North Ronaldsay is the most obviously Scandinavian of the Orkneys. Every place-name is Norse, and the island dialect is the one most closely akin to the ancient Norn and the most difficult for the uninstructed visitor to grasp. The island name derives from the Old Norse Rinansay, once thought to indicate a connection with St Ninian. This is most unlikely, and if there is any connection at all it must have been a very indirect one, just possibly the result of a later 'Ninianic' revival. The island is mentioned several times in the Orkneyinga Saga. It is almost certain that the *Bu* farm of saga times was near Kirbist in the tunship of Busta (*Bolstathr*) adjacent to the best land and close to the lairds' house of later times. Many croft and farm-names relate to topographical features, such as Breck (slope), Gravity (hollow or depression), Ancum (meadow-land), Howar (mound), Clett (rock); there are also names which refer to aspects of the settlements themselves such as Conglabist (cluster) and Sugarhouse (south garth house).

The imprint of the estate system which developed under Scots rule, and particularly of the improvements made by the Traills when proprietors of the estate last century, is clear upon the land. Most obvious is the neat squaring of the fields, a result of the planking about mid-century. Here and there on the foreshore, old kelp burning pits are to be seen, for instance near Howar. The lairds encouraged, or rather forced, their tenants to engage in kelp burning by subdividing the land into plots of less than economic size. This policy caused the total population of the island to rise to a peak of 522 in 1831, an increase of 100 in 40 years, giving a density of 130 to the square mile.

Other signs of the old estate system include the fine stone-built laird's mill in the south of the island. This is still in full working order, and was in operation until about 1965. It replaced a post-mill, Scotland's last working windmill, which went out of commission about 1900. Only its stump remains. There was also a water mill on the east shore, using the tiny stream which flows from the Loch of Hooking. In the past, grain was the principal product of the island. The mansion of the Traills, Holland House, also survives. It was not a lavish house, and the Traills were not permanently resident. Its large home farm was created out of a number of crofts by eviction. Though a small-scale affair compared with Highland evictions, this caused great bitterness and distress; it was almost certainly beneficial to farming standards.

Today, North Ronaldsay is still an estate island, and the land is farmed by tenants, many of whom come under crofting regulations by virtue of the small size of their holdings. There are 67 crofts all told, and three farms. Most crofts are small: 21 have less than 10 acres of land, 31 have 10–19 acres and 15 have 20–49 acres. Not all are inhabited, and some are worked together. The three larger properties are Holland and Treb, worked as a unit of 255 acres, and Howar, once the residence of the lairds' bailie, 74 acres. Most of the land is under grass, and the primary activity is the raising of beef cattle for export via Kirkwall. At present there are about 370 cattle in the island, including a few milkers for domestic use. One has the impression that farming is not carried on very intensively, mainly because of the large number of small crofts.

North Ronaldsay is unique in that its foreshore is grazed by about 2,000 Orkney native sheep. These animals were swept out of the rest of Orkney by nineteenth-century improvements. They are strange short-tailed creatures liable to moult in springtime, with a variety of coloured fleeces, though grey seems to predominate. They are confined to the foreshore by a 15-mile perimeter wall, built last century when the land was planked. All the sheep run together but they belong to each property on the island in numbers proportionate to annual rents and are distinctly marked by punches in the ears. Their food is mainly seaweed, and this gives a unique flavour to their mutton; one wonders whether this could be marketed in the 'delicatessens' of the south. Once a year the sheep are gathered to be sheared, dipped and marked; large pounds may be seen on the shore for this purpose. Each tenant has responsibility for maintaining a section of the perimeter wall, and this task becomes more onerous year by year because of the continuing depopulation.

North Ronaldsay is connected with the rest of Orkney and the world outside by the weekly Orkney Islands Company ship, which uses the recently improved pier in the south-west of the island. Since 1967 there has also been a twice-weekly Loganair passenger service; and there is a small-boat link with Sanday. About a dozen telephones are installed and there are a school and a resident doctor. Two shops are replenished by the weekly boat. Since 1966 most properties have had mains water, drawn from the Loch of Ancum, but there is as yet no mains electricity. Since the island has no peat ground, coal is the only fuel available; this is delivered annually by the National Coal Board. There are good roads, the result of improvements made by the Traills and more recent official support. A surprising array of motor vehicles is most strikingly displayed at Sunday morning church or near the pier when the ship is expected. Life is thus quite comfortable and not very isolated.

Because of the lack of natural havens or even of a bay sheltered in all weathers, the islanders have had little connection with the sea which surrounds them. Today there are about six lobster boats (prams) based in the island. The island has however received a great many wrecks in its time; it is so low-lying that it was almost impossible to see it in the days before lighthouses, and the channel between it and Fair Isle was a busy one in the great days of the northabout route. The first light was lit on the extreme eastern point of the island in 1789, but was not high enough, so that wrecks continued. A 100ft unlit beacon, capped by a great masonry sphere, was next erected, and is still to be seen. The modern lighthouse is 184ft high and is the second tallest in Scotland. Its top commands a fine view of the whole island and is the first and last object which the visitor by ship sees of North Ronaldsay.

This then is Orkney's farthest island. About 130 people now live on it but the number is decreasing, mainly through the emigration of young people. Before the second World War the island held 350 people, and a decline of this magnitude makes the provision of such services as regular ships and aircraft ever more costly. What the future holds it is impossible to say, but following the trend throughout Orkney it would appear to include some further depopulation and an amalgamation of crofts into more efficient units, probably on an owner-occupied basis. Only outstanding efficiency in farming can guarantee the survival of a community on North Ronaldsay into the twenty-first century.

9   SHIPPING AND AIRWAYS

S TEAMERS and motor vessels have served the islands regularly for almost 150 years. Most of the ships belonged or still belong to the ancestor companies of the modern North of Scotland Orkney and Shetland Shipping Co Ltd, so that an account of the ships becomes mainly a company history. Company records were destroyed in an air raid on Aberdeen in World War II, and such an account must depend very much upon the painstaking research of Gordon Donaldson in a number of Scottish ports.

ORKNEY SHIPS

The tiny paddle steamer of 378 tons, *Sovereign,* which inaugurated the regular run between Leith, Aberdeen, Orkney and Shetland in July 1836 belonged to the Aberdeen, Leith, Clyde and Tay Shipping Co, with headquarters in Aberdeen. This company, a direct ancestor of the modern North Company, had. originated in 1790 as the Leith and Clyde and amalgamated in 1810 with the Aberdeen, Dundee and Leith to form what was known for short as 'the Aberdeen, Leith and Clyde'. It kept this name until 1875 when it became the North of Scotland and Orkney and Shetland Steam Navigation Co; it became a limited·company in 1919. Then, as steamers finally gave place to motor ships, the name was changed again to its present form. At first the service was provided in summer only; there was little winter demand and in any case paddle steamers could not operate regularly in winter in these waters.

The company acquired its first screw steamer *Queen*, 448 tons, in 1861 and this vessel, as more and more lighthouses were established, began regular sailings to the northern isles in winter as well as summer. Its very first run, from Leith to Lerwick by way of Wick and Kirkwall, was in November. From this time the service expanded in a remarkable manner, and a pattern of sailings very much like that of today emerged. Thus in 1883 ships sailed from Leith on Monday, Wednesday and Friday in summer and called at Aberdeen the same day. The Monday ship reached Stromness on Tuesday morning and Scalloway in west Shetland on Tuesday evening. The Wednesday ship reached Kirkwall on Thursday morning and Lerwick on Thursday night. The Friday ship called at Wick and Kirkwall on Saturday morning and Lerwick on Saturday night. The vessels were back in Aberdeen on Friday, Saturday and Wednesday respectively. The speed of these services is remarkable; there was almost no restriction upon the hours a seaman, stoker or ship's officer might be required to work, and by tradition this was an age of hard steaming.

Between 1867 and 1871 three new ships were added to the company's fleet, making it extremely well equipped for the tasks it was performing. The fleet consisted of *St Magnus*, 618 tons, the company's last paddle steamer; *St Clair*, 641 tons, and *St Nicholas*, 787 tons, both iron screw steamers. Before the first World War these were reinforced by *St Rognvald*, 1,053 tons, *St Giles*, 407 tons and *St Ninian*, 787 tons. After 1867 the company's new ships were named after saints having connection with north-east Scotland and the northern isles. There was one exception to this policy, *Earl of Zetland*.

THE PENTLAND FERRY

The Pentland Firth crossing between Stromness and Scrabster had at first no connection with the ancestors of the North Company. It was inaugurated by John Stanger, a Stromness shipbuilder, and in 1856 mails were first carried on this route by the wooden paddle steamer *Royal Mail*, 103 tons. The mails contract next passed to George Robertson of Stronsay who worked the route with the screw steamer *Express*, 217 tons. In 1877 the contract went to the Highland railway company whose line had reached Thurso in 1874. They operated with the steamer *John O' Groat* until 1882, when the present company took over. At first, the North Company used the steamer *St Olaf*, 232 tons, then the first *St Ola*; this name is the local form of Olaf, and commemorates the Norwegian king and saint who is alleged in the Orkneyinga Saga to have converted Orkney to Christianity in 995. This tiny ship, only 231 tons, served Orkney for fifty-nine years before being replaced in 1951 by the present *St Ola*, a motor ship of 750 tons.

During the second war the Pentland ferry became a veritable lifeline to the multitude of servicemen and women who were stationed in Orkney. It led to Thurso railway station, from which the single track eventually took one home, far from the chill boredom of an Orkney winter. Two vessels worked from Stromness, *St Ola* which carried mainly civilians and *Earl of Zetland*, the company's first motor ship, brought into service in 1939. A third ship *St Ninian* worked between Longhope and Scrabster and was well known to naval personnel at the great Lyness base. In the war years the *Earl* carried over half a million passengers across the Firth and *St Ninian* 900,000; each ship steamed more than 100,000 miles. Of these historic ships only the *Earl* survives; she works the North Isles of Shetland from Lerwick.

PRESENT-DAY FLEETS

Today, the North of Scotland Company, now a member of the Coast Lines group, works two routes to Orkney using five of its fleet of seven ships: from Leith and Aberdeen to Kirkwall and Stromness, and from Scrabster to Stromness.

The first of these routes is worked by MV *St Ninian*, 2,244 tons, which continues her voyage to Shetland; MV *St Rognvald*, 1,024 tons, which was built specially for the Orkney cattle and cargo trade, and MV *St. Magnus*, 1,637 tons, which carries cargo only. Most Orkney cattle and sheep are exported by this route. Passenger traffic declined considerably during the 1960s, from over 3,000 in 1962 to 1,100 in 1967.

The Pentland Ferry is worked by MV *St Ola*, 750 tons, which is based in Stromness. This is the route by which most passengers and vehicles enter and leave Orkney and the volume of traffic is increasing. In round figures, about 12,000 passengers and 5,500 vehicles were carried annually in the late 1960s. A fifth ship, MV *St Clement*, 816 tons, works both the Scrabster-Stromness and Stromness-Aberdeen-Leith routes. She is familiar to visitors as a relief car-carrier in summer.

L

Ships bearing the names of unusual saints give a special flavour to Orkney harbours. Orkney's connections with the various saints varies from close to tenuous. Magnus and Rognvald are Orkney names par excellence, and ships bearing these names have traditionally served Orkney as part of their regular duties. The present *St Magnus* is the fourth ship of that name, *St Rognvald* the third. St Ninian or Nynia was formerly believed to have had connections with pre-Norse Christianity in Orkney and Shetland, and ships of this name have usually served both island groups. *St Clair* does not derive directly from a saint but from the family of St Clair who came from a village of that name in Normandy in the thirteenth century to found the great Sinclair family of Caithness and Orkney. Earls of both counties sprang from this distinguished line. It is unfortunate that the present *St Clair*, third ship of this name, never calls either in Orkney or Caithness.

NORTH ISLES SERVICES

A final word must be said about the service between Kirkwall and the North Isles of Orkney. This began in 1865 when John Stanger of Stromness put into service the wooden screw steamer *Orcadia*, 101 tons. Previously there had only been intermittent communication between the North Isles and Mainland by sailing craft. *Orcadia* called at Stronsay, Sanday and Eday on her first run, and later the service was extended. The little ship steamed at 8 knots and carried 30 people in her cabin, an unheard-of luxury for North Isles passengers. From the very first year of operation the route was popular with holiday-makers, and the ship was also used for special excursions, to Fair Isle for example. The success of this venture caused Robertson to have a new *Orcadia* built in 1867; by now he was managing director of the Orkney Steam Navigation Co. This new ship had to be lengthened in 1884 to accommodate increased traffic; she worked the island route until 1931.

Between the two wars the steamers *Earl Thorfinn* and *Earl Sigurd* were added to the company's fleet. After the second war the problem was to replace these vessels, which were coal-burning and increasingly expensive to run. Shipbuilding costs rocketed upwards and the company was quite unable to finance construction of a new ship. The Highland and Islands Shipping Services Act of 1960 offered government help under such circumstances, but even with this the company felt unable to maintain the North Isles service, and the North of Scotland Company felt unable to take it on. The solution was to form a new company with government-nominated chairman and vice-chairman and named the Orkney Islands Shipping Co. In 1962 the new company chartered a third *Orcadia* from the Secretary of State for Scotland; this was a modern motor ship, specially built for the North Isles service. The *Earl Thorfinn* was then scrapped. *Sigurd* continued her almost legendary career as the last steamship on regular service in British waters until July 1969 when the 250 ton motor ship *Islander* sailed into Kirkwall with great ceremony to replace her.

Islander was also specially built for the North Isles service with the help of a loan from the Secretary of State. She is primarily a cargo ship, designed with containerisation in mind. For many years the North Isles ships have carried their miscellaneous cargoes in small containers; the standard pattern is too large for these local purposes. She has space for 80 cattle below decks. Passenger accommodation is limited to 12, each person having a reclining chair and a table; it is expected that in future most North Isles passengers will choose to travel by air.

A service between Stromness and the islands around Scapa Flow is provided by a third company, Bremner & Co, using the small MV *Hoy Head*, supported by MV *Watchful* in summer.

LIFEBOATS AND LIGHTHOUSES

No account of shipping around the coasts of Orkney could possibly be complete without reference to the lifeboatmen who have long been famed for their feats of courage and superlative seamanship in wild winter seas, and to those who man the lighthouses.

There are four lifeboat stations in Orkney, at Scapa and Stromness in Mainland, on the North Isle of Stronsay, and at Longhope (Brims) in the South Isles. Some measure of the service rendered by Orkney lifeboats is given by the total number of lives saved by each; the Stromness boat rescued more than 800 men in its first century of operation, and this is not by any means an exceptional record.

The tragic loss of the Longhope lifeboat *TGB* with all eight members of her volunteer crew on the night of 17 March 1969 underlined the risks which lifeboatmen and their families face every time they answer a distress call. The *TGB*, whose strange name commemorated the initials of an anonymous donor, was called to the assistance of a Liberian ship, SS *Irene*, which was in difficulties off South Ronaldsay. About 10 pm, in a furious sea, with visibility reduced almost to nil and a force nine gale blowing from the south-east, *TGB* capsized near the Pentland Skerries. SS *Irene* grounded and her crew were rescued by breeches-buoy. Next afternoon the lifeboat was found upturned off the coast of Walls, quite close to her base. She has since been refitted and now serves again in the Aran Islands off the west of Ireland. At Longhope a new volunteer crew was at once forthcoming and began training to man a new boat, the 52ft *Hilton Briggs* that was brought to the station on 22 May 1970.

Stromness is the base in Orkney for the Commissioners of Northern Lighthouses, an equivalent body in Scotland to Trinity House in England. Their motor ship *Pole Star* serves lighthouses and beacons around the coasts of northern Scotland, Orkney and Shetland. The ship and its supporting base provide about thirty Stromness families with a livelihood.

In the winter half of the year the relief of lighthouses in North Atlantic waters can be a hazardous, sometimes even an impossible operation for the *Pole Star*. In April 1970 the three keepers of Sule Skerry, a tiny rock 30 miles west of Orkney, had eventually to be lifted off by helicopter after a vigil of 64 days during which their supplies almost completely ran out. Such conditions are not unusual in the history of Orkney lighthouses.

SHIPPING PROBLEMS

A discussion of farming, or indeed of almost any other aspect of Orcadian life, leads almost inevitably to a discussion of transport problems, especially shipping charges.

The North Company is not subsidised in any way, except for its mails contract. It has faced continual increases in labour, fuel and maintenance costs and has also had to accumulate capital to replace ageing ships. In consequence its charges have steadily crept upwards and there are fundamental questions that concern both the company and the Orcadians : whether the services provided are those which Orkney needs at the present time and whether and how they should be subsidised.

The most serious gap in the present service is the lack of a roll-on, roll-off ferry connection between Orkney and the mainland which could reduce handling costs of goods being transferred to the main British road system. A second serious deficiency is the lack of a quick ferry for the 27 mile crossing between Caithness and Orkney. *St Ola*, which sails daily between Stromness and Scrabster, spends nearly seventeen hours out of every twenty-four alongside Stromness pier. The speed of the vessel and, more significantly, the time taken to load and unload cargo, especially vehicles, by ship's crane are responsible for this kind of timetable. In summer particularly there is a need for a ferry to ply between Orkney and the Scottish mainland several times a day, chiefly for short-stay visitors with cars.

With a view to creating a faster service, the possibility of re-opening the historic route between South Ronaldsay and John O'Groat's was much discussed in the middle and late 1960s. Several surveys and reports were prepared, notably that by Kinnord Associates, and it became clear that to develop the alternative route would be enormously expensive. Further, since the total potential traffic would support only one ferry, a grave blow would be dealt to the port of Stromness. After considering the evidence, and bearing in mind the urgency of the matter, the Highlands and Islands Development Board announced their firm decision in October 1969 that the present Stromness-Scrabster route should be redeveloped, to be worked by a roll-on, roll-off ship. The new vessel will carry 85 cars and lorries and make the crossing in about an hour and a half. It is expected to be put into service in 1974.

The question of subsidy is more difficult. Orkney has never asked for preferential treatment but has striven to keep its disadvantages of insularity and distance from markets to a minimum. It has seemed recently that each new increase in freight charges, however necessary from the company's point of view, has widened the gap between Orkney farmers and those on the mainland to the disadvantage of the former.

In 1968 the North Company announced that it would have to raise its charges by 10 per cent from mid-1969. This raised a storm of protest and dismay both in Orkney and Shetland, and led to a request from both island communities for a government subsidy to tide them over the period of adjustment; in Orkney, this period was seen as extending to cover the opening of an improved Pentland Firth ferry service. The request was granted by the Minister of State, on condition that 25 per cent of the total sum required was raised from Orkney and Shetland rates. Authority for this unprecedented arrangement was found in the 1968 Transport Act, which states that 'if help from public funds is to be made available to secure that rural services are provided or continued, the local community should take its part in determining what services are to be considered as essential, and should contribute to the cost . . .'

The sum required to meet the 10 per cent increase was £100,000. It was calculated that since part of the sum to be raised from the rates would be offset by a rate support grant, the net result would be a 5d (2p) rate increase in Orkney, equivalent to about 10s (50p) a year on an average family farm. This very reasonable offer was accepted in Orkney but was fiercely resisted in Shetland.

Subsidy, from whatever source, can only be a short-term solution to the freight problem. Rising freight rates reflect economic and social changes which are not only national but also continent- and world-wide. All that subsidies can do is to provide a period of grace in which adjustments can be made to changing conditions, by the shipping company and by Orkney itself.

The profitability of Orkney farming is also affected by the high freight rates and a changeover in exports from live beef stock to prepared carcases might yield better returns with lower transport costs.

AIR TRANSPORT

Air services supplement the available sea transport and compete very strongly for the islands' passenger traffic, both external and internal. Two kinds of air service are provided: BEA links Kirkwall with Glasgow, Edinburgh, Aberdeen and Inverness and also with Shetland; while the Orkney firm of Loganair, which is associated with the North Isles shipping company, flies small passenger aircraft daily between Kirkwall and Westray, Papa Westray, Sanday, North Ronaldsay and Stronsay, and is steadily extending its service.

BEA use large aircraft such as Viscounts, which are expensive to fly, especially in winter when they may be nearly empty; hence there are few flights. Timings are such that it is impossible to fly south from Orkney and return the same day. This arrangement suits visitors to the islands, but it most certainly does not suit Orkney businessmen who have to attend meetings in Inverness or Aberdeen. A more frequent service using smaller aircraft is needed but BEA is not at present able to provide such a service. One obvious solution would be for BEA, which at present has the monopoly, to allow Loganair to fly scheduled services with small aircraft as far south as Aberdeen. Large BEA aircraft could profitably concentrate on the considerable traffic from the south of passengers who are not primarily concerned with early or same-day return flights. In the late 1960s BEA carried about 20,000 passengers into and out of Kirkwall annually; of these some 2,000 travelled to and from Shetland, while seventy per cent of the total were carried between April and October.

Loganair began operating in 1967. Its service is the lineal descendant of the pre-war inter-island service provided by the old Highland Airways. The plane used was a twin-engined Britten-Norman Islander, the type of machine which was to win the 1969 London-Sydney air race. The plane carries eight passengers, and in the first two years of service carried 14,000 people 175,000 miles, making 8,000 take-offs and landings. The two Loganair pilots became famous for their skill in defying winter storms. Sometimes, when bad weather made it impossible for the large BEA aircraft to land in Orkney, the Islander flew to Wick and picked up stranded passengers.

The Loganair service has revolutionised personal travel for North Isles people. Because the ships carry cargo, their progress between Kirkwall and the islands is necessarily slow; the plane provides very rapid direct communications which are especially welcome in the stormy and short days of winter. The number

183

of passengers carried by air first exceeded that carried by ship in the winter of 1967–8.

Loganair also provides a charter service, and this at once became so popular that a second aircraft, an Aztec, had to be based in Orkney in 1968. In addition to business flights, holiday trips to formerly inaccessible places such as Fair Isle are now popular.

10 KIRKWALL AND STROMNESS

K IRKWALL is not only the capital of Orkney. It also brings together in its streets and buildings all the history and all the life of Orkney, past and present. In Norse times it was Orkney's only town and so it remained until the rise of Stromness in the seventeenth and eighteenth centuries; but Stromness never took away anything of Kirkwall's importance, though it temporarily surpassed the old town in population. Kirkwall remained the centre of power and influence in the islands, and its buildings show it. Kirkwall is representative in a unique way of its county.

Kirkwall has grown so much in recent years that it is hard for the visitor to discern the original layout of the town. For a concise account of this layout, which still exists, one may turn to Murdoch Mackenzie, writing in 1750: 'Kirkwall stands along an Arm of the Sea . . . and consists of one Street three Quarters of a Mile long, in which there are about 300 Families. All the Houses are built of Stone; some of them tolerably handsome both within and without, and, for the most Part, have a small Kitchen-garden behind. A Brook crosses the Street towards the north End, over which there is a Bridge of one Arch, with a parapet wall on either Side.' This single street is now the main thoroughfare of Kirkwall which runs from the harbour to St Magnus Cathedral; it is called Bridge Street, Albert Street and Broad Street in different parts of its length, and was and is the commercial heart of the town. Its alignment is roughly north-south.

There is a second section to the old town, that which belonged in times past to earl and bishop. This section, called the Laverock, consists of St Magnus itself and the Earl's and Bishop's Palaces, together with buildings nearby, which still have the air of a cathedral precinct. In front of the west doors of St Magnus is an open space called Kirk Green, once the town's market-place. Here

185

were held the three annual fairs which Kirkwall was entitled to hold under its royal charter of 1486. Lammas Fair was the most important. It continued into modern times but has now been replaced by the County Agricultural Show, held on the outskirts of the town on the second Saturday in August. A one-day event is better suited to the needs of family farmers than one which used to last a fortnight.

Between the two sections of the old town stood the great castle of Henry Lord Sinclair, the last vestiges of which were cleared away by town improvements in the mid-nineteenth century. The name Castle Street records the existence of the vanished stronghold; so does a plaque set high in the wall of a building at the corner of Castle and Broad Streets.

The Street continues its winding course beyond the cathedral as Victoria Street. Most of the houses are older than Queen Victoria's day, and it would appear that all the names for the main street are modern inventions.

The winding course of the Street follows the original shoreline of the Peerie (little) Sea, the 'Arm of the Sea' referred to by Mackenzie. Until relatively recent times Kirkwall had its harbour on this small inlet, not on the sea coast proper where the modern harbour stands. Houses were built gable-end to the Peerie Sea, and long narrow properties ran back from the Street to its shore. These properties, little wider than lanes, can be seen from some of the narrow passages that run from the main street towards the Peerie Sea. Below the cathedral especially, a distinct break of slope may be located; this was the original shoreline. Whether there were ever piers at the end of the properties, as at Stromness, is not clear. None appears on the earliest known picture of Kirkwall which dates from 1766.

The original town is now embedded in a matrix of newer buildings. No significant additions were made until the 1820s, when King Street was laid out roughly parallel with the main street on its inland or eastern side. At the same time the infilling of the Peerie Sea began, or at least gathered momentum, so that by mid-century the old Street was a considerable distance from its shore. Town improvements after 1850 included the making of Junction Road on this man-made land, parallel with the original

186

street. Later Great Western Road was added even further out, and it too is now some way inland.

In its natural state the Peerie Sea was almost shut off from the sea proper by a narrow peninsula of sand and shingle called an ayre. Ships entered through a channel at its western end, called an oyce. When a new road to Stromness was built in 1858, the ayre was used to carry it out from Kirkwall and the oyce was bridged. Henceforth the Peerie Sea was closed to navigation, and it became Kirkwall's dead sea, considered a legitimate receptacle for urban rubbish, until the improvements of 1973.

In the latter part of the nineteenth century there was much overcrowding of existing buildings and some small extension in area. In the old town, the 'Bridge of one Arch' over the Papdale Burn was removed, and the stream was piped. A plaque from the bridge was set high up in the wall of the town hall, built in 1874 opposite the cathedral. The point where the Papdale Burn once entered the Peerie Sea is now marked by Burnmouth Road. In this same period, prosperous Kirkwall merchants, ships' chandlers, grocers, tailors and professional men left the congested Street, and built fine stone houses for themselves on the south-eastern

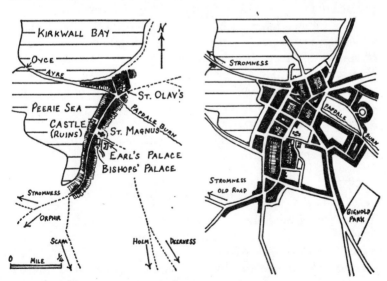

Growth of Kirkwall, from (*left*) the eighteenth century to (*right*) the twentieth. The second map shows the burgh about 1935

edge of the town up above the cathedral. Here also was built the episcopalian church of St Olav.

In the present century there was little building between the two wars, but in the 1950s and 1960s came something of an urban explosion. Both private and municipal housing spread out rapidly south and eastward and filled in the spaces between the roads to Scapa, Holm and Deerness. The population increased to over 4,000, then remained steady. More recent expansion has mainly been the result of rehousing. Simultaneously there was considerable commercial expansion on the made ground between the original single Street and the Peerie Sea. Here a new power station was built, using water from the Sea for cooling purposes. The original straggling shape of the old town was now hidden among all the new building, though it may be picked out clearly from the air.

Two injections of wartime building came to interrupt this development. Immediately below St Magnus Cathedral is a hangar-like structure which was built for the RNAS in World War I and later housed the first electricity power station. Larger and far more unsightly is the old Fleet Air Arm station at Hatston, just across the ayre to the west of the town. This consists of ranges of black wooden huts which are used for council housing, hangars which have been put to some limited industrial use, and an array of concrete runways and roads. The general effect is ugly and depressing. Wartime accommodation for women of the WRNS, which consisted of wooden huts, was at last removed from just behind the cathedral in 1969. The remaining wartime buildings impart a curious feeling to the visitor of returning to the immediate post-war period. It is to be hoped that soon they will all be cleared away.

ST MAGNUS CATHEDRAL

The place of supreme interest in Kirkwall is undoubtedly St Magnus Cathedral, and it forms a good starting point for a walk through the town. St Magnus has been much described, and a small booklet is available by Rev Harald Mooney (1963) which gives much interesting architectural, historical and ecclesiastical detail. The cathedral stands in a unique legal position for two reasons. First it belongs to the burgh, not to the Kirk of Scotland. This arises from the fact that it was built by Earl Rognvald on his own private land. It was therefore his own personal property, and that of all subsequent earls including King James III of Scotland, who made himself earl in person. He granted it to the burgesses of the Royal Burgh of Kirkwall by his charter of 1486, and in their hands it has remained ever since.

Equally strange is the fact that the Kirk of Scotland which holds services in St Magnus is not a cathedral body. It has none of the church dignitaries and ceremonial which one associates with cathedrals in England, for example. For the Kirk, St Magnus can be no more than a parish church.

A first view of St Magnus from outside is likely to produce several immediate impressions. On a sunny day particularly the colours of its stonework are very striking, Reds, browns and yellows dominate, with some pale grey and various intermediate shades. In places the colours have been used with deliberate effect, as in the west front facing Kirk Green, the arches of the western portico and a small thirteenth-century doorway in the south transept. Elsewhere different colours have been mixed with scant regard for the overall effect; there has in fact been much patching.

A second impression is indeed of considerable restoration. Though there were considerable repairs from early in the nineteenth century, the present excellent condition of the structure dates from a great restoration (1913–30) made under a bequest from G. H. M. Thoms, Sheriff of Caithness, Orkney and Shetland. Both exterior and interior were completely renovated. Some paintings of the work in progress are hung in the town hall. They are the work of Dr Stanley Cursiter, Queen's Limner in Scotland and catch the colours of the stone and the northern character of Orkney light in a remarkable manner.

St Magnus is also a small building, only 226ft long, but beautifully proportioned. Visitors should not expect a Durham, a York or a Lincoln; the scale here is quite different. However, once inside the impression of smallness is lost because of the perfect balance between length, width and height. After a short while one begins to think of it as a large and lofty building. Inside, the superb reddish colour of the stone dominates every other impression; for this reason, black and white photographs are completely unsatisfactory.

An examination of the nave, transepts, tower and choir shows the cathedral to have been long in building. Indeed, at least 350 years elapsed from its traditional date of foundation by Earl Rognvald, under the expert guidance of his father Kol, in the year 1137, to its completion. That part of the choir nearest to the transepts, the transepts themselves, and the eastern six bays of the nave were finished quite quickly, and a temporary west end built so that services could be held. Reconstruction of the transepts to their present form and extensions of the choir eastward and the nave westward were carried out in stages and were not completed until the early fifteenth century. The tower is a fourteenth-century feature, the spire twentieth. It replaced an unpleasing squat pyramid of seventeenth-century vintage.

When the partly finished cathedral was ready for use, the mortal remains of St Magnus were brought to it from Thorfinn's Christ Church in Birsay, until then Orkney's premier church. These relics seem to have vanished about the time of the Reformation. However, in the eighteenth century some bones were discovered in a rectangular pier on the north side of the choir, close to the original position of the high altar, and these were generally thought to be the lost relic. In 1919 a second set of bones and a skull were found in the pillar opposite. Anatomical study of the two sets suggests that the second are the remains of St Magnus. It seems almost certain that the bones first discovered were those of Earl Rognvald, the cathedral's founder.

In 1968, when Orkney commemorated the five hundredth anniversary of its union with Scotland, carved wooden figures of the three men responsible for the cathedral's foundation were placed behind the altar. These are Kol, who conceived the whole idea of the cathedral, Earl Rognvald his son who, with his father, put the idea into practice, and Bishop William 'the Old', close colleague of the two builders and the first Bishop of Orkney.

From the top of St Magnus tower there is an excellent panorama of Kirkwall, with views which, on a clear day, extend from the North Isles to Scapa Flow.

THE PALACES

Immediately to the south of the cathedral stand the palaces of bishop and earl. The Bishop's Palace is by far the older building, though much of what one sees today dates from Bishop Reid's reconstruction of 1541–58. He added the round Moosie Tower which faces the cathedral. Earl Patrick Stewart also made some alterations to the building, probably before 1600. This is not therefore the actual building in which King Hakon Hakonsson died in 1263 after his disastrous show of strength against the Scots, but it undoubtedly stands on the same site. Indeed, it is very probable that some stonework in the lower parts of this building belong to the earlier one.

The episcopacy was abolished in Scotland in 1689, so that this palace has long stood empty, serving as a convenient quarry for building stone.

Earl Patrick's palace is a very different, altogether more elegant building in the renaissance style. It was built in the darkest days of Stewart tyranny out of the exactions laid upon rich and poor alike and by forced labour 'without either meat, drink, or hire'. In a few short years between the completion of the palace about 1600 and the hanging of its founder, it must have been a centre for pomp and revelry the like of which Orkney had never imagined. 'Amid the blaze of festal light,' wrote Daniel Gorrie, 'with trenchers smoking on the board and great fires roaring up the chimneys of the hall, the gloom of an Orkney winter would sit lightly upon the spirit of the luxurious earl. "He had gude plenish-ing of beds and buirds", as we learn from the quaint testimony of Bishop Graham, and the whole appointments of the palace appear to have been on a scale of royal splendour . . . In the turreted chambers, now "tenantless save to the crannying wind", the ladies, who graced the court of the Orkney Earl, have haply sipped their cups of malvoisie, or listened to the soft minstrelsy of virginal and viol.' Earl Patrick never went out, even to church, without fifty musketeers and 'other gentlemen of convoy and guard'. At dinner, the various courses were heralded by trumpeters.

The palace forms three sides of a rectangle facing the Bishop's Palace. Apart from the road, the space between the two buildings is occupied by lawns and a grove of trees, the largest in Orkney, well sheltered from the wind by the surrounding buildings. Inside the palace, notable features include the great thickness of the walls and the many signs of defence, the great kitchen, which is some indication of the high living intended, and the first-floor banqueting hall with its fireplace and adjacent turreted chambers. Again in the words of Gorrie: 'In its combination of strength and elegance the residence of Earl Patrick Stewart was equally well adapted for war and wassail, for purposes of outrage and scenes of revel . . . it possessed from the first all the features of a robber's stronghold though adorned with the elegancies of a palace.'

KIRK GREEN, THE STREET AND THE HARBOUR

Opposite the west front of the cathedral stands Tankerness House, a fine sixteenth-century mansion which for more than 300 years was the town house of the Baikie family, merchant lairds whose country estate lay in the Tankerness district beyond where Grimsetter airport is now laid out. Over the doorway are the arms of Gilbert Fulzie and his wife Elizabeth Kinnaird. Fulzie was the last archdeacon of the cathedral before the reformation of 1560. The house stands on the site of two cathedral buildings, the archdeanery and sub-chantry, and may possibly incorporate parts of them.

For many years Tankerness House stood empty and decrepit while the burgh council debated what to do with it. Demolition was actually proposed, and it is very much to the credit of the council that this disaster was prevented and the house beautifully restored, ready for the quincentennial celebrations of 1968. It is now a museum where there are already many interesting exhibits and plenty of room for the archaeological treasures which in past years have been taken out of Orkney. If these can be prised out of museums in Edinburgh and elsewhere, Tankerness House will be a very notable museum indeed and a great attraction for visitors. Behind the house is a very fine garden sheltered by a high wall, a veritable oasis of greenery and colour in summer.

Several other buildings of merit stand in this area. Between Tankerness House and the Moosie Tower is a range of houses of sixteenth-century origins which were restored in 1968–9 after a long period of neglect. Somewhere hereabouts Bishop Reid 'taught school' in what was to become Kirkwall Grammar School. The presence of this school was formerly noted in the street-name School Wynd, now renamed Tankerness Lane, which runs past Tankerness House towards the Peerie Sea.

The town hall stands on the site of the cathedral provost's house. It is an entertaining building in the Scots baronial variant of the Victorian style, with impractical turrets. Nearby a house still survives built gable-end to the street, and at least one other merchant laird's house may be identified.

This was the earl's and bishop's town. Between it and the Kirkwall of humbler folk stood the great castle, now hardly a memory. The approximate alignment of its walls on the south side is given by Castle Street. Some of Earl George's cannon balls were found during the clearing away of the ruins last century. Parts of the castle foundations may still be seen in cellars of buildings on the site.

The ancient division between an upper and lower town is still symbolised each Christmas and New Year's day by the strenuous ritual of the Ba' Game. This is mass football played between the men of the harbour and Street end of town and those of the Laverock and Victoria Street end, the Uppies and Doonies or Up-the-Gates and Down-the-Gates. Nowadays four games are played, by boys in the morning and men in the afternoon. The Mens' Ba' is likely to involve up to 150 men in four hours of furious play, the object being to force the ba' (ball) either into the harbour or up the street to a goal at the Old Castle.

The Ba' Game probably has its origins in mass games played in Norse times; such a game is described in the Saga of Gisli the Outlaw. Few visitors ever see it, and those who do are usually astonished by the proceedings. An American newspaper man who watched the 1969 New Year's Ba' described it in his paper under the headline: 'Orkney holds savage New Year rite. Mass mayhem called Ba' rages four hours in street.' His account summarises the character of the game very well:

> 'Once thrown the ba' seemed to disappear into the swirling, pushing, steaming, kicking, groaning mass of humanity and was seldom seen again unless one of the players, assisted by super-

M

193

natural beings, extricated himself . . . sympathisers, relatives and onlookers stood by ready to comfort the wounded with a dram of the local brew strong enough for both external and internal use.'

Beyond Castle Street corner one enters 'the Street' with its solitary 'Big Tree', survivor of three; it is said that the railings were put round it to dissuade Mr Gladstone from chopping it down; he had the reputation of being a keen tree-feller. Apart from the new shop fronts, people's dress and the motor cars, the street looks much as it did a century ago, and parts of Daniel Gorrie's description of 1868 read in a surprisingly up-to-date way.

'The greater portion of the mile-long street is so exceedingly narrow that there is only space for a strip of causeway between the pavement on either side. This curious style of street-building might suit the time when pack-ponies carried their burdens like camels . . . but the narrow defiles between rows of houses, where "two wheel-barrows tremble when they meet", are ill-suited . . . to increasing traffic. It takes skilful steering on the part of drivers to avoid collisions, and a runaway cart spreads consternation like a war-chariot . . . there is also an odd intermingling of elegant new banks and time-worn edifices . . . some of the large and commodious buildings huddled together and hidden from view in back courts were, in former times, the abodes of leading families in the islands, who spent the winter months amid the gaieties of the Orcadian capital.'

The Street is one of the finest pedestrian precincts in Britain, where cars are an intolerable intrusion. It has not yet been spoiled by unsuitable or tasteless building, though there have been some unfortunate shop front developments in recent years. At all costs the unity of this fine street must be conserved—which does not mean that no changes can be made—and it urgently needs to be made traffic-free, especially in the holiday season.

For a town with a population of less than 5,000 the array of shops along the Street is striking. There are many old-established family businesses, and the chain-store revolution has hardly begun. Woolworths and Boots have arrived but not Marks and Spencer; many Kirkwall people think this last would meet a real need in the town. There are relatively few signs that Kirkwall is a seaport, many that it is the centre of a farming community. Even the

Customs House also accommodates the North of Scotland College of Agriculture.

Towards the north end of the Street, a sharp bend indicates the position of the old bridge over the Papdale Burn and a little visual detective work will reveal where the stream course once ran. The name Papdale given to the valley which runs inland at this point indicates the presence of Celtic 'fathers' in pre-Norse times. Presumably it was their church which caused the Norsemen to call this place Kirkjuvagr (church bay). Following the custom of the times, the Norsemen when they also became Christian probably built their church on the Celtic site. This Norse church was dedicated to St Olav; it was thoroughly reconstructed in the sixteenth century by Bishop Reid.

Some vestiges of St Olav's church may be found by turning up a narrow passage called St Olav's Wynd on the east side of Bridge Street. The passage now lacks any visible proof of identity, but may be located by the savings bank on its corner. Here may be found a sixteenth-century stone archway set in a quite modern wall. This marks the approximate position of the old church, parts of which are thought to be incorporated in a house north of the wynd.

Bridge Street leads out past the Kirkwall Hotel to the harbour. Most of the piers date from 1859–65, with later additions. A considerable variety of shipping may be seen. The North of Scotland ships from Aberdeen and Leith call regularly at one side of the main pier on their way to and from Lerwick, while *Orcadia* and *Islander* serving the North Isles use its opposite side, an arrangement which facilitates transhipment. The whole economy of Orkney, and most of its problems, may be observed at first hand on this pier. Droves of beef cattle and flocks of sheep may be seen, either coming in from the North Isles or awaiting shipment south along with the variety of import cargoes and of cargoes bound for the islands. A feature of the latter is fertiliser in bags and petrol in drums; there are no bulk handling facilities in the smaller islands. A floating bank may be seen, usually in the evening. It belongs to the National Commercial Bank of Scotland and takes banking services to communities too small to support a regular branch.

West from Bridge Street, there is a large stone building facing the harbour with steps up from the road. This was once the granary where the earldom skats were collected for export and is called the girnel. It dates from the seventeenth century. A kiln once stood at the west end of the building to dry grain before shipment; the corner into Junction Road is still marked Kiln Corner on the Ordnance map, though the name is no longer in common use. A small pier opposite the girnel is called the Corn Slip. Further west, buildings run out along the ayre towards Ayre Mill, built 1865 and now the Kirkwall egg-packing station.

Old houses on Shore Street, Kirkwall, demolished to make way for oil tanks

East from Bridge Street, some very old properties, gable-end to the harbour, have been cleared away and replaced by an oil-tank depot. It is generally thought that this area between the shore, Bridge Street and the Papdale Burn is the oldest part of Kirkwall. Further east, Shore Street becomes Cromwell Road and runs out to the site of Cromwell's fort at Weyland Park, where there is now the coastguard station and the territorial army camp.

STROMNESS

The monopoly of Kirkwall over all commerce and all crafts, guaranteed by the regulations governing Royal Burghs, was broken during the eighteenth century by the upstart town of Stromness. The legal contest between the ancient Burgh striving to maintain its privileges and the new and growing trading community in Stromness, whose members found themselves hamstrung by obsolete regulations and well able to manage their own affairs, became a classic test case, and its resolution in 1758 in favour of Stromness began a new era of town development throughout Scotland.

Today, Stromness looks like an ancient town and is certainly more picturesque than Kirkwall; it is in fact one of the most visually attractive towns in Britain. The initial impression of great antiquity is misleading, however. A walk along the mile-long main street reveals few buildings older than the eighteenth century; one near the pierhead has the date 1716 carved above its door, and appears to be one of the oldest. Significantly the parish church dates only from 1717, though most of what one sees today, leaving aside the reconstructions of 1967–8 into a youth centre, dates only from 1814. Further examination of the street, and such narrow passages leading from it as the Khyber Pass, reveals that a very high proportion of the buildings date from the period of the Napoleonic wars. There is a limited Victorian and Edwardian development near the pier, and a small number of newer houses outside the limits of the old town. The story of Stromness is clearly written in its buildings.

Until early in the seventeenth century Stromness was merely the name of a parish. The town on the inlet of Hamnavoe did not then exist, although that excellent natural harbour had been much used since Norse times and probably earlier. In contrast to Kirkwall's location, Hamnavoe faced the South Isles, which were either barren and poor like Hoy, or late to develop because of persistent raids from across the Pentland Firth. Once established Kirkwall attracted what little commerce there was.

By the year 1603 French and Spanish merchant vessels were using Hamnavoe for shelter. Soon after this, some younger sons of local landowners built houses near the shore, hoping to profit from visiting ships. However, by 1670 only thirteen houses seem to have been built. In the century following there is much indirect evidence that Stromness was growing and becoming prosperous, for a large number of Stromness men are recorded as buying estates in Orkney in the style of Kirkwall's merchant lairds. Then came the celebrated test case against the monopoly of Kirkwall, beginning in 1743.

A first chink in the impregnable armour of the Royal Burghs

had already been made, when in 1690 it was agreed that merchants might trade outside the limits of the burghs in return for payment. This insistence on payment on the part of the burghs was perfectly reasonable from their point of view. They had contracted with the king to pay one-sixth of the total land tax of Scotland each year, and in order to raise this sum they had to keep a firm hand on their means of payment, namely trade.

The union between Scotland and England in 1707 created an anomalous situation for the burghs, in that on the one hand all citizens of the United Kingdom were guaranteed the legal right to trade where they wished, and on the other, the monopoly of royal burghs was reaffirmed. Clearly there was now room for manœuvre, or so the citizens of Stromness thought.

In 1717 Kirkwall obtained the right to tax all traders throughout Orkney and Shetland; its request to do so was stimulated mainly by the rise of trade at Stromness. In 1719 Stromness, under the leadership of one 'Hary Graham, one of their [Kirkwall's] burgesses in Stromness or Kairston', agreed to take responsibility for a fixed proportion of Kirkwall's annual tax, this single payment to replace taxes levied directly by Kirkwall on individual Stromness merchants. This compromise lasted until 1743, when Stromness refused to pay its share on the grounds that the sum demanded was excessive. A ruinous legal battle ensued which lasted for fifteen years. Eventually Stromness had the satisfaction of having its claim for exemption upheld by the ultimate authority of the House of Lords, but the victory was dearly bought. Alexander Graham, son of the 'Hary' Graham who had negotiated the first compromise arrangement with Kirkwall, and who had led and partly paid for the fight on behalf of the Stromness merchants, was forced into bankruptcy and seems to have died in poverty. The monopoly of royal burghs had been successfully challenged; the cost of challenging them had also been demonstrated, and the lead given by Stromness was not followed for some time. Alexander Graham's house still stands in Stromness at 8 Graham Place.

Stromness continued to develop as a principal way-station on sea routes which led around the north of Scotland. An important trade developed between the ports of Northern Ireland, the Clyde and Mersey on the one hand, and north European ports on the other. In one direction went British coal and salt, in the other such items as timber, tar products and iron ore. This northern route was favoured because of its relative freedom from pirates who infested the English Channel in Jacobite times, and later because of its distance from French bases. The so-called northabout route was physically very hazardous. Seas were liable to be very stormy indeed, except in midsummer. Coasts were totally without lights, save for the occasional flickering beacon of a wreckers' party, and there were no charts. Ships from the south kept to the west of St Kilda, called at Stromness for water and stores, then beat around the north of Shetland to minimise the chances of running ashore at night. As it was, many were lost by storm and grounding, and for this reason small vessels only were used, their loss being less ruinous to their promoters.

It was out of these navigational hazards that Murdoch Mackenzie's celebrated charts of Orkney emerged in 1750. A set of these may be seen in Kirkwall Public Library. They give an excellent picture of the Orcadian landscape, besides navigational information, and are well worth detailed scrutiny. Many of the hilltop cairns of piled stones were put up as markers for Mackenzie's triangulation. Mackenzie produced his charts ten years after the first survey of the north-west Scottish coasts and islands by Rev Alexander Bryce. Out of the navigational perils of the northabout route also sprang the Lighthouse Board on Northern Shores, established in 1786. One of the first four beacons set up by this body before 1790 was on North Ronaldsay. This low-lying island at the northern extremity of Orkney was almost impossible to see at night or in poor weather, and had wrecked many ships. In 1794 a light was placed on the Pentland Skerries, graveyard of vessels trying to navigate the Pentland Firth at night, and in 1801 on Start Point in Sanday, where eleven wrecks occurred between 1796 and 1798.

Stromness shared the North American rice trade with Kirkwall for a short time. Nineteen American vessels called at the port in the three years 1757–60 and paid duty of £14,000. At the pierhead in modern Stromness stands a large stone-built warehouse said to date from this period. The lucrative rice traffic was lost by Stromness when Kirkwall managed to persuade the Americans that its location was the more convenient. But Kirkwall's victory was short-lived, because at the conclusion of the Seven Years War in 1763, when the Channel became safe again, the traffic abandoned Orkney altogether and went to Cowes in the Isle of Wight.

THE HUDSON'S BAY COMPANY

A plaque beside Login's Well near the southern end of the main street in Stromness records that vessels of the Hudson's Bay Company obtained water here from 1670 until 1891. In fact the first certain record of a company ship calling at Stromness dates from 1702 but it appears likely that the practice of doing so was already well established. Stromness was a convenient base for the company's ships bound for northern Canada, because of its excellent harbour, good water and victuals and its northerly position. It may be worth noting that no base comparable with Stromness existed in Shetland until the growth of Lerwick in the twentieth century.

Each year, Hudson's Bay vessels came to Stromness in early June and remained about two weeks preparing for the trans-Atlantic voyage. In the mid-eighteenth century it was customary for three vessels of 150–400 tons to make this voyage each year, returning to Stromness in November. Cargoes taken to the Bay included such products of European civilisation as guns, powder, shot, clothing and axes, which were traded for furs, especially beaver.

The company favoured Orcadians for service in northern Canada, because they were prepared to work longer for less pay than southern recruits and were noted for their good behaviour and sobriety. Between sixty and a hundred men were employed at any one time, usually on five-year contracts. Most came from the Stromness district and at one stage nearly three-quarters of the company's men in Canada were Orcadians. Most men went as labourers, possibly as craftsmen, but a few achieved posts of considerable responsibility in the company's service; during the whole period of recruitment no fewer than ten Orcadians became governors or chief factors and another eighteen district masters or chief traders. About 1750 the company's agent in the town was paying out up to £3,000 in wages annually. No wonder the farms were neglected.

Under the terms of its royal charter, granted in 1670, the Hudson's Bay Company was required to explore and prospect its vast territory in northern Canada. One of its most distinguished explorers was Dr John Rae, of Hall of Clestran in Orphir, who made five epic journeys into the Arctic between 1846 and 1854 and added 1,135 miles of new coastline to the charts. It was Rae who established the fate of Sir John Franklin's last expedition in search of the northwest passage; Franklin had watered his ships *Erebus* and *Terror* from Login's Well in 1845 on his way north. John Rae lies buried in the churchyard of St Magnus Cathedral; inside, near the east end, he is commemorated by a striking monument.

The Company used Stromness regularly until 1891 and continued to order stores there until 1914. By the mid-nineteenth century the number of men taken on had dropped to 35–40. After the merging of Hudson's Bay with the Canadian North West Company a policy of employing Canadians was favoured, and opportunities for Orkneymen to find relatively lucrative work in the Canadian north gradually declined. However, advertisements still appear from time to time in *The Orcadian* newspaper for young Orcadians to go to Canada in the Hudson's Bay service.

THE DAVIS STRAIT WHALERS

About 1760 Stromness began to supply stores and men to whaling vessels bound for Davis Straits and other rich whaling grounds around the North Atlantic margins. Whalers left Stromness in March to hunt whales near the edges of the melting ice. At this time whales were very numerous in Greenland waters and were hunted mercilessly, large and small, male and female being indiscriminately slaughtered. By the 1830s the numbers of whales had been much reduced, and whalers stayed later and later into the autumn, risking destruction by ice in order to make up their profits.

Writing in 1841, Rev Peter Learmonth, Minister of Stromness, recorded that 'For a long period, a number of whalers have called here to obtain their full complement of men for the whale-fishing at Davis' Straits; but lately, the number has considerably decreased. There have been engaged, for the last seven years, on an average, 292 men annually. The number at one time was much greater'. Whaling lingered on as a relatively minor occupation for Stromness men until 1914.

The demands of the Hudson's Bay Company and of the whalers upon the men of Stromness were augmented from time to time by those of the naval press-gang. In consequence there was a persistent imbalance between the numbers of men and women in the town; in the mid-eighteenth century the proportions were 12 men to 21 women.

THE NAPOLEONIC WARS AND AFTER

For Stromness the years 1795–1821 were golden years, when the northabout route was busier than ever before and Hamnavoe was full of ships. The town's population grew rapidly to reach a peak of 2,236 in the census year of 1821, the only occasion on which it exceeded Kirkwall (2,212). There was much overcrowding, for building failed to keep pace with increasing population. Stromness was made an independent Burgh of Barony in 1817, with its own magistrates and council; one of the first things this body did was to enrol a police force to control the riotous seafarers who terrorised the townspeople while bringing great profit to innkeepers. Soldiers were quartered in the large, long building which stands near the south end of the street; to fill the idle time they were employed building walls on Brinkies Brae.

After the war, Stromness suffered a gradual decline, which has continued to the present time. The northabout route became much less busy when the English Channel was re-opened to peaceful shipping. Of the war years Rev Peter Learmonth wrote :

'The shipping belonging to Stromness has of late years greatly increased, and is at present in a very prosperous condition. The kind of vessel which is preferred is the schooner, which is found best suited for the trade in which it is employed. The owners seldom or never insure their vessels, and many of them have succeeded well. The number of vessels belonging to the town is 23; 2 of them brigs, 18 schooners; 3 sloops. Their tonnage amounts 2,132 tons.'

Stromness retained its importance as a port as long as sailing vessels needed shelter while waiting for favourable winds; and it is worth emphasising that the transition from sail to steam was a very gradual one. Steamers when they came favoured Kirkwall rather than Stromness because of the better harbour facilities provided there after reconstructions, beginning in 1865.

MODERN STROMNESS

Stromness derived some temporary benefit from the upsurge of herring fisheries in the northern isles late in the nineteenth century, and curing yards were built at Ness, south of the town, as at other places in Orkney. The 1901 census figure was inflated to 2,450 by the presence of the herring fleet in harbour on census night; the resident population of the town was only about 1,650. Unfortunately the herring industry was extremely uncertain. In some years it was almost wildly profitable, in others ruinous, and perhaps the most permanent benefit accruing from it was the improvement in navigational aids which the increased shipping encouraged. Near Stromness, the lights on Graemsay (1851) and at Ness Point (1895) date from this period. Besides the erratic herring, some cod and lobster were landed at Stromness. Lobster landings are recorded as early as 1815.

By 1914 Stromness had been reduced to a chance haven for passing vessels and a quite minor fishing port. Its commercial traffic had almost ceased. From these setbacks the town has never recovered. Its population now seems to have stabilised at about 1,700 but its age structure is disturbing; in 1961, 17·8 per cent of the people of Stromness were aged 65 and over, compared with 14·5 per cent in the whole of Orkney and 13·7 per cent in Kirkwall. The town has yet to find a new role for itself within the life and economy of Orkney.

Before leaving this account of the changing fortunes of Stromness, a word needs to be said about the town's unique layout. From the first, it was the aim of every member of the trading community to have a waterfront to his property. In consequence, long and narrow properties, called quoys, were laid out extending back from the shore. The first house on each quoy usually stood gable-end to the water, and most soon had a private pier. As trade and with it population grew, further building took place on the quoys, still as near the water as possible. An access passage was left between the first and second houses, and when in course of time it became necessary to make a street parallel with the shore, these access passages were joined up to produce the narrow and irregular main street one sees today. Originally it was even narrower in places, but some demolition was done early this century to open the street to motor traffic. In the golden years of the Napoleonic wars more building took place on the quoys, extending up the lower slopes of Brinkies Brae, and between the new extensions access lanes were run, such as the Khyber Pass. The seemingly chaotic layout of the town is misleading. In terms of the purposes for which the town was built and the conditions, especially the transport conditions, of the times, the layout is perfectly rational. It does create a modern traffic problem; the overall effect is uniquely attractive.

M OST visitors to Orkney have a limited time at their disposal, and this chapter is designed to help them use it to the best advantage. The visits described follow the order of earlier chapters, and in cases where items of interest from more than one chapter occur in one locality they are mentioned together.

The map (page 12) provides a guide to the location of the places mentioned, but a larger scale map is a desirable accompaniment to the exploration of the landscapes and monuments of Orkney. The Ordnance Survey seventh series one-inch sheet no 6, Orkney Islands (Kirkwall) covers the islands from Eday in the north to northeastern Hoy; sheet no 5 covers all the northern islands and no 7 runs from the latitude of northern Hoy to south of Thurso in Caithness. The relevant quarter-inch geological sheet is no 3, the one-inch sheets nos 117 and 118 (South Isles), 119 and 120 (Mainland and Stronsay), and 121 and 122 (North Isles).

THE NEOLITHIC: A VILLAGE AND BURIAL CAIRNS

Skara Brae

The site stands near the southern corner of the Bay of Skaill in Sandwick. It is in the care of the Ministry of Public Buildings and Works and there is a resident custodian. A description by Professor Gordon Childe is on sale at the site.

Like Pompeii, the village we now call Skara Brae was engulfed by a natural calamity, in this case burial by windblown sand. The event seems to have been very sudden though burial was not at first complete; the excavations revealed huts and passages blocked with sand, and in one passage a scattering of beads showed where a woman had broken her necklace squeezing through a narrow doorway in her flight. The huts contained a rich collection of relics and there was no sign of subsequent pillaging. The refugees appear to have returned and camped in the half-buried site; the remains of their fires and the bones of the deer they cooked were found at three levels above that of the buried hut floors. Gradually however they abandoned the village completely, since all remains die away at higher levels. Centuries later, the Norsemen seem never to have known there was a village buried beneath the sandhills they named Skara or Skerroo Brae.

Photographs of the site seldom give much idea of its setting. Skaill Bay is a broad sweep of sand backed by dunes, which bar the outlet of a shallow valley and hold back a small loch. Higher ground rises at each end of the bay. The corner near Skara Brae is somewhat sheltered by a low headland, in the lee of which fishing boats usually lie at anchor even in wild weather.

The site consists of the unroofed remains of ten huts in a remarkably good state of preservation. These are roughly rectangular in plan, with low covered passages running between them giving access to each through low door-spaces. The whole is constructed with great skill in thin slabs of unmortared flagstone. Inside the huts are the remains of primitive stone furniture— remarkably modern in appearance—resembling cupboards and sideboards, together with stone bed-frames, small tanks (thought to have been used to keep shellfish fresh) and central hearths.

When excavated the whole site was found to have been cocooned in a mass of its own rubbish, including food remains. From these deposits it has been deduced that the inhabitants had many cattle and sheep; that they found difficulty in wintering their cattle and therefore slaughtered many calves each year, probably in autumn; that they had horses and were hunters of red deer and wild boar; and that they collected vast quantities of shellfish but probably did no other fishing. Their clothes and the roofs of their houses were probably made from skins; they had bone and stone tools for piercing skins but none for making textiles. There is absolutely no sign of any kind of trade or exchange with other communities, and no metal objects were found. This seems to have been a self-sufficient group, and it probably enjoyed quite a high standard of living for the time, at least during the summer. Possibly it was a kinship group since House 1, closest to the shore, is larger than the others and seems to have been the head-house of the community. It is interesting to note also that the bed to the right of the door in each hut is larger than that to the left, and presumably belonged to the man. This arrangement is almost identical to that which existed in Hebridean black houses until the present century and would seem to denote a patriarchal organisation of society.

Many interesting problems await solution at Skara Brae. First there is the dating problem. It has proved impossible to say exactly when the site was first occupied, because the successive groups of occupants seem to have used the stone from earlier buildings to make their own. Thus, materials from long-vanished huts are probably to be seen now in the newest. Doubts also linger about the true age of what is exposed to view. Certainly the community's culture was neolithic, but does the village as it appears today really date from 2000 BC? It seems not impossible that neolithic groups survived for a very long time in the northern isles after more recent cultures had been established in Britain. The remains are still very remarkable.

Second, was Skara Brae built on the shore? On grounds of common sense it seems unlikely that a people whose chief interests lay in flocks and herds and who did not fish would choose a windy coastal site in preference to a more sheltered inland location. We know the sea has encroached here in modern times because the site was only exposed to view in 1850 by a great storm, and since then the waves have advanced right up to the ruins and would by now have destroyed them but for a Ministry sea-wall. Moreover, we have a measure of the speed of encroachment. Skaill Mill close to Skara Brae was built in 1700 about 50 yards from the shore; the waves are now undermining it.

An examination of local geological conditions may help to suggest a reasonable hypothesis. A zone of structural weakness associated with faults runs inland from Skaill Bay in a south-easterly direction and the very existence of the bay results from marine erosion working landwards along this zone. The modern outline of the bay represents the position now reached by the encroaching sea, an encroachment that has probably continued since the sea reached its present level after the Boreal period. If the rate of encroachment indicated by the Skaill Mill site has in fact been maintained since 2000 BC the site of Skara Brae must have originally been at least 800 yards from the shore, in the shelter of a wide belt of dunes.

Maeshowe and Onston Cairns

Maeshowe has been described as the most magnificent chambered tomb in western Europe. It stands on gently sloping ground near Tormiston farm 3 miles from Finstown on the main road to Stromness. From outside it appears as a large grassy mound 115ft in diameter and 24ft high standing near the centre of a circular ditch and bank. It has been calculated that this ditch yielded enough earth to raise the mound and this seems more probable than the notion, which is sometimes put forward, that the turf cover of the cairn is the result of natural soil formation.

The site was skilfully chosen by an architect with a good eye for country. The howe can be seen from a surprisingly large part of the west Mainland plain, and this seems to be so obviously intended that one may suppose that here lay the 'metropolitan area' of neolithic Orkney, dotted with settlements and grazed by flocks and herds, and with occasional patches of cultivation. The immediate setting of the howe is also remarkable. An area of tumbled glacial mounds or drumlins extends into the central plain from the Binscarth valley above Finstown. Maeshowe stands where these fade away, a kind of man-made advance-guard for an army of natural hillocks. It looks as though one such hillock was levelled and used as a foundation for the howe.

Maeshowe is in the care of the Ministry of Public Buildings and Works. The custodian lives at Tormiston, and there is a printed guide on sale at the site. Entrance to the heart of the mound is through a passage 36ft long and 4ft 6in high. Inside, there is a spacious chamber 15ft square, beautifully built in drystone and corbelled in overlapping courses to about 12ft. Above this, a modern domed roof has been built and concealed lights installed. The original roof was removed during the 1861 excavation. A notable feature of the structure is the use of true megaliths, giant slabs of flagstone placed vertically to support the roof and laid horizontally to form the entrance passage. The alignment of the entrance and central chamber is roughly north-east to south-west. There seems to have been no ritual requirement about the direction in which such tombs should be built; but perhaps by chance, the entrance passages of Maeshowe and Onston lie along almost the same compass point.

To left and right and also opposite the entrance, burial cells open off the central chamber. All were empty when the tomb was excavated a century ago, and the reason for this is to be seen on the walls. Some time in the twelfth century, vikings broke into the howe and robbed it of a great treasure, or so they tell us in the runic inscriptions which they cut on the walls. Howe-breaking seems to have been a favoured pastime of men of spirit in that wild and superstitious period.

The inscriptions were made by several groups at different times probably between 1150 and 1153, and together form the finest collection of runes gathered in any one place. For some years following the initial excavation of Maeshowe in 1861, it was believed that the tomb itself was Norse, and only gradually was it realised that the runes had been inscribed in a building that was already ancient. The viking age may seem very distant in history to us, yet when the runes were cut, Maeshowe was already three-quarters its present age.

The letters are deep and clear-cut. One section records that the axe used belonged to one Gauk Trandillson from the southland. This individual is known with fair certainty to have lived about 150 years earlier in the south of Iceland, and his axe must therefore have been a treasured possession of one of the vikings, perhaps an heirloom. A set of runes tells of the visit of 'Jerusalemfarers' or Crusaders to the Holy Land, who are known to have set out from Orkney in 1151. Another set dated from 1153 says that Earl Harald and his men were snowbound in the howe and that two members lost their wits, which was 'a great hindrance to their journey'. In addition to the runes, the viking howebreakers carved a small 'dragon' or 'lion' on one of the great stone uprights. This figure has been related by Professor Shetelig to carvings in Urnes church in Norway dating from the early twelfth century.

Maeshowe is still an awesome place and an air of mystery lingers about it. Clearly it must have been built for some great line of rulers who were probably both the religious and secular leaders of their people. Perhaps they were the ruling caste of a

N

group, missionaries as well as conquerors, to whom the people of Skara Brae and similar villages were tributary. Beyond these surmises we know very little.

Onston cairn is much smaller. It stands two-and-a-half miles from Maeshowe on a little peninsula jutting into the Loch of Stenness. When excavated in 1884 by R. S. Clouston it yielded the largest collection of neolithic pottery ever found in Scotland. From the remains of twenty-two earthenware vessels, six were reconstructed sufficiently to reveal the salient features of what has since become known as Onston Ware. They may be seen in the National Museum of Antiquities in Edinburgh.

Onston is an example of the 'stalled' type of cairn, which reaches its finest development in Rousay; but it also has affinities with the 'chambered' type, most perfectly represented by Maeshowe. Possibly Onston is transitional between the two styles, though this has not been conclusively demonstrated. Entrance is by a 14ft passage from the north-east. The main chamber, aligned at right-angles to the entrance, is 21ft long and relatively narrow, in the style of stalled cairns. Four vertical slabs of flagstone stand out from the walls to form eight burial recesses, which may once

Interior of Onston cairn

have had upper storeys. One has a threshold slab, worn as though trodden by many feet. Clearly it cannot have been worn thus in its present position; possibly it came from the house of the important personage who was buried here. Opposite the entrance there is a small cell, rather like the side-chambers in Maeshowe. As in Maeshowe there are Norse runes cut in the stone.

Rousay Island

Stalled cairns reach their most perfect development in Rousay, an island which may be reached by motor boat from Tingwall pier in Rendall or from Evie pier. The Orkney Tourist Organisation supplies information about entry to the cairns, which are kept locked.

On Rousay, the largest of all stalled cairns is Midhowe, a mile beyond Westness house in the almost deserted Westside district. Westness is a fine house of the mid-eighteenth century, set in a small wood. It stands higher up the hillside than, and some distance south of, the site of the home of the Norse chief Sigurd of Westness mentioned in the saga, of which nothing remains on the surface. Midhowe cairn, once a great grassy mound, was opened in the years 1932–3 by Mr Walter Grant, then proprietor of Trumland, under the expert guidance of Dr Callender of the Edinburgh Museum of Antiquities and Mr Hewat Craw.

Midhowe is enormous. It consists of a drystone structure 35yd long and 14yd wide. The outer wall is double, 18ft thick, and decorated in herring-bone fashion. This gives rise to the question of whether the tomb was originally exposed to view, the turf covering being merely the product of nearly forty centuries of natural colonisation by plants, with consequent soil formation. This same question is also suggested by decoration in the walling of some other cairns, for example that on Wideford Hill near Kirkwall. However, it is also suggested that such tombs derive from a Mediterranean tradition of burial below ground, which would suggest that the earth cover was probably added as soon as the tomb had been built, symbolising true underground burial.

Entrance was by a passage from the south-east, now roofless. The central chamber is no less than 76ft long, and being only 7ft wide has the appearance of a corridor rather than a true

211

chamber. Eleven pairs of large flat flagstones placed vertically divide this corridor into twenty-four burial compartments—twelve on each side. The excavation revealed 25 burials, comprising 17 adults, 6 adolescents and 2 children. There were also the remains of several oxen and sheep, pigs and red deer, various birds and many limpet shells. Some fragments of pottery were of the Onston type. Otherwise, there were almost no artifacts.

So important is Midhowe in the development of prehistoric archaeology that an enormous hangar-like structure has been built over it by the Ministry of Public Buildings and Works to protect it from the weather. There is lighting from roof windows, and overhead gangways give access to all parts of the excavation. Unfortunately, in sunny weather the roof windows produce a strong greenhouse effect, so that the interior is almost unbearably hot and stuffy, and the excavation itself may be suffering damage from the heat, through drying-out of the stonework. It is difficult, however, to imagine how else this remarkable monument could be kept open for public inspection. Finally, a tip for photographers: almost the only way to photograph the central chamber without including a great amount of Ministry girder-work is to lie prone on the cross gangway at its western end.

Those who enjoy a little gentle hill walking in association with the study of prehistoric monuments should strike uphill from Midhowe to the summit of Mansemass Hill, and follow its relatively level crest-line to Ward Hill above Westness. On a clear day, the views are magnificent. Eynhallow, the holy isle of medieval Orkney, deserted now, lies midway across the sea channel between Rousay and the green shores of Evie. The ruins of its small medieval church can just be discerned. The fine northern cliffs of Mainland jut out strongly into the Atlantic and are almost always fringed by the breakers. Away beyond Mainland, the hills and sheer cliffs of Hoy are visible.

Looking south and east, the low brown cone of Gairsay, also deserted, stands sentinel at the entrance to Wide Firth leading up to Kirkwall, the buildings of which are clearly visible. Beyond are the low levels of east Mainland, continued northwards by the equally low outlines of Shapinsay and Stronsay.

Looking inland over Rousay itself, one appreciates the highly strategic location of Westness immediately below a gap in the central Rousay uplands through which one may take a short cut to the north coast. The view in this direction takes in the rarely seen Muckle and Peerie (large and small) Waters, and extends across the still-populous valley of Sourin to the isle of Egilsay, dominated by the tall round tower of its church. At this distance the tower looks rather like one of the old stone-built chimneys which dot the hills in the former lead-mining districts of northern England. Westray blocks the northern horizon and looks larger and closer than one expects; its western cliffs are spectacular. Eday is dark and forbidding, presenting its unpopulated moorland side. Sanday is so low-lying as to be hardly visible, but in sunlight there are bright yellow glimmers from its extensive dunes.

From Ward Hill, the walk may be continued roughly in a direct line to Yarso cairn. This stands on one of the striking natural hillside terraces into which the southern face of Rousay has been ice-hewn and weathered. Such terraces are characteristic of the sides of low hills cut from the Rousay Flags, and seem to be the result of strongly differentiated hard and relatively soft layers being worked upon by moving ice, probably late in the Ice Age.

Yarso is a small stalled cairn. When excavated, it yielded the mortal remains of no fewer than twenty-one persons. The skulls were of neolithic long-headed folk, and yet pottery fragments suggested at least some connection with later bronze age times. The remains of thirty-six red deer were also unearthed in the tomb.

Following the natural hillside terraces towards Trumland pier, landing-place for the boat from Tingwall, one passes Blackhammer cairn, another fine example of the stalled type. This stands immediately above the road. Finally, on this remarkable walk, one may see the notable two-storeyed tomb of Taiverso Tuick standing on a low ridge-end and commanding a mignificent view across Wyre and Gairsay towards Kirkwall.

Taiverso Tuick may be regarded as the most remarkable neolithic tomb in Orkney after Maeshowe. It was accidentally discovered in 1898 when the then proprietor and builder of Trumland House, General Burroughs, caused a lookout seat to be erected at this point. Part of the upper chamber was then disturbed, but fortunately no further damage was done. Excavation was carried out by the Ministry of Public Buildings and Works in 1937, and the remarkable character of the tomb was then brought to light.

In its complete state, Taiverso Tuick contained two burial chambers, one above the other but without any connection. The lower chamber and its access passage were subterranean. The passage was 19ft long, the chamber 12ft long by 5ft wide. Vertical stone slabs divide it into four compartments, one at each end and two opposite the entrance, leaving a kind of antechamber at the end of the entrance passage. Little remains of the upper chamber, which was larger than the lower. It is noteworthy that, whereas the lower chamber is entered from the south-east, access to the upper was from the north-west. Both chambers were enclosed within a single circular wall, so there can be no doubt that the whole structure was planned as a whole. Finds in the lower chamber included several interments and some Onston pottery.

Nothing now remains to be seen of Rinyo, the neolithic village in Rousay similar to Skara Brae. There was some excavation after World War II, and the site was then filled in to protect it from the weather. The position of Rinyo is marked approximately by the farm Bigland, south of Faraclett Head in the northeast of the island.

Hoy's Dwarfie Stone

The Dwarfie Stone in Hoy, above the col on the road from Linksness pier to Rackwick, and long an object of local legend, may be the oldest of all Orkney's neolithic tombs. It is in fact an example of a rock-hewn tomb of neolithic date, unique in Orkney and until very recently thought to be unique in Britain.

A large rectangular sandstone boulder, 28ft by 14ft in plan and 6ft high at its unburied end, has been hollowed out to make a passage with two side-chambers. The top is now open, though how it came to be so is unexplained. Nearby is a large stone which once sealed the entrance. The identification of this monument as a cut-out variant of Maeshowe came only in 1935 through the work of Mr C. S. T. Calder of the Royal Commission on the Ancient Monuments of Scotland. The Dwarfie Stone has still an air of mystery about it. It lies in a wild and empty valley beneath the forbidding Dwarfie Hamars (crags) from which it must long ago have been plucked by moving ice. Like Maeshowe it can be picked out from afar when one knows exactly where to look for it.

IRON AGE BROCHS

Gurness, Midhowe and Borwick

The two largest and best-preserved brochs so far excavated stand facing each other across Eynhallow Sound. These are Gurness in Evie and Midhowe in Rousay.

Gurness broch stands on the northern point of Aikerness, a low sandy headland commanding good views along the sound. Excavation began with a trial shaft in 1929. At first, the site gives an overall impression of a great confusion of low walls and fallen stone, from the midst of which the massive circular wall of the broch rises to a height of about 12ft. A large roughly circular ditch encloses the broch to landward; on the seaward side part of the ditch has been removed by marine erosion. Inside the broch there is also an impression of confusion, produced by numerous partitions, some built in drystone, some made from flagstone slabs in a technique that was much better developed at Skara Brae.

The official pamphlet and site-plan help to reduce this apparent confusion to some kind of order. From the plan, it will be seen that the broch tower is the primary structure and that a whole succession of buildings was added, nearby, inside and outside, at later dates. The sequence of buildings at Gurness in fact summarises events of the broch and post-broch period very clearly.

First came the broch itself, built sometime in the first century AD when raiding and reprisal were at their height. Its term of service as a defensive work, at least in its original form, seems to have been rather short, though it was maintained in some kind of defensive state for some time, and indeed extra works were added for the protection of its entrance. Then, in more settled times, probably during the second century AD, the people whose refuge it had once been built layer upon layer of domestic buildings inside and around it. Its interior was divided radially into living compartments by stone partitions, and there seem to have been two internal storeys, access to which was by two new stairways set in the wall. At some stage a small foundry was established. The surrounding ditch was filled in, and building extended across it. Repeated use of the site continued until the early viking period, when several long-houses were added. Examples of these have been disentangled from the ruins and rebuilt clear of the broch.

Entrance to the broch is through the original access passage, in which a door fitting can still be seen. Small cells open off the passage on either side and lead into a ground-level intra-mural passage which can be followed for some distance. This passage is unusual; brochs normally have no galleries below first-floor level. The passage at Gurness may in fact have been a fatal error in design, because the broch seems to have partially collapsed quite early in its history. There is a well of fresh water near the centre of the broch, into which it is still possible to descend.

Midhowe broch is an equally large and spectacular example. Like Gurness, it stands on the shore, and close to the Midhowe stalled cairn previously described. Excavation was begun in 1930 by the proprietor of Trumland, the late Mr W. G. Grant, who later handed it over to the Office of Works for preservation. Reference has already been made to Mr Grant's work in connection with the excavation of the neolithic cairns on Rousay. It is probable that no landowner has ever had so many notable ancient monuments on his property; certainly none has done more to unravel their mysteries and to preserve them for posterity.

Midhowe, as its name implies, is the central one of three brochs. The other two remain to be excavated, and are to be seen as grassy mounds nearby. It is astonishing that three such large structures should have been built so close together; even more remarkable is the presence of no fewer than fifteen along the shores of Eynhallow Sound. The site of Midhowe is exceptionally well chosen; the broch stands between the two trench-like sea inlets of Stenchna Geo and Geo of the Brough, and at high tide is surrounded on three sides by the sea. A massive double ditch and bank protect the landward approach. The sea has encroached a few yards since iron age times, and in so doing has stripped away some of the conglomeration of later buildings which surrounds the broch. A Ministry sea-wall now prevents damage to the broch itself.

The broch rises to 14ft in places. Its diameter is 59ft and the walls are up to 15ft thick. Entrance is by a passage from the seaward side. From this passage, a small intra-mural chamber opens to the right; this has fine corbelled beehive roofing. To the left, another chamber gives access to a passage within the wall, as at Gurness, and as at Gurness also, this seems to have promoted an early partial collapse of the tower, for at some stage an attempt has been made to pack it with stones, and external buttressing has also been added.

Inside, at first-floor level a doorway is to be seen which leads to the first fifteen steps of the original broch stair. There is as always a central well, which still contains fresh water. Otherwise, the interior is a chaos of flagstone slabs put up to divide the broch into living quarters after its military function had become obsolete. Signs of hearths are to be seen.

Outside, an even greater confusion of structures is evident, but to the north of the broch there is one of special interest, now protected from the weather by a glass cover. Here was found a smelting hearth, with stones cracked by fire and a quantity of iron slag. Oddly enough, apart from this clear evidence of iron age culture, no iron objects were found during the excavations. There were a few tiny items of bronze. It is true that iron objects are likely to have rusted away in the damp Orkney climate, but nevertheless one has the strong impression that, for most people in the so-called Iron Age, household equipment was no better than neolithic.

There are many broch sites worth a visit which are not preserved with clinical tidiness by the Ministry of Public Buildings and Works. The author's favourite is the broch of Borwick, on the west coast of Mainland just over a mile south of Skara Brae. It is most easily reached by taking the minor road to the cliff edge at Yesnaby, 6 miles north of Stromness. From this point, magnificent clifftop walks are to be had both southward and northward.

Heading north, and keeping as close as possible to the clifftop, one passes splendid examples of natural arches and a blow-hole or 'gloup', marked by a cairn, at the bottom of which the ocean may be heard pounding its way inland along a line of weakness in the rocks. From the northern slopes of the low hill of Borwick,

o

the narrow inlet of the same name comes into view, formed by the waves attacking a geological fault-line which runs away south-east from this point. This major fault intersects with another fault at the head of the 'wick' or inlet, to produce a narrow 'nose' of cliff on which stands the broch. Immediately to the south a tiny stream runs down to a beach where boats must have been drawn up from the earliest times. Near the stream is the nettle-covered outline of a fisherman's or kelp gatherer's hut.

The Borwick broch is partly exposed from beneath a grassy hillock. Its wall is in fair condition on the landward side, and it may be entered through a low passage. Inside there is an uneven mound of grass-covered stones, fallen from the tower or possibly the remains of secondary structures. Part of the wall on the seaward side has fallen over the cliff, further evidence of encroachment by the sea. Nearby there are signs of circular radially partitioned 'wheelhouse' structures, probably somewhat more recent than the tower itself.

Excavation has not yet been done at enough broch sites for it to be clear whether the broch was a spontaneous invention, which it appears to have been, or whether it was evolved in stages from earlier structures. The problem of brochs can be pursued in the Ministry guides to Mousa and Clicknimin in Shetland, obtainable from HMSO, and the chapter on the subject by J. R. C. Hamilton in Dr Wainwright's *Northern Isles*. An excellent model of a broch, cut away to show the interior arrangements, is in Tankerness House museum, Kirkwall.

THE NORSE AGE

From the Norse golden age several notable buildings or sites remain. St Magnus Cathedral, the most notable of all, and the Bishop's Palace have already been noticed in the chapter on Kirkwall. The runic writing in Maeshowe has also been noted. Five others are particularly noteworthy.

Brough of Birsay

Earl Thorfinn lived the last peaceful seventeen years of his eventful life on the Brough of Birsay. The Brough is a small tidal island at the north-western tip of Mainland, 20 miles from Kirkwall and 14 from Stromness. It is accessible only at low water by a causeway, recently improved. When the tide is rising this is covered at a most remarkable speed, and it is absolutely essential to know the state of the tide before crossing to the island. High water at Birsay is an hour in advance of Kirkwall, the times for which are published daily in *The Orcadian*.

The Brough is a most attractive place, especially on a fine clear northern day. It consists of one great tilted slab of flagstone with cliffs to seaward and a gentle slope facing inland. The excavated site stands near the foot of the inland slope, but high enough to command wide views along the cliffs of north Mainland and south along the wide sweep of Birsay Bay to Marwick Head and the cliffs of Hoy. There is an extensive prospect into the heart of west Mainland, where it will be remembered are the place-names ending in -ston, probably settlements of Earl Thorfinn's retainers. This is a fine base for a sea-earl, whose dominions were held by sea power and who needed always to be on guard against raiders from the sea.

Before excavations began, all that was visible was a ruined church, known locally as Peter Kirk and sometimes St Colm's (after St Colm of Buchan and Caithness, not St Columba as has often been thought).

The site is very complicated, and in order to disentangle the various parts it is useful to consult the excellent Ministry guide by Mr C. A. R. Radford. Earl Thorfinn's Christ Church is a good starting point from which to begin exploring. To modern eyes this seems a very small building, yet in fact it is 55ft long, 10ft longer than St Magnus in Egilsay, which seems now to be quite a large church. The effect of smallness is produced by the low height of the walls which reach only to about 7ft. Its layout was of nave, choir and apse. There are signs that a western tower may have been intended. The altar which now divides apse from choir is a later addition, probably thirteenth-century. Near the centre of the nave a grave was discovered containing a wooden coffin and the disarticulated remains of a man. This grave is thought to have been used first to bury St Magnus, but after his remains were taken to Kirkwall it is very possible that this, apparently the only grave inside Orkney's most venerated church, was used to rebury its founder, Earl Thorfinn himself. The church stands inside a walled rectangular enclosure, the Norse cemetery.

Near the shore stand the remains of Earl Thorfinn's hall, looking across to the palace of the Stewart Earl Robert on Mainland. It is difficult to distinguish the Norse hall from earlier and later structures, because the same stones have been used over and over again. The hall was large and well-appointed for its day and had heating arrangements and a bath-house. It stands over the outlines of an earlier hall. Sometime after Thorfinn's death his hall was burned and over it were built a number of dwellings used by clergy.

About fifty years after Thorfinn's death his Christ Church was raised to the dignity of a cathedral and became the seat of a bishop. North and west of the church may be seen the rectilinear pattern of a bishop's palace arranged around a courtyard. When this palace was built various modifications were made to the church itself, notably the addition of two altar recesses at the east end of the nave. The first recorded bishop was William, who took up his charge about 1108.

In addition to these buildings of Earl Thorfinn's day and later there are some much earlier remains of great interest. Fine examples of viking long-houses dating from the first phases of Norse colonisation stand on the hill above the church, And, from an even earlier time, there have been some exciting discoveries, though there is now little to be seen. Underneath Thorfinn's minster are the foundations of a Celtic church, while a Celtic Christian burial ground partly underlies the Norse cemetery. Here was found the celebrated Birsay Stone, a replica of which stands at the head of a triple grave wherein were buried, one may suppose, the three notables shown on the stone. There is believed to have been a Celtic Christian monastery on this, the most holy site in Orkney.

The Round Church in Orphir

This tiny church of which only the apse and the outline of the circular nave remain is probably the oldest surviving church structure in Orkney. It stands near the earls' drinking hall in Orphir, half-way on the coast route between Kirkwall and Stromness and close to the shore. Its location clearly suggests an earl's work, and its plan, derived from the Holy Sepulchre in Jerusalem, suggests that Earl Hakon had it built after his pilgrimage to the Holy Land. This would place its date between 1116 and 1123.

It is tantalising to find that this building was complete until the eighteenth century, when most of it was pulled down to make room for a new parish church. This newer church has itself been demolished; it was built against the apse of the round church. The circular nave had a diameter of 20ft and stood 15ft high at the centre; light was admitted by a roof window. The only building in Britain which gives much idea of what the Orphir church must have been like is the chapel in Ludlow castle, but that is considerably larger; the closest parallels are to be found in Prague.

Egilsay: St Magnus Church

A visit to the islands of Egilsay and Wyre starts at Tingwall pier and may be combined with a visit to Rousay. Arrangements for a boat need to be made in advance; this may be done through the offices of the Orkney Tourist Association in Kirkwall or Stromness.

Egilsay is rather like an arrow-head in plan, the arrow pointing south. It is about three miles long and has at present 45 inhabitants. The ground rises to a low central ridge upon which, near the centre of the island, stands the church of St Magnus. Its round tower is visible from afar (one may pick it out from the main road between Kirkwall and Finstown) and must have stood in earlier times as an ever-present reminder of the power, temporal and eternal, which had been planted in these heathen isles.

St Magnus consists of a rectangular nave about 30ft long and 15ft wide, with a narrower chancel 15ft long. The round tower at the west end stands 48ft high, and was originally about 15ft higher. The stone walls are very thick, especially at the base of the tower, and the appearance of the exterior has been enhanced by the decorative use of squared blocks. The chancel is barrel-vaulted and above it there is an apartment known as the 'grief' house. This name derives from the Old Norse word for sanctuary, and it is noteworthy that the Orphir round church used to be called the 'girth' house. It is possible that a gallery once continued the level of this upper apartment around the nave, but no trace remains. The round tower is one of two known to have been built in Orkney, the other being in Stenness and long since demolished. It has misleadingly been compared with the round towers of East Anglia; in fact its connections are clearly Irish. The apartment over the chancel is also an Irish feature.

St Magnus church, Egilsay

It is impossible to date St Magnus church precisely from architectural evidence alone, except to say that it is twelfth century. Bearing in mind its dedication to the young earl who was slain nearby in 1116 and the subsequent development of a 'Magnus Party' in Orcadian affairs, one is fairly safe in ascribing its foundation to the agency of Bishop William the Old in the years 1135–8. Egilsay may in fact have been his residence before the bishopric was moved to Birsay.

Another point of interest here concerns the island name Egilsay. When place-name study was developing in Orkney, it was generally thought that this church was Celtic; thus Daniel Gorrie in his *Summers and Winters in the Orkneys,* written in the second half of the nineteenth century, refers to it as 'the old Celtic-Scandinavian Kirk'. A derivation of Egilsay from *eaglais,* the Celtic word for church, was therefore proposed. It became clear

222

subsequently that almost every place-name in Orkney was Norse and it was then thought unlikely that the Norsemen would use a Celtic word to name an island. A derivation from the Norwegian personal name Egil was suggested, and this is generally accepted.

It is perhaps unfair to dismiss the first explanation of the name out of hand. The strategic situation of Egilsay must have commended it to the Celtic Christian papae and it is perfectly possible that a Celtic church was built on this island, at this very spot. If the Norse invaders were pagans, which they almost certainly were, they may have had no suitable word for the building they found here, which was visible from afar and after which they wished to name the island. Under these circumstances, admittedly hypothetical, use of the Celtic word for church could have resulted.

Wyre Castle and Church

Wyre is a smaller island than Egilsay but of very similar shape. Its present population is 36. Its name derives from the Old Norse *vigr*, meaning spearhead. This same island name may be found in the Norwegian county of Sunmøre and probably records the fact that the first Norwegian of note to settle here came from that part of Norway. There is a third island with this name off Iceland, perhaps settled by another member of the same family.

On the high ground overlooking Wyre Sound and with good views in every direction stands the excavated castle of Kolbein Hruga, a notable chief of the mid-twelfth century and descendant of Earl Paul I. Kolbein was undoubtedly one of that class of gødings or best men established by Thorfinn the Mighty, a class which became progressively more influential in Orkney affairs in the Norse period. This castle is mentioned twice in the sagas. In the Orkneyinga Saga it is recorded from about 1150: 'At that time there lived in Wyre in the Orkneys a Norwegian called Kolbein Hruga, the most haughty of men. He had a good stone castle built there that was a safe stronghold.' In King Hakon's Saga we read of the last Norse earl slain eight years later in a Thurso cellar and his murderers taking refuge in Wyre castle, where they were presently besieged. 'But it was a very unhandy place to attack', and so friends of the contestants arranged a temporary peace.

223

Kolbein's castle consists of a square keep surrounded by a deep ditch. The keep is very small compared with later Norman versions, the sides being about 25ft long. There are signs of at least one upper floor. In the ground-floor chamber a water tank is cut into the stone floor. A number of later buildings may be made out around the keep, but the purpose of these is unclear. The inner side of the ditch is faced with stone. All the stonework is of a very high standard of workmanship. Entrance to the castle was from the east. The keep had a door at first floor level from which a ladder could be lowered to admit welcome visitors.

North of the castle is the farm called Bu of Wyre. This name shows it to have been from the beginning of Norse settlement the house of the principal family on the island, and it was undoubtedly Kolbein's farm. East of the castle at the foot of the natural knoll on which it stands is a small roofless church of late twelfth-century date. Kolbein Hruga's son was the distinguished Bishop Bjarni who succeeded to the See of Orkney about 1190. The church is probably Kolbein's work, built at his son's behest. It is romanesque in style and represents the adoption by an important landowner of architectural ideas brought into Orkney by Kol and Rognvald.

Winksetter in Harray

One farm building survives which can be ascribed with fair certainty to the late Norse period. This is Winksetter, located under the Harray hills. The name denotes the 'seat' or dwelling of a man named Wing. A persistent tradition attaches to this house, that it was long ago inhabited by the second son of a Norwegian king.

Winksetter may be approached by car from the main road from Finstown to Dounby or on foot over the moors from the old road through the parish of Rendall. This second alternative is to be strongly recommended on a fine day for its sweeping views over Wide Firth and the islands on the one hand and the central plain of west Mainland on the other, with unexpected glimpses of the peaks of Sutherland beyond Hoy and the Pentland Firth. In the deep cleft of Syradale a small waterfall may be discovered, an unusual sight in Orkney.

The old house has long been used as a byre. The roof has

fallen in and some recent subtractions and additions have been made to the original structure. Nevertheless the original layout may still be made out with a fair degree of certainty. The house is long and rather low in proportion, and placed lengthways down a gentle slope, so that slight down-stepping is necessary between the main rooms. The general alignment is roughly east-west.

The western section of the building was a byre originally. Entrance to the house proper is through this by a doorway in the north-east corner. Inside there are three rooms connected by doorways on the north side. The first two rooms seem somewhat cramped. This is because a cross-wall of relatively recent date has been built across the middle of one long room, the fire-house of the original dwelling. Inspection of this cross-wall shows it to be clearly intrusive; removing it in the mind's eye, a room unusually spacious for an old Orkney house is revealed.

In the first room, there is a well preserved quern-ledder or alcove in the south-west corner. This is a stone shelf on which stood a mortar and pestle used for grinding grain. The corner is neatly rounded to allow free movement for the grinder's arm. Underneath is a lithie or tethering-place for a calf, and to the left a hen-roost is built into the wall. In the next room, beyond the original position of the free-standing fire-back, the north wall exhibits a rich array of stone-built cupboards and two goose-nests close to the floor. The nest beside the door has been filled in; ankles must have been tempting targets for its inmate. Close to the west door there is a sae-bink or water-jar shelf, also neatly rounded. Opposite on the south wall is a window of gun-loop design. Some interior details are illustrated on page 72.

The next cross-wall is original. It divided the fire-house from a living room once double its present length, for the end wall of the house is also intrusive. Here also there are stone-built cupboards and a large recess built out on the north side where ale was kept. The floor of the whole house is flagged, and it is evident that the eastern room was partly dug out of the hillside in order to achieve a level floor. This is most unusual in old Orkney houses.

A narrow 'close' separates the main house from a former byre; this close is still remarkably sheltered, and its western end, facing the prevailing winds, is blocked by rough walling. Once there were at least two additional buildings, including one with a kiln at its end, but these have totally disappeared.

The impression is of a dwelling of some substance, and one is led to ask, can this structure really date back to Norse times? The answer depends upon assessing the balance of probabilities; there is no direct evidence.

' First, the building has a number of features known to be early. The thickness of the walls, down-stepping and gun-loop window are all strongly reminiscent of Icelandic houses of the fourteenth century or earlier; there is no reason to suppose them later features in Orkney. Second, the location of the building is remarkable. It is surprising to find so elaborate a dwelling in the remote fast-nesses of the Harray moors. Who might have built it in such a place, and for what purpose?

Ancient rentals show that Winksetter became earls' property in the time of Earl William Sinclair, 1434–71. Henceforth it was held by a succession of tenants on three-year leases. These tenants would not have built such a house themselves, and it seems un-likely that any earl had it built for them. The house seems there-fore certainly to antedate Earl William. How much older may it be?

The tradition that a Norwegian king's second son lived here may help to answer this question. As it stands the tradition is undoubtedly incorrect; and yet, during the period of direct Nor-wegian administration which followed King Hakon's expedition of 1263, Orkney was governed by one Hakon Jonsson, whose grandmother was a daughter of the Norwegian king. Hakon Jonsson himself had certain theoretical claims to the throne, which he formally relinquished in 1388. He may have been the man referred to by tradition. He was in Orkney for only a short time about the year 1369.

Why should Hakon Jonsson build this elaborate house in so remote a spot? In terms of the modern cultivated landscape this is inexplicable, but in Norse times much of central west Mainland was a hunting waste reserved for earls' use; Winksetter stands at the end of this tract nearest to Kirkwall and to the earls' hall in Orphir. It could have been a hunting lodge.

On balance it is reasonable to think that Winksetter is a Norse building. It may be the oldest surviving domestic dwelling in

Orkney from the Norse period. Unfortunately its state is ruinous. It is to be hoped that steps will be taken to preserve it before it is too late.

TUNSHIPS

Few visible remains survive of the old tunships, though their names remain on modern maps, and are locally in common use. The planking of the farms in the nineteenth century and the wholesale attack on the old wastes by twentieth-century ploughs have run the tunship lands one into the other. Some slight impression of what the separate tunships used to look like may be had in the Beauquoy district of Birsay or Heddle in Stenness; in both cases there is still an impression of farmlands set among moorland. But of course no sign of the intricate strips of the old runrig system can be seen. To see a tunship landscape in anything like its primitive condition one has to travel to Shetland, parts of the Highlands or the Hebrides.

Here and there an old tunship dyke may be picked out, of the kind which once separated the farmland from the common or one tunship from the next. A good example runs along the hill above the minor road from Finstown northwards towards Redland, another is to be seen at Yesnaby.

OLD ORKNEY HOUSES

In one or two places, tightly bunched groups of houses still survive from the days before the plankings and the associated dispersal of the farms. An example is Lettaly in Rendall, close to the pass through the hills into Harray called the Chair of Lyde. The narrow lanes between the old long-houses give a good impression of what an old Orkney 'tun' must have looked like a century and a half ago.

Small ruined houses in remote places were often the homes of tenants driven off the farms by improving landlords. Some were able to squat on the commons before these were divided. Examples are to be seen at many places; in Birsay they line the bare slopes of Skelday Hill, and in Rousay one comes upon them high on the moorland 'steps' above the cultivated district of Westside.

Old house in Firth, Mainland

A number of Orkney houses survive in fair condition, in addition to Winksetter which is exceptionally ancient. The best example is Midhouse in Harray, which has since 1968 been under the care of a Kirkwall committee who intend to develop it as a rural museum. Midhouse stands beside the Burn of Corrigall a short distance to the south-east of Dounby. Here may be seen a fine example of a long-house with flagstone 'fitted furniture', a barn with its threshing doors opposite each other and a complete kiln, a byre with flagstone stalls and a place high up in one corner for a horse's feed. Midhouse is a most interesting site. In addition to the house there is a small grinding mill and an iron age broch which remains to be examined.

Another small example of an old house with good interior detail occurs in Firth near the farm of Redland. Here may be seen a quern recess in one corner, flagstone cupboards, a stone bed set in the wall and an adjacent ale-cupboard.

Other interesting old houses include a very derelict specimen in Kirbister, Harray, which still retains its roof; Mossetter in Rendall near the Loch of Brockan, and another on the small island of Cava in Scapa Flow. Orkney is dotted with roofless ruins, in most of which nothing remains of any interest; but here and there the persistent explorer may still find the remains of a

228

wall-bed, quern recess or flagstone cupboards hidden among the nettles of summer. Until recently there was little interest in these things, and much remains unrecorded.

MILLS

Only one complete example remains of the many small water mills which Orkney landlords once had on their properties. This is the Click Mill in Harray, which used the waters of the little Burn of Lushan. It stands near the B 9057 and is in Ministry care. The mill is a small drystone structure with a turf roof resting on thin flagstone. The millpond, which is now drained, stands beside it. This mill, which is in full working order, was built about 1800 but it represents a type centuries old, spread through many parts of Europe. In western Norway, almost identical mills dating back to medieval times were put back into commission during the second World War, when commercial flour became scarce.

In contrast, the Barony Mill in Birsay represents a class of much larger and more recent mills built by principal landowners, to which their tenants brought their grain; most of what they brought remained there as rent. The Barony Mill stands beside the A 967 a mile east of the Earls' Palace. It was built in 1873 beside older mills which are now derelict. This is the last Orkney mill to remain in commercial operation, milling both home and imported grain. One of its notable products is beremeal, which is exported to Shetland and the Hebrides. In 1968 some 300 bolls of bere, 10 stone apiece, were shipped from this mill. In the vicinity, a field or two of bere may be seen growing in most years. It ripens in advance of other grains in this northern climate. The Click and Barony mills are illustrated on page 90.

The remains of many mills of both kinds are to be found in the Orkney countryside, and need to be recorded by sketch, measurement and photograph before they fall into irretrievable ruin. The future of at least one large mill should be secured for posterity. The Barony Mill is safe from destruction as long as it remains in operation. Another fine example still in working order is Tormiston Mill near Maeshowe. This was privately refurbished and opened as a restaurant and craft shop in 1972.

PLACES TO VISIT

Orkney has many splendid clifftop walks, two of which have already been mentioned : the most spectacular of all, from Rackwick northward to the Old Man of Hoy and St John's Head, and that from Yesnaby northward to the Broch of Borwick on the west Mainland coast.

There are many others. By walking southward from Yesnaby a remarkable succession of bays and headlands, deeply cut inlets or geos, natural arches, caves and sea-stacks may be seen, the latter including Yesnaby and North Gaulton Castles, both very fine examples. By walking south to the crest of Black Craig, a little way short of the low ground of Breck Ness, a magnificent panorama of Hoy and Scapa Flow is brought into view. To the north, there are fine cliffs at Marwick Head and on the Brough of Birsay, and along the north coast of Mainland all the way to Costa Head. In Deerness there is a superb stretch of cliff coast between Sandside Bay and Mull Head, with a fearsome 'gloup' or collapsed sea cave about a mile south of Brough of Deerness.

On the North Isles, Rousay has fine cliffs on its western and northern coasts, and the western cliffs of Westray are well worth a visit; they command extensive southward views of Rousay and west Mainland. The cliffs of South Ronaldsay are the finest in the eastern South Isles, while in Hoy, a walk southward from Rackwick towards Sneuk Head, Little Rackwick and The Berry is in some respects as spectacular as the northward walk.

Many of these cliffs are bird cliffs, and should in consequence be approached with respect. The keen ornithologist should obtain local and up-to-date advice about specially rewarding locations.

BIBLIOGRAPHY

For many years, books dealing with various aspects of Orkney life, history and landscape have been published by the Kirkwall Press, occasionally in Stromness. It has been normal practice to print only a small number of copies of each title, with the result that most are out of print. Second-hand copies are very hard to find and some have lately become much sought after by collectors. All may be consulted in the Orkney Room at Kirkwall public library.

The general prehistoric and archaeological background is most comprehensively dealt with in *The Northern Isles*, edited by the late Dr F. T. Wainwright. J. Storer Clouston's *History of Orkney* is the best single work on the Norse and early Scots periods. Hugh Marwick's *Orkney* is a good general account of the islands as they were in the early 1950s. John Firth's *Reminiscences of an Orkney Parish* is a fascinating account of country life in an Orkney about to cross the threshold into modern times. Daniel Gorrie's *Summers and Winters* is a readable and accurate account of the islands in the second half of the nineteenth century. Magnus Spence's *Flora Orcadiensis* is the primary work on Orkney botany, and Robert Rendall's *Orkney Shore* the most comprehensive work on marine natural history. *The New Orkney Book* (Shearer and others), though designed as a resource book for schools, is of interest to the general reader and contains rather compressed articles by a team of local authors on a variety of Orcadian topics. It is interesting to compare this with *The Orkney Book*, edited by John Gunn, which was produced for the same purpose more than half a century earlier. All these titles are included in the following alphabetical list.

ALMGREN, B. and CAGNER, E. *The Viking*. London, 1966
ANDERSON, J. (ed.) *Orkneyinga Saga*, translated by Hjaltalin and Goudie. Edinburgh, 1873. Facsimile edition, Edinburgh, 1973.

231

BIBLIOGRAPHY

ARBMAN, H. *The Vikings*. London, 1961

BAILEY, P. J. M. 'Field studies in Orkney', *Journal*, Institute of Education, University of Newcastle upon Tyne, vol. 22, 1970

BALFOUR, D. of Balfour and Trenaby. *Odal Rights and Feudal Wrongs. A Memorial for Orkney*. Edinburgh, 1860

BARCLAY, R. S. *The Population of Orkney 1755–1961*. Kirkwall, 1965

BARRY, G. *History of the Orkney Islands*. Edinburgh, 1805

BEN, Jo. *Descriptio Insularum Orchadiarum, 1529*, translated in Marfarlane, W. *Geographical Collections relating to Scotland*. Edinburgh, 1908

BERRY, R. J. 'Genetical changes in mice and men', *Eugenics Review*, vol 59, 1967

BERRY, R. J. 'History in the evolution of *Apodemus sylvaticus* (mammalia) at one edge of its range', *Journal of Zoology*, vol 159, 1969

BRØGGER, A. W. *Ancient Emigrants. A History of the Norse Settlements in Scotland*. Oxford, 1929

BRØNDSTED, J. *The Vikings*. Harmondsworth, 1960

BROWN, G. M. *A Time to Keep*. London, 1968

BROWN, G. M. *An Orkney Tapestry*. London, 1969

BROWN, M. and MEEHAN, P. *Scapa Flow*. Harmondsworth, 1969

BUCHAN, S. *Stromness: A Boom-Town of the 1880s?* Unpublished MA dissertation, University of Aberdeen, 1961

CAMPBELL, A. J. *Fifteen Centuries of the Church in Orkney*. Kirkwall, 1938

CHARLESWORTH, J. K. *The Quaternary Era, with special reference to its glaciation*. London, 1957

CHILDE, V. GORDON *Skara Brae: A Pictish Village in Orkney*. London 1931

CHILDE, V. GORDON 'A Stone Age settlement at the Braes of Rinyo, Orkney', *Proc. Soc. Antiquaries Scot.*, vol. LXXXI, 1946–7

CLOUSTON, C. *Meteorological Observations taken at Orkney*. Kirkwall, 1861

CLOUSTON, J. STORER *The Orkney Parishes*. Kirkwall, 1927

CLOUSTON, J. STORER *History of Orkney*. Kirkwall, 1932

COULL, J. R. *Report of the Survey of the Islands of Westray and Papa Westray*. Scottish Development Department, Edinburgh, 1965 (limited distribution)
232

COULL, J. R. and WILLIS, D. P. 'The air service in the North Isles of Orkney', *Geography*, vol 55, 1970

CRAVEN, J. B. *History of the Church in Orkney, I–IV*. Kirkwall, 1893–1912

CURSITER, J. W. (compiler) *List of Books and Pamphlets relating to Orkney and Shetland*. Kirkwall, 1894

DASENT, G. W. *The Orkneyingers' Saga*. London 1894

DIETRICHSON, L. *Monumenta Orcadica*. Christiania, 1906

DONALDSON, G. *Northwards by Sea*. Edinburgh, 1966

DREVER, W. P. *Udal Law and the Foreshore*. Kirkwall, 1914

DREVER, W. P. *Udal Law in the Orkneys and Zetland*. Kirkwall, 1914

EDMONSTON, T. *Glossary of Shetland and Orkney Dialect*. Kirkwall, 1866

ELLIOTT, R. W. V. *Runes*. Manchester, 1959

FEACHAM, R. *A Guide to Prehistoric Scotland*. London, 1963

FIRTH, J. *Reminiscences of an Orkney Parish*. Stromness, 1922

GEIKIE, A. 'On the Old Red Sandstone of Western Europe', *Trans. Royal Soc. Edinburgh*, vol 28, 1879

GORRIE, D. *Summers and Winters in the Orkneys*. London, 1868

GUNN, J. (ed.) *The Orkney Book*. London and Edinburgh, 1909

GUNN, J. *Orkney. The Magnetic North*. London, 1941

HEDDLE, J. G. F. M. and MAINLAND, T. *Orkney and Shetland*. Cambridge, 1920

HENDERSON, L. *The Picts*. London, 1967

HOSSACK, B. H. *Kirkwall in the Orkneys*. Kirkwall, 1900

LACAILLE, A. *The Stone Age in Scotland*. London, 1954

LINKLATER, E. *The Ultimate Viking*. London, 1955

LINKLATER, E. *Orkney and Shetland*. London, 1965

LOW, G. *Tour through the Islands of Orkney and Shetland*. Kirkwall, 1879

MACARTHUR, R. H. and WILSON, E. O. *The Theory of Island Biogeography*. Princeton, 1967

MACKENZIE, J. *The General Grievances and Oppressions of the Isles of Orkney and Shetland*. Edinburgh, 1836

MACKENZIE, M. *Orcades: or a Geographic and Hydrographic Survey of the Orkney and Lewis Islands in Eight Maps*. London, 1776

BIBLIOGRAPHY

MACKINTOSH, W. R. (ed.) *The Orkney Crofters: Their Evidence and Statements . . . before the Crofters Commission.* Edinburgh, 1888

MACKINTOSH, W. R. *Around the Orkney Peat Fires.* Kirkwall, 1914

MACQUEEN, J. *St Nynia: A Study of Literary and Linguistic Evidence.* London, 1961

MARWICK, H. *The Orkney Norn.* Oxford, 1926

MARWICK, H. *Merchant Lairds of Long Ago.* Kirkwall, 1939

MARWICK, H. *The Place-Names of Rousay.* Kirkwall, 1947

MARWICK, H. *Orkney.* London, 1951

MARWICK, H. *Orkney Farm Names.* Kirkwall, 1952

MARWICK, H. *Ancient Monuments of Orkney. Official Guide.* Edinburgh, 1952

MARWICK, H. *The Place-Names of Birsay*, edited by Nicolaisen, W. F. H. Aberdeen, 1970

MATHER, J. Y. 'Boats and boatmen of Orkney and Shetland', *Scottish Studies*, vol 8, 1964

MAWER, A. *The Vikings.* Cambridge, 1913

MILLER, R. 'Orkney: a Land of Increment' in Miller, R. and Watson, J. W. (eds.), *Geographical Essays in Memory of A. G. Ogilvie.* Edinburgh, 1959

MILLER, R. and LUTHER-DAVIES, S. *Eday and Hoy. A Development Survey.* University of Glasgow, 1968

MINISTRY OF PUBLIC BUILDINGS AND WORKS *Guides and Leaflets.* HMSO, Edinburgh
  Childe, V. Gordon *Ancient Dwellings at Skara Brae, Orkney,* 1950
  Radford, C. A. R. *The Early Christian and Norse Settlements at Birsay, Orkney,* 1959
  Simpson, W. D. *The Bishop's Palace and the Earl's Palace, Kirkwall, Orkney,* 1965

MITCHISON, R. 'Two Northern Ports', *Scottish Studies*, vol 7, 1963

MOIRA, B. L. C. and MOIRA, R. E. with SARGENT, M. *Kirkwall and Stromness Survey Report.* Kirkwall, 1959 (limited distribution)

MOONEY, H. *St Magnus Cathedral, Kirkwall.* Kirkwall, 1966

MOONEY, J. *Eynhallow. The Holy Isle of the Orkneys.* Kirkwall, 1923

MOONEY, J. *St Magnus, Earl of Orkney.* Kirkwall, 1935

MOONEY, J. *The Cathedral and Royal Burgh of Kirkwall.* Kirkwall, 1943

O'DELL, A. C. *Orkney* in Stamp, L. Dudley (ed.), *The Land of Britain*, Part 4. London, 1939

O'DELL, A. C. 'The Northern Isles of Scotland' in Steers, J. A. (ed.), *Field Studies in the British Isles*. London, 1964

Orkney Agricultural Discussion Society *Journal*, 1925–39

Orkney Antiquarian Society *Proceedings*

PEACH, B. N. and HORNE, J. 'The glaciation of the Orkney Islands', *Quart. Journ. Geol. Soc.*, vol. 36, 1880

PETERKIN, A. (ed.) *Rentals of the Ancient Earldom and Bishoprick of Orkney*. Edinburgh, 1820

PETERKIN, A. *Notes on Orkney and Shetland*. Edinburgh, 1822

PIGGOTT, S. (ed.) *The Prehistoric Peoples of Scotland*. London, 1962

RENDALL, R. *Mollusca Orcadiensis*. Kirkwall, 1956

RENDALL, R. *Orkney Shore*. Kirkwall, 1960

ROBERTSON, J. *Uppies and Doonies*. Kirkwall, 1968

ROLLO, D. *History of the Orkney and Shetland Volunteers 1793–1958*. Lerwick, 1958

Royal Commission on the Ancient Monuments of Scotland, 3 vols. Edinburgh, 1946

SAWYER, P. H. *The Age of the Vikings*. London, 1962

SCOTT, M. A. *Island Saga. The Story of North Ronaldsay*. Kirkwall, 1968.

SHEARER, J., GROUNDWATER, W. and MACKAY, J. D. *The New Orkney Book*. London, 1966

SHETELIG, H. (ed.) *Viking Antiquities in Great Britain and Ireland*, 6 vols. Oslo, 1940–54

SHIRREFF, J. A General View of the Agriculture of the Orkney Islands. Edinburgh, 1814

SIMPSON, W. DOUGLAS *The Celtic Church in Scotland*. Aberdeen, 1935

SISSONS, J. B. *The Evolution of Scotland's Scenery*. Edinburgh and London, 1967

SMALL, A. 'The historical geography of the Norse and Viking colonisation of the Scottish Highlands', *Norsk Geografisk Tijdsskrift*, vol 22, 1968

SPENCE, M. *Flora Orcadiensis*. Kirkwall, 1914

Statistical Accounts of Scotland. Edinburgh, 1793 and 1842

TACITUS *Agricola*, translated by Mattingly, M. Harmondsworth, 1948

BIBLIOGRAPHY

TAYLOR, A. B. (ed.) *Orkneyinga Saga*. Edinburgh, 1938

THOMSON, D. C. and GRIMBLE, *I. The Future of the Highlands.* London, 1968

THOMPSON, D. P. *Orkney through the Centuries. Lights and Shadows of the Church's Life in the Northern Isles.* Kirkwall, 1956

TROUP, J. A. and EUNSON, F. *Stromness*. Stromness, 1967

TUDOR, J. R. *The Orkneys and Shetlands. Their Past and Present State.* London, 1883

Viking Society publications

WAINWRIGHT, F. T. (ed.) *The Problem of the Picts.* Edinburgh, 1955

WAINWRIGHT, F. T. (ed.) *The Northern Isles.* London, 1962

WALLACE, J. *A Description of the Isles of Orkney.* Edinburgh, 1693

WATSON, W. J. *The History of the Celtic Place-Names of Scotland.* London and Edinburgh, 1926

WEST, R. G. *Pleistocene Geology and Biology.* London, 1968

WILSON, G. V., EDWARDS, W., KNOX, J., JONES, R. C. B. and STEPHENS, J. V. *The Geology of the Orkneys.* Edinburgh, 1935

ZEUNER, F. E. *The Pleistocene Period: its Climate, Chronology and Faunal Successions.* London, 1959

ACKNOWLEDGEMENTS

I wish to thank the following for their help in the writing of this book : the Geographical Field Group, and especially my friend Dr Philip Wheeler who first introduced me to Orkney; Eileen Churchill, Principal of the Northumberland College of Education at Ponteland who made my field courses at Ness Battery 1966–8 possible; the many Northumberland College geography students who lived and worked with great good humour in Mainland, Hoy and the North Isles during those years; the Orkney Field Club, whose members were most generous of their time and expert assistance, and especially the late John Scott of Onston and secretary Elaine Bullard of St Ola; Evan Macgillivray MBE, formerly County Librarian and Ernest Marwick of Kirkwall, who made many valuable suggestions and were kind enough to read parts of my typescript; the editor of *The Orcadian*; Professor Emrys Bowen of Aberystwyth for advice on the Picts and the Celtic church; the Headmaster of Kirkwall Grammar School and the Rector of Stromness Academy for details of their two schools; Mr F. G. Cursiter of the Board of Management of Orkney Hospitals for notes on the history of Balfour Hospital; several official bodies, notably the Highland TA and VR Association, the North of Scotland Hydro Electric Board, the Telephone Manager for the Aberdeen Area and the Department of Agriculture and Fisheries for Scotland; John Dewar of Planair, Edinburgh, for help with air photographs; Real Photographs Ltd of Southport for finding photographs of HMS *Hampshire* and *Royal Oak*; the Ministry of Public Buildings and Works for permission to reproduce their photograph of Maeshowe; finally, David Orme of the University of Leicester Department of Geography, who drew the maps and George Clements of the School of Education who processed my own photographs and produced modern negatives with infinite care and patience from the fine glass plates of Thomas Kent.

237

INDEX

Page numbers in italic indicate illustrations

INDEX